The Human Element:
Employee Communication in Small to Medium-sized Businesses

Tamara Gillis, ABC, Ed.D

Sponsored by

IABC
RESEARCH FOUNDATION

IABC INTERNATIONAL ASSOCIATION OF BUSINESS COMMUNICATORS
One Hallidie Plaza, Suite 600 / San Francisco, CA 94102, USA

TABLE OF CONTENTS

LIST OF FIGURES

LIST OF TABLES

ABOUT GEVITY

Thousands of small and mid-sized businesses nationwide leverage the flexibility and scalability of Gevity's human resources (HR) solution to help them maximize the return on investment in their people. Essentially, Gevity serves as the full-service HR department for these businesses, providing each employee with support previously only available at much larger companies. Gevity delivers the Gevity Edge™, a comprehensive solution comprised of innovative management and administration services, helping employers to streamline HR administration, optimize HR practices, and maximize people and performance. This solution enables both businesses and their employees to achieve their full potential, giving them an edge over competitors. Gevity's unique approach features Gevity OnSite™, experienced HR Consultants based in local markets backed by nationwide resources and easy-to-use technology, including Gevity OnLine™ and Gevity OnCall™. For more information, call 1.800.2GEVITY (1.800.243.8489) or visit gevity.com.

EXECUTIVE SUMMARY

According to the Small Business Administration (2006) Office of Advocacy estimates, in 2005 "small firms with fewer than 500 employees represented 99.9 percent of the 25.8 million [U.S.] businesses." In 2006, the Business Register of Statistics Canada reported that more than 99 percent of employer businesses were small businesses with less than 500 employees (Industry Canada, 2007b). In 2005 99.9 percent of the estimated 4.3 million businesses in the U.K. were small to medium-sized enterprises (250 or fewer employees), according to the U.K. Department of Trade and Industry Small Business Service.

Whether employees are working together on the manufacturing floor to produce a product, sharing information between departments to complete a project, or teaming to produce business strategy in the board room, it is the ability to build relationships based on trust that propel the collective success of the company.

This study of employee communication practices in small businesses examines research data compiled by Insightrix Research Services for the IABC Research Foundation. The information contained here is in response to the project titled "Best Communication Practices in Small Firms," commissioned by the IABC Research Foundation and the Gevity Institute.

While there is a great deal of research on employee communication or internal communication in large companies and organizations, there is little information about how small businesses or small firms apply these theories, practices and measures to create a compelling organizational culture and an engaged workforce.

This study includes a literature review that constructs the concept of employee communication in small enterprises, followed by the results of a survey that captured the perceptions of business professionals responsible for communication practices in small enterprises, case studies, and concluding commentary regarding recommendations for developing and improving employee communication practices in small enterprises.

The recommendations from this study provide valuable insight for small business owners, communication professionals and researchers interested in further study of employee communication in small businesses.

The goal of this project was twofold: to identify current and emerging employee communication practices and to address the impact of effective internal communication on small businesses.

The primary research questions in this study were:

- What are the common employee communication practices among small businesses?
- What are emerging employee communication practices among small businesses?
- What is the cost-effectiveness of communication practices in terms of impact on productivity and profitability for small businesses?
- What is the organizational impact (on employee retention, business growth, etc.) of employee communication practices in small businesses?

There are many key findings in this research project. Research on the practice of organizational communication and large companies indicates a connection between communication and return on investment (Watson Wyatt, 2003). Research in this study suggests connections between greater profit margins and employee communication within small to medium-sized enterprises (SMEs).

There is mounting evidence that communication plays a role in engaging and retaining employees, both of which contribute to the profitability and productivity of an organization.

From the review of literature related to employee communication practices and small to medium-sized enterprises, the following findings are apparent:

- Measurable links exist between company productivity and employee communication, at least in studies conducted with large businesses.
- Communication plays a role in engaging and retaining employees, both of which contribute to the profitability and productivity of an organization.
- Companies with highly engaged employees are more profitable, accounting for 1 to 10 percent of earnings (Hammonds, 2005).
- Direct, two-way communication and staff interaction foster employee engagement.
- Business potential can only be realized if employees are fully aware of the company goals and their role in reaching those goals, and are motivated and committed to achieving those goals.
- Employee loyalty increases when managers exercise direct communication and consultation.

- Effective communication improves employee retention and reduces turnover rates.
- Staff loyalty is a result of setting goals and encouraging open and clear lines of communication across the organization.
- The person responsible for communication activities for the small to medium-sized businesses is the owner or manager, who is also responsible for other key aspects of the business' success.
- As businesses grow in size, communication activities are often delegated to human resource personnel or to marketing/sales personnel, for whom employee communication is not the primary concern.

From the survey results, the following findings are apparent:

- Direct face-to-face employee communication practices are identified by respondents as the most valuable for building employee engagement and increasing productivity.
- Electronic communication strategies are becoming more valuable to small businesses, but they remain an emerging practice for most.
- Many small to medium-sized businesses do not have a dedicated budget for communication.
- Many SMEs do not have a strategic communication plan that includes internal communication.
- A large proportion of the businesses surveyed did not measure the effects of employee communication tactics on their profitability.
- Because small to medium-sized businesses do not measure communication effects, there is little direct evidence to connect communication activities to return on investment.

From the in-depth interviews conducted with small businesses, owner/manager commentary supports the following principles:

- Positive relationships between owners and managers, defined by communication practices, were credited for employee engagement and productivity.
- Small businesses rely more heavily than larger businesses on face-to-face communication practices due to their small populations and proximity to one another.

- Electronic and print communication practices supplemented and reinforced the messages and face-to-face communication exchanges.
- The growing pains of expanding the employee population or the addition of multiple locations increase SMEs' need for more formal and planned internal communication practices. This can be frustrating for organizations that want to maintain the "feel" and spontaneity of the small organization. These growing organizations need to plan internal communication more than ever: to ensure that messages are delivered and received in a common manner across the organization, and to identify and confront any barriers to understanding and reaching company goals before they become problems.

In summary, after analyzing the literature, the survey results and the commentary by SME owners and managers in the case studies, the following recommendations with implementation suggestions are provided for small businesses that wish to capitalize on employee communication as a resource for business success:

- Improve direct, two-way communication between management and employees.
- Cultivate a culture that values communication—in all directions within the company.
- Develop career-long communication opportunities.
- Create opportunities for informal communications.
- Connect marketing with internal communications.
- Improve communication research techniques that connect employee communication to the company bottom line.

In conclusion, the findings and recommendations from this study provide evidence for the development of internal communication strategies that, when practiced consistently and measured, will have an impact on employee behavior and productivity, which ultimately can be measured by profitability and reputation variables. These strategies are compelling for small businesses that wish to retain their size or those small to medium-sized enterprises in the throes of growing pains. Internal communication practices that encourage open two-way communication and recognize the contributions of employees in achieving company goals will provide endless value to small to medium-sized enterprises.

CHAPTER 1 / Introduction

This study examines internal or employee communication practices within small businesses. The information contained here is in response to the project titled "Best Communications Practices in Small Firms," commissioned by the IABC Research Foundation and the Gevity Institute.

Research regarding employee communication practices in small and medium-sized enterprises includes the study of a combination of disciplines: communication, human resources, organizational development and business development to name a few. A literature review and survey comprise the majority of this study. Additional case studies were also compiled from research and interviews. The study findings reveal a number of initial conclusions and recommendations for small business owners.

The primary goals of the research project were to determine:

- Common employee communication practices.
- Emerging employee communication practices.
- The cost-effectiveness of communication practices in terms of impact on productivity and profitability.
- Organizational impact (on employee retention, business growth, etc.).

To fulfill the objectives of this project, a literature review of international sources was compiled to provide a body of knowledge on current and emerging employee communication strategies in small businesses. The literature review guided the survey design for the quantitative portion of the research.

A primary finding of this study links employee communication practices with greater business success: Positive employee relations—effective communication programs and practices—are central to productivity and to subsequent business success. The following report highlights the key findings as well as a number of practices that complement and strengthen communication within a small business.

The literature review, coupled with the survey findings, provides insights regarding organizational impact on small enterprises. An overarching principle exhibited through the literature review and survey findings is the power of positive productive relationships in the workplace and trust built from a foundation of effective communication programs and practices that contribute to productivity and business success.

CHAPTER 2 / Study Design and Research Protocol

Strategy and return on investment (ROI) are critical concepts in both private and public enterprises, large or small. For small organizations in particular, there are no resources to waste on tactics that do not contribute to achieving goals. When considering the role of communication in creating a rich and productive organizational culture, it is critical that the practices are strategic and that they support business goals.

This study was designed to identify the best practices of small organizations that have created open, effective internal communication channels necessary to nurture successful organizational cultures. Additionally, this report identifies trends in communication that will affect communication and business success in the future.

Many factors affect communication within an organization, such as culture, multiple locations, the nature of work, shifts, industry, the number of employees, etc. (Schaefer, 2005). Given this diversity, there is no *one-size-fits-all* solution to the communication problems of small businesses.

Small businesses sometimes charge someone in marketing or human resources with the responsibilities of internal communication (Grunig, 1992). In this situation, strategic internal communication can be overlooked in favor of simply addressing the communication needs related to the department's other work responsibilities. If a communication professional is employed, the pace of small business often dictates that internal communications are more reactive than proactive. For the smallest of businesses, micro-businesses, the responsibility of employee communication rests with the owner or manager—along with all of the other daily business practices.

RATIONALE / For small businesses, time, funds and energy are precious inputs that need to be invested, not simply used. It's essential for decision makers to allocate resources to communication strategy development because these practices have a measurable impact on the success of a business.

Many studies are available on the internal communication strategies of large multinational companies, but there are few such resources for small to medium-sized enterprises. This study is intended to help fill that gap by addressing the internal communication strategies of small enterprises.

Mapping communication trends helps steer internal communication strategy to meet future needs. The effects of a strong communication strategy may take time to benchmark and measure. Implementing a strategy now that will address future needs is a smart use of resources.

A literature review was conducted with data spanning 20 years; trends, changes and patterns in communication theories can easily be determined through this analysis. The literature review also revealed extensive research correlating communication practices with profitability and productivity.

THE SURVEY / Based on a review of current and emerging employee communication strategies in general, and the concerns of small enterprises, a survey was developed to collect data regarding the practices and contributions of employee communication to the success of small enterprises.

The survey was administered three ways: first, with a small business panel provided by Carpe Diem Consultants Inc.; second, with the IABC membership; and third, with a panel provided by Global Market Insight. An e-mail was sent to each potential respondent with a link to the survey. Clicking on the link opened a browser window containing the online survey. Using unique identification numbers, which are embedded in the URL, each respondent was only allowed to complete the survey once. Respondents had access to save and resume functions, which allowed them to exit the survey and re-enter at the question they last completed. This was particularly useful for those respondents who were interrupted while completing the survey or who had to sign off to get information or data not at hand. To encourage participation, e-mail reminders were sent regularly to those who had not yet completed the survey.

The survey instrument was designed by Insightrix as a fact-seeking and informative tool to learn about communication practices and their effects on productivity and ROI for small businesses. The intent of the survey was to collect and gauge best practices in employee communication in small businesses.

The survey included open- and closed-ended questions. The open-ended questions in particular give insight into the use of new and emerging technologies and the array of tactics currently in use.

According to Insightrix representatives, "Each question on the survey was analyzed by appropriate demographic variables including number of employees, sector, type of organization, gender of CEO and location of main office."

Findings from the literature review and survey are included in this report. The Appendix includes the unabridged compiled data from the study. Differences that are considered to be statistically significant have an alpha value of 0.05 or less, meaning that there is less than a 5 percent chance that the results could have occurred by chance.

THE POPULATION / The population that participated in the survey included 609 companies defined as small to medium-sized enterprises (SMEs). The population included businesses differing in location and industry. The respondents were owners and managers of small businesses who were generally responsible for the communication practices of the company.

These respondents represented the following positions: 28.9 percent of respondents were owners, 27.4 percent were managers, 22.5 percent were senior managers and 17.2 percent were employees.

The majority of respondents (81.8 percent) were responsible for managing communication for their organization, while 18.2 percent were not. Respondents who identified themselves as "employee" were least likely to be responsible for managing communication (50.5 percent), compared to 88.3 percent of other respondents.

Respondents who indicated that they worked for a company with 50 or fewer employees totaled 48.8 percent, while 26.9 percent said their company has 51 to 200 employees, and 24.3 percent said more than 200 employees comprised the company.

The population of the study represents a variety of industries or sectors. The percentage of respondents representing the professional, scientific and technical services sector was 38.1 percent. Eleven percent represented the manufacturing and food processing sector, 8.7 percent represented finance and insurance, and 8.5 percent worked in the information sector.

Corporations accounted for 59.9 percent of the respondents' companies. Proprietorships represented 17.6 percent of the population. Partnerships accounted for 15.9 percent of the companies, and 1.3 percent identified their companies as cooperatives.

Approximately three quarters of respondents said that their CEO or company leader was male, while 24 percent said the company leader was female.

Approximately three quarters of respondents indicated that their main office was located in the U.S. Another 14.6 percent said their main office was in Canada, 4.3 percent said Europe and 1.6 percent said Asia. Eight respondents said their main office is in Mexico, six respondents said Australia, three respondents said South America and one respondent represented Africa.

Almost 40 percent of respondents said that their business has offices, plants or stores, including the main office, in only one site. Those whose businesses had two sites totaled 16.8 percent, 30.8 percent had three to 10 sites and 10.4 percent had 11 to 50 sites. Only 2.3 percent of respondents indicated that their business has more than 10 sites.

The majority of respondents (88.8 percent) indicated that no portion of their workforce is unionized, while 8.4 percent said that all or a portion of their workforce is unionized.

THE CASE STUDIES / A series of case studies supplements the literature review and survey, providing in-depth information on best practices. These case studies were developed through in-depth interviews with representatives of small businesses who have been successful in developing effective employee communications to sustain their businesses.

Survey results conclude the report in the Appendices.

CHAPTER 3 / Literature Review

Research in the area of employee communication or internal communication as part of the organizational communication discipline is rich in regards to theory and practices used by large companies and organizations. Entire interdisciplinary journals and books are dedicated to examining these practices from internal perspectives of human resources management and management theory to applied practices of employee communication, employee relations, employee engagement and organizational behavior.

This review of literature summarizes the nature of small business along with current practices of employee communication in general. An operating assumption of this review is that concepts and strategies used by large organizations also apply to the operations of small enterprises but at a different scale. In the end, this literature review will construct employee communication within the framework of small enterprise (businesses/firms).

WHAT IS SMALL BUSINESS? / The answer to this question should be simple: A small business is a business that is small. But it is not that simple.

The common criteria used to define *small business* or small enterprise include gross annual revenues, dominance in the industry sector and number of employees.

The U.S. Small Business Administration (SBA) defines a *small business* as "one that is independently owned and operated and which is not dominant in its field of operation" (NFIB, 2000, p. 7). Under the SBA definition, a small business may be a sole proprietorship, a corporation or any other legal form. To be considered a small business in the U.S., a business must have an operation in the U.S. that contributes to the U.S. economy and does not exceed the numerical size standard for its industry.

The SBA uses the North American Industry Classification System to identify industry and sector for comparison of enterprises across North America (Mexico, Canada and the U.S.) and set size standards. A business is considered small if it is not greater than the size standard for its classification, i.e., 500 or fewer employees for a manufacturing enterprise, 100 or fewer employees for a wholesale trade business, or US$750,000 or less in revenue for agriculture.

The Great Place to Work Institute, a research and management consultancy based in the U.S. with international affiliates, produces an annual index of excellence titled "Best Small and Medium Companies to Work for in America." The Great Place to Work Institute defines small companies as those with 50 to 250 employees (GPWI, 2006).

Industry Canada defines a small business as one with fewer than 100 employees if the business is a goods-producing business and fewer than 50 employees if the business is a service-based enterprise. Medium-sized enterprises are those with less than 500 employees. Statistics Canada defines small and medium-sized enterprises as established businesses with 0 to 499 employees and less than CAN$50 million in gross revenues.

On 6 May 2003 the European Commission adopted a new recommendation regarding the definition of SMEs. "Small enterprises are defined as enterprises which employ fewer than 50 persons and whose annual turnover or annual balance sheet total does not exceed 10 million Euro" (2007, p. 14). Medium-sized enterprises are defined as employing less than 250 people with an annual turnover of less than or equal to €50 million or an annual balance sheet total that does not exceed €43 million.

Holmes and Gibson (2001) developed the following definition of small business that was accepted by the Small Business Coalition, an informal grouping of 27 industry associations in Australia with an interest in small business issues:

> A small business is a business which is independently owned and operated, with close control over operations and decisions held by the owners. Business equity is not publicly traded and business financing is personally guaranteed by the owners. The business will have less than twenty employees. (p. 17)

In a study of the influence of internal and external factors on employee relations practices in small businesses in Ireland, MacMahon (1996) reported that 67 percent of the small business owners assumed personal responsibility for personnel management. All of the companies exhibited centralized decision making, a simple organizational structure and a tendency to select employees based on their ability to "fit in." Communication practices were described as flexible and informal. Twenty-five percent of the sample reported no formal established method of communication. Structured methods were viewed as a threat to the employment relationship and capable of drawing attention to power inequities that are otherwise unchallenged. However, this lack of "personal distance" between management and employees could potentially result in issues being taken much more personally. Similarly, performance evaluations were viewed as counterproductive. MacMahon (1996) reported that incentive programs that could increase productivity and profitability were hampered by external factors, like competition with larger businesses.

In a study of employee relations in small businesses in the U.K., Matlay (1999) found that owners or managers of micro-businesses are more prone to use informal, highly personalized management styles with informal employee communication practices and strategies. Communication practices are highly influenced by owner/manager preferences.

Matlay concluded that micro-business owners or managers played a critical role in the overall management of their businesses, and they were not willing to delegate the business functions of human resources management and employee relations. According to Evatt, Ruiz and Triplett (2005), "a small business owner is responsible for making decisions, solving problems, preventing them and finding opportunities in 12 areas: production of the product or service; hiring and firing; marketing and advertising; quality control; planning; sales; funding and financial forecasting; administration; research and development; bookkeeping and takes; employee management; and cash flow" (p. 61).

Inherent in these definitions of small business are the following characteristics (Bolton, 1971; Broom, Longenecker & Moore, 1983; Matlay, 1999; Holmes & Gibson, 2001; Evatt, Ruiz & Triplett, 2005):

- Management and ownership are held by the same individuals.
- Business decision making and operations reside with a few key individuals in the organization, with the owners controlling key business strategy.
- The equity in the business is not publicly traded.
- The owners of the business are personally responsible for the finances of the enterprise.
- The number and level of formal contractual relations (including employees) are kept to a minimum level to achieve the business goals.

Since the population for this study represents small businesses on an international level, a working definition for small business gleaned from this review of definitions and used for this study is *companies that are independently operated with 200 or fewer employees.* This working definition includes micro-businesses, small businesses and some medium-sized businesses.

A leading assumption about small businesses, derived from the definitions reviewed, is that within a small enterprise, the owner, president or chief executive officer directly performs or is directly responsible for the functions that are normally performed by a management team in a larger business, i.e., research and development, human resources, finances, marketing, *organizational communication,* strategic planning, sales, et. al.

EMPLOYEE COMMUNICATION / Organizational communication is a function of management, and employee communication is that management function that spans an employee's life with an organization. It begins with recruitment, hiring and orientation; progresses through the life of an employee with the company; and concludes with the exit interview upon retirement or resignation from the enterprise. The Society for Human Resource Management (2004) considers communication among the "Critical 4 Cs" criteria for a successful and positive productive workforce: "Commitment, Culture, Communication and Compensation."

> In legal terms, an employee is a person hired to provide services to a company on a regular basis in exchange for compensation. An employee who does not provide these services is part of an independent business.
>
> In reality, employees are the frontline troops who provide products and services that define corporations, organizations and government entities. They are the lifeblood that allows businesses to grow, and the powerful intellectual capital that gets traded alongside company stock shares in the marketplace. When employees leave the office at the end of the day, they act as their corporations' and organizations' ambassadors in the community (Gillis, 2004, p. 8).

Employee communication is defined as a management tool and motivational force (Roxe, 1979). The most important aspect of personnel management, employee communication encompasses the free flow of concepts, instructions and ideas between employer and employee (Siegel, 1978). Effective employee communication consists of the right information and the right message delivered in a clear manner; it is two-way and essential to the health and productivity of a business (Smith & Mazin, 2004; McAleese & Hargie, 2004). It is the process of exchanging information and creating understanding and behaviors within an organization that reinforce the organization's vision, values and culture among employees, who can then communicate the company's message to external audiences.

Employee relations as an organizational strategy includes general communication activities as well as the concerns of employee retention, employee engagement, employee loyalty, employee satisfaction and employee performance. According to Grunig's (1992) study of excellence in organizational communication, the employee communication function is either led by public relations officers or human resources officers—with larger organizations favoring the public relations approach and smaller organizations favoring the human resources approach. The human resources office is traditionally responsible for communicating to employees about benefits and company orientation.

Effective communication entails the reception and comprehension of messages as well as their broadcasting. It involves listening, understanding and empathy. Effective communication relies on message clarity and feedback. Personal communication facilitates message accuracy. Communication awareness programs that address diversity in regard to interpretation, timing and priority avoid information overload (Rimler & Humphreys, 1980).

In a global study, Gay, Mahony and Graves (2005) identified four critical challenges for employee communication, regardless of business size:

1. **"Motivating employees to align with the business strategy**—creating a line of sight between employees and organizational strategy.
2. **Leadership and management communication**—educating and engaging leaders and managers in their role in employee communication.
3. **Managing information overload**—breaking through the communication 'clutter.'
4. **Measuring the ROI of internal communication**—linking communication to business results" (p. 15).

These findings confirm the results from the 2003/2004 Watson Wyatt Worldwide Communication ROI Study.

Employee loyalty "is generated when employees, unhappy with the status quo, are constantly reaching to deliver the kind of value and service that develops increasingly loyal customers" (Reichheld, 2001, p. 3). According to the Bain & Company Loyalty Acid Test, "small teams have the highest levels of employee loyalty. ... So keep the size of your teams small, and give employees the tools they need to build strong relationships with customers" (p. 4). This is good news for small businesses. According to Carol Kinsey Goman, loyalty has two dimensions, internal and external. "The internal dimension...includes emotional bonding, mutuality, affiliation and caring.... The external dimension has to do with the manifestations of loyalty—the behaviors that people see" (Allen, 1989).

Employee retention is the concept of creating a work environment that encourages employees to remain with the company. Among the best employee retention strategies according to SHRM are promoting qualified employees, offering competitive merit increases and salary adjustments, and providing career development opportunities. Low employee retention results in tangible and intangible losses to the company, i.e., customer loyalty; poor morale; and high turnover, recruitment and training costs.

The Institute for Employment Studies defines *employee engagement* as "a positive attitude held by the employee towards the organization and its values. An engaged employee is aware of business context, and works with colleagues to improve performance within the job for the benefit of the organization. The organization must work to develop and nurture engagement, which requires a two-way relationship between employer and employee" (Robinson, Perryman & Hayday, 2004).

Employee satisfaction or job satisfaction is "a pleasurable or positive emotional state from the appraisal of one's job or experiences" (Locke, 1976, p. 1297). Empirical evidence links effective employee communication as an element of quality of work life and overall employee satisfaction to the overall financial performance of businesses (May, Lau & Johnson, 1999; Lyon, 2001).

Organizations with high communication effectiveness leverage the employee/manager relationship to enhance formal communication processes. Leadership clearly articulates its vision and ties communication initiatives to business objectives. Managers receive information in advance so they have time to absorb and understand it before presenting it to employees (Vogt, 2004, p. 24). Organizations with high communication effectiveness constantly measure and refine their programs (p. 25).

The greatest benefit from effective employee communication is a knowledgeable workforce that is satisfied and productive, which leads to positive interactions with customers, investors and the community.

EMPLOYEE COMMUNICATION STARTS AT THE TOP One cost-effective means of improving employee satisfaction with organizational communication is to improve the communication of senior executives and managers (Pincus, 1994; Gray and Robertson, 2005; McCown, 2005).

"Senior executives, especially the CEO, provide leadership to align the organization with its vision. They set the direction, and their behavior determines the tone and culture—how vision will be achieved" (Gray and Robertson, 2005, p. 26). It is not surprising then that employees want to hear the company's direction from their leadership.

According to Gray and Robertson (2005), employees want to hear from their CEO or executive management about the following "big picture" topics:

- The future of the organization.
- Overall corporate strategy.
- Top-line financial results.
- Major changes.
- Feedback from the board of directors (or, in the public sector, government).
- Major stakeholder issues.
- Responses to media attention. (p. 27)

Effective communication makes that connection with employees and engages them in the journey of the business strategy. In small to medium-sized businesses, owners and unit managers are poised to make this connection with their teams and employees. Their success in accomplishing this task depends on their ability and readiness to accomplish it.

MANAGERIAL COMMUNICATION AND EMPLOYEE COMMUNICATION

As new technology continues to improve and increase the opportunities for communication within organizations, studies are reinforcing the role that immediate managers play in keeping employees informed and connected to the company's business strategy (Williams & Dong, 1999; Larkin & Larkin, 1994; Therkelsen & Fiebich, 2003; Smith & Mazin, 2004; Whitworth & Riccomini, 2005). The results of a study reported by Whitworth and Riccomini (2005) indicate that managerial communication effectiveness correlates to employee job performance. While many other channels can convey information to employees, the manager can provide both information content and context for the employee. Context includes a sense of perspective on how the unit's work contributes to the organization's success. Managerial communication includes "taking big picture issues and discussing how they affect the immediate work group and individual employees. It means engaging in a dialogue with employees to make sure that there's common understanding" (p. 20).

A unique characteristic of small business is the strong interpersonal relationships between employees and owners (Carland & Carland, 1990; Matlay, 1999; Therkelsen & Fiebich, 2003). Managerial communication includes interpersonal communications to exchange information regarding defining tasks, articulating satisfaction with employee performance, sharing praise and criticism to improve productivity, and listening to employees with genuine interest and within an environment that is open and encouraging (Carland & Carland, 1990).

According to Matlay (1999), "The critical role that owner/managers [of micro-businesses] usually played in the day-to-day operation of their firms brought them into direct contact with most, if not all, of their employees" (p. 294) and reflected in the successful operation of the business.

Managers are leaders within companies who have the ability to guide, instruct, motivate and encourage employees. They are encouraged to practice enthusiasm, welcome staff inquiries, be attentive listeners, maintain an open door policy, recognize individualism and support independent decision making (Burstiner, 1998). Managers have the ability to shape organizational culture through their articulation of overall business strategy, sharing the culture through communication with staff and measuring performance (McAleese & Hargie, 2004).

Small business owners need to be well-versed in the principles of personnel management to improve employee retention, employee engagement, productivity, morale and satisfaction (Balderson, 2000; Burstiner, 1998). Effective managerial communication practices help reduce the incidence of misunderstandings and mistrust as well as provide the foundation for conflict resolution.

The manager-employee communication process begins with the first few days: Orientation activities as well as the delegation of a coach to assist the new employee in his or her transition improve employee satisfaction and employee engagement (Siegel, 1978; Burstiner, 1998; Smith & Mazin, 2004). The orientation period should familiarize the employee with company rules and regulations and all aspects of the job and the company. Communication must be reciprocal to ensure comprehension and engagement in the business.

Managerial communication is one of many channels on which to build a broader employee communication or internal communication program. According to Whitworth and Riccomini (2005), after the manager, the three most credible sources of organizational information are the company intranet, the business executive and external mass media.

PLANNING A SUCCESSFUL EMPLOYEE COMMUNICATION PROGRAM

The formal communication program of a company includes many communication opportunities. As discussed above, face-to-face communications between managers or owners and employees continue to be a critical component to building trusted employee communications. Meeting employees' preferences for information delivery is a key to building trust and maintaining employee engagement.

In a study of employee communication preferences conducted from 1997 to 2004, Sinickas (2005) concluded that employees prefer "a combination of electronic and other sources, or just face-to-face sources, depending on the subject matter. Electronic channels that actively 'push' information to employees' attention (e-mails and e-newsletters) are more highly preferred on most subjects than the passive 'pull' sources where employees have to choose to go search for information (intranets, web sites). About three-fourths are unwilling to give up printed employee periodicals in favor of exclusively electronic ones" (p. 31).

According to the 2002 Fleishman-Hillard survey of employee communication practices and the 2002 Mercer Human Resource Consulting "People at Work" survey, communication is vital to employee retention. Manager accountability for communication is critical. *Best Practices in Employee Communication* included the use of innovative technologies to engage employees and the use of staff feedback. These findings further support the use of multiple communication channels in the employee communication mix. Print newsletters and intranet sites are the most common communication forms, along with e-mail, voice mail, television, and audio and video streaming. Incentives, training and two-way communications are valued.

As shown above, a successful employee communication plan relies on a number of communication opportunities to meet diverse employee preferences.

An internal public relations plan is a total communication effort designed to inform and influence various internal publics through mutual understanding. This internal communication process lays the groundwork for increased productivity as well as external initiatives and generally consists of six steps:

1. Goal setting
2. Identification of the audience
3. Schedule planning

4. Choosing tactics

5. Budgeting resources

6. Evaluating progress

Adhering to a structured communication plan with identifiable objectives and strategies for implementation provides a foundation for measurable employee communication.

A proactive planned approach to employee communication involves adopting a philosophy of prevention, engaging in two-way communication, embracing change, recognizing interdependence, involving employees in planning and decision making, and displaying supportive power relations (Rimler & Humphreys, 1980).

Employee communication programs typically include:

- Print publications, such as company handbooks and policy manuals, benefits brochures/booklets, newsletters, and bulletin board postings.
- Face-to-face communication between employees and supervisors and other senior staff that spans the gamut from informal conversations to staff meetings and large-group meetings like town hall gatherings.
- Audiovisual channels, such as mass mediated voice mails, company video, closed circuit broadcasts and news telephone hotlines.
- Electronic channels, including the company intranet and external web site, mass e-mails, e-newsletters, blogs, and podcasts.

Company publications are an effective means for the dissemination of information to all employees at the same time (Roxe, 1979). For small businesses, print publications may include letters sent to the employee's home to convey general information and newsletters that define company culture (Smith & Mazin, 2004). Formal informational documents, including job descriptions, a handbook of personnel policies and a grievance procedure manual, reinforce verbal communication and foster a sense of employee value (Burstiner, 1998; Balderson, 2000; Smith & Mazin, 2004).

Owners/managers need to practice face-to-face communication at the onset of the employee relationship during orientation. They should use written materials containing personnel policies and company information to supplement personal contact (Beckman, Good & Wyckham, 1982).

Bedi (1996) contends that employees' perceptions of policies and initiatives are vital to establishing healthy dialogue and swift, curative action. Imperative to the communication process is dialogue in both the hierarchical and grassroots directions. Since employees sometimes remain silent during meetings for fear of reprisal or ridicule, methods are needed to increase honest employee feedback as a gauge of employee reaction to company policies and activities.

Beyond the face-to-face communication between managers and employees, employee forums are highly motivational. Feedback from staff and a free flow of information, in turn, benefit management and employees (Roxe, 1979).

By fostering employee engagement through direct, two-way communication and interaction with existing staff, setting goals, and encouraging open and clear lines of communication, managers can develop staff loyalty. Suggestion systems, performance evaluations and reward plans are effective employee relations tools for sustained two-way communication and employee engagement. Suggestion systems ensure upward communication, acknowledge employee concerns and encourage employees to share ideas on improving the enterprise. Follow-up on employee suggestions will show employees that their ideas are valued. Performance reviews must include a reward for achievement as well as constructive criticism (Siegel, 1978; Roxe, 1979; Beckman, et al. 1982; Smith & Mazin, 2004; Krotz, 2005).

Electronic communications cannot substitute for face-to-face communication with a manager or supervisor. E-mails and blogs are similar to conversations and small group discussions, but face-to-face communication is superior because of the immediate feedback and the personal expressions of body language and facial expressions (Gray, 2006).

Employees can share information regarding the operations of the business on the company intranet, an internal private network (Murgolo-Poore & Pitt, 2001). Since sensitive information is on the intranet, security is of the utmost importance. Company intranets are used to empower employees to maximize their potential; to enable employees to learn about the company, the competition and other functions of the business; and to enable employees to access and manage personal benefits information (SCM, 2002).

In a survey of North American businesses in 2004, both large and small, Edelman Change and Employee Engagement Group found that few companies were experimenting with newer tools such as blogs and wikis, but intranet investment remained high and the use of instant messaging in the workplace was on the rise. In just two years, Edelman followed up with the study in 2006, and much had changed. While face-to-face communication was rated as the most effective channel to communicate with employees, nearly all respondents reported knowledge of blogs, podcasts and wikis. E-mail was ranked as the most frequently used communication tool within companies, while intranets were noted to be highly valued for sharing information and promoting best practices. The use of blogs in internal communication is on the rise. Smith and Mazin (2004) prescribe limited use of e-mails and memos due to the impersonal nature of the media.

A comprehensive employee communication program includes a plan to measure how employee communication activities affect the company's business goals. Inherent in creating a culture of communication and knowledge sharing is an environment for feedback. Elements of such a culture include:

- Leaders who listen, respect employee contributions and engage employees in problem solving.

- Employees who work well in teams, have strong interpersonal communication as well as technical skills and who are trained in problem solving.
- Information flow systems that ensure open communication in all directions, value feedback and have high levels of interaction between employees (Shuler, 1999).

Employee feedback, surveys, grievance procedures and suggestion boxes are a few means for exchanging information, measuring employee satisfaction and developing an environment of trust (Smith & Mazin, 2004).

Employee focus groups and employee advisory committees can be useful forums for testing messages and getting feedback on campaigns during the development phase as well as in the summative measurement phase of an employee communication program (Lawson, 2004).

Surveys and regular monitoring of employee attitudes keep potential grievances in check by ensuring continued dialogue with employees. Surveys also demonstrate management's concern and interest in the opinions and ideas of staff. Immediate follow-up ensures positive relations, and respondent anonymity promotes trust and honesty.

A CLEAR LINE OF SIGHT

Increasingly, organizations are looking inward to assess how effective communication can be used to improve corporate performance. Internal communication processes influence employee perceptions and behavior and can therefore be used to align employees with business goals and priorities. An organization's potential can only be realized if employees are fully aware of its goals and are motivated and committed to achieve them. Since employees are a key information source for customers, they need to be effectively engaged in the communication process if they are to represent the organization well to others (Kapel & Thompson, 2005). A communication audit can help a company improve how it manages internal communication, ensuring the employee brand aligns with external branding efforts.

Organizational strength is derived from the depth of knowledge that dedicated employees retain (Insightlink Communications, 2004). Company management must understand and effectively manage *employee loyalty* as opposed to mere *retention* by emphasizing responsibility rather than job function; providing opportunities for learning, development and growth; and encouraging holistic company participation as well as conducting both informal and formal performance evaluations. Clarity and openness of communication are essential to the administration of these principles. Legitimizing corporate strategy through consistency between communication and action is essential to promoting and sharing the company's vision.

There is a disconnect in most companies between strategy formulation and strategy execution. According to Kaplan and Norton (2005), on average, 95 percent of a company's employees are unaware of or do not understand the company's strategy. If employees are unaware of the strategy, they cannot assist the organization in implementing it effectively.

Bado (2002) maintains that to engage employees and incite interest in profitability, performance information must be shared in an exciting and interesting manner. Abstract financial figures should be communicated through a practical, creative and interactive approach. Specifically, 1) connect the "numbers" to real-life experiences; 2) get creative by making it fun, interactive and engaging; 3) build a line-of-sight from daily work to the big numbers; and 4) play mini-games with visual scoreboards.

According to Kaplan and Norton (2005), one approach to developing business alignment is to adopt the Balanced Scorecard and its associated tools to help managers better communicate strategy to their employees and to guide and monitor the execution of that strategy. Some companies, of course, have achieved better, longer lasting improvements than others. The organizations that have managed to sustain their strategic focus have typically established a new corporate-level unit to oversee all activities related to strategy: an office of strategy management (OSM).

The OSM coordinates an array of tasks:

- Communicating corporate strategy, ensuring that enterprise-level plans are translated into the plans of the various units and departments.
- Executing strategic initiatives to deliver on the grand design.
- Aligning employees' plans for competency development with strategic objectives.
- Testing and adapting the strategy to stay abreast of the competition.

The OSM does not do all the work, but it facilitates the processes so that strategy is executed in an integrated fashion across the enterprise. Although the companies that Kaplan and Norton studied use the BSC as the framework for their strategy management systems, the lessons of the OSM are applicable even to companies that do not use it.

Effective communication affects the bottom line for companies that use communication as a strategic business tool. Aligning the process of employee relations with business strategy fosters employee ownership and ultimately, profitability (McAleese & Hargie, 2004; Hammonds, 2005).

According to the 2002 Fleishman-Hillard survey of employee communication practices and the 2002 Mercer Human Resource Consulting "People at Work" survey, documenting communication's contribution to bottom-line results was the most sought-after result of communication strategies or imperatives.

In the 2003/2004 Communication ROI Study, Watson Wyatt Worldwide (2003) illustrated that organizational communication can drive business results. The results of the study of predominantly large organizations showed that companies with the most effective employee communication programs provided a 26 percent total return to shareholders from 1998 to 2002 and were associated with lower turnover rates than other organizations. The study identified nine communication dimensions that can be directly linked to an increase in company value; three are associated with the largest increase in value: "driving managers' commitment to effective communication, having a formal communication process in place and creating a clear 'line of sight' between business objectives and employees' jobs" (Yates, 2004, p. 8).

Lyman (2003) reports that a strong trust-based relationship between employees and management built on open communication has resulted in "superior financial performance" for the 100 Best Companies to Work for in the U.S.

> For every year that the "100 Best" list has been published in the U.S., the Great Place to Work® Institute has sought independent analyses of the financial performance of publicly traded 100 best companies compared with other companies contained in various market indices.... The 100 best experience significantly higher levels of financial performance, and in general have about half the turnover of other companies in their industries. (p. 27)

Whitworth and Riccomini (2005) state that "The better the managers' communication, the more satisfied the employees were with all aspects of their work life," which ultimately translates to higher performance and an impact on the bottom line for the company (p. 18).

According to Hammonds (2005), employee engagement scores are directly linked to profitability and account for 1 to 10 percent of company earnings. Employee performance must be connected to profitability indicators, such as customer loyalty, quality and employee replacement costs.

Effective organizational communication, regardless of organization size, starts with formal communication processes, leveraged by technology and employee preferences for communication media, coupled with a rewards program that uses employee feedback to ensure that employees see how their daily work activities contribute to the overall success of the organization.

INTERNATIONAL PERSPECTIVES

Employee communication is a universal concept that translates across cultures.

From a study of small businesses in the U.K., Marlow (1997) contends that best communication practices are informed by larger businesses. However, to understand the extent of any similarities between employee communication practices in large and small businesses, it is vital to study small enterprises. For instance, Marlow reported that owners and managers of small businesses demonstrate limited knowledge of human resource procedures and communication techniques, which would seem to indicate a difference between the practices in large and small organizations.

Communication practices that are common to larger companies pose risks for smaller ones due to the personal and informal nature of the small business. Formal practices are likely to result in employee resentment and alienation (MacMahon, 1996).

In a study of employee practices in small businesses in New Zealand, Massey (2004) reports that small businesses have both positive and negative attributes. Management practices in small businesses were assessed as informal, short-term and nonstrategic in comparison to the practices of large businesses. However, small businesses have an edge over their large business counterparts when it comes to their informal employee communication practices and flexibility. Most important, small businesses need to be considered on their own terms and not as "merely immature large firms" waiting to grow out of their small business stage.

In China, both altruism and a collective persona inform Asian human resource strategies and provide an example for initiatives in the West. Whiteley, Cheung and Zhang (2000) report that businesses in China hold frequent and regular meetings between managers, department heads and supervisors. Employee feedback is highly valued, and agreement documents signify the worker's commitment. Specialized departments educate employees in company culture and strategy; publish newsletters; and conduct workers' forums and performance appraisals. Broad career paths, training, employee engagement, job security and explicit job descriptions were highly integrated into human resource strategy.

In 2004, Leininger reported that China was facing a local labor market with double-digit turnover rates and high salary increases. Leininger argues that key drivers for improving employee retention rates are: clear communication, high job satisfaction, inspired leadership and management, effective performance management systems, and a positive work environment (p. 38).

Anton (1980) attributes fewer work stoppages, mutual understanding and higher productivity to employee participation in decision making, understanding of employee contributions to organizational success and two-way communications. Employee participation manifests in different models, country by country, due to differing political, economic and social environments. Positive outcomes of employee participation include improved communication, job enrichment and semi-autonomous work groups that positively impact the organizational goals, including financial goals.

EMERGING EMPLOYEE COMMUNICATION ISSUES FOR SMES / From the literature reviewed for this study, the following issues were identified as emerging issues of concern for small to medium-sized businesses:

- Multiculturalism and diversity.
- Communication technology.
- Nontraditional work arrangements.

- Work space design.
- Trust in the workplace.
- The effects of management trends.

MULTICULTURALISM AND DIVERSITY

As small and medium enterprises begin to grow and increase staff diversity, a number of issues emerge: multicultural communication, generational communication and gender communication issues. The U.S. Bureau of Labor Statistics reports that by 2008, 41 percent of the American workforce will be members of minority groups.

Sensitivity to differences in communication styles, cultural concerns, and work styles includes acknowledging gender, generational and multicultural differences. Owners and managers need to understand and appreciate these differences, avoid stereotyping individuals based on differences, and encourage meaningful communication and knowledge sharing among staff (Vanfossen, 1996; Sanders, 1996; Srinivas, 2005). Diversity training sessions are encouraged as a means to educate managers and employees and to create a more culturally sensitive and productive workplace. The need for training and orientation programs is imperative in major corporations and small businesses alike (Ursy & White, 2000; Owens, 2005; Hammonds, 2005). Employee interaction, language training, orientation, mentoring, conflict resolution, sounding boards, cultural awareness and fostering a company culture of tolerance are a few suggestions.

The U.S. Department of Education reports that a high number of Americans who experience difficulty with English are of workforce age. Benico (2005) suggests the following as best practices in easing the confusion in communicating benefits to a multicultural workforce: language translation of relevant materials; benefits discussion groups that are open to family members, including younger persons who are more likely to be fluent in English; and using bilingual employees as a resource to translate and interpret both written documents and discussions of meetings.

Communication among employees in an atmosphere instilled with the values of tolerance and respect builds a positive group dynamic that contributes to the overall functioning of the business (Carland & Carland, 1990).

In 1994, Wainwright Industries was one of only six small businesses ever to be honored with a Malcolm Baldrige National Quality Award. Wainwright Industries provides all its employees with a basic skills training program focused on interpersonal relationships and the values of respect and dignity for all people (Barrier, 1995). Wainwright relies on a suggestion system that in 1994 yielded 54 implemented recommendations per employee. Wainwright's managers are committed to responding to suggestions within 24 hours if at all possible, and to implementing accepted suggestions within 72 hours. These programs have cultivated a culture of respect and organizational improvement from the grass roots.

COMMUNICATION TECHNOLOGY

The rise of uses for social media—such as blogs, IM, podcasts and wikis—in employee communication models is an issue for both large and small businesses. Managers/owners and communicators are including these media, considering the implications of controlling these media, and allowing them to grow to meet employee communication needs and business strategies (*The Business Communicator*, 2006).

An intranet to communicate securely and reliably within the company is strongly advised at the point of growth where decision making is no longer a singular or expedient process (Komando, 2005).

NONTRADITIONAL WORK ARRANGEMENTS

The 2004 U.S. Bureau of Labor statistics confirmed that 27.5 percent of U.S. full-time employees had flexible work schedules, i.e., virtual workers, telecommuters and flex workers. According to Schaefer (2005), flex time affords significant savings to small businesses in terms of absenteeism due to stress, burnout and family responsibilities. In addition, job satisfaction, morale, productivity, energy and creativity are increased. Work arrangements may vary from a range of start and end times, compressed work weeks, telecommuting, remote employees, and part-time or job sharing schedules.

Assumptions are often made about staff who take on these nontraditional work arrangements. In a study by Kandath, Oetzel, Rogers and Mayer-Guell (2003), significant differences between remote and nonremote workers were found concerning organizational identification, behavior, attitudes and work patterns. These researchers contend that communication is a key factor to employee engagement with remote workers. Remote workers are not merely an extension of the office staff; managers need to consider the implications of mediated communication on interpersonal communication and conflicts, trust building, commitment, efficiency, and cultural difference. Remote workers become a subculture of the normal organizational culture. Training managers to be sensitive to communication issues across the organizational culture and subcultures shows promise for increased productivity and engagement of remote employees.

Flex work arrangements present specific communication challenges. To offset the lack of social interaction and information sharing for flex workers, regular meetings should be scheduled, and contact should not be limited to e-mail. Management is faced with the responsibility of monitoring, assessing, and updating flex arrangements and must adopt a system based on trust and respect. The focus must shift from the work process to the outcome. Lack of employee input in determining work schedules and policies on flex time that are inconsistent or poorly documented can lead to resentment, decreased morale, employee turnover and legal ramifications. In the latter regard, overtime and occupational health and safety issues must be adequately addressed and communicated (Smith & Mazin, 2004; Business Communicator, 2002).

Communication presents a challenge particularly with telecommuters, off-site workers or virtual offices. New technology, like social media and intranets, supports the dissemination of communication materials by breaking spatial barriers to enhance the exchange of information.

WORK SPACE DESIGN

Kahler Slater Architects Inc. (2006) defines "a well-designed workspace as one that supports a company's strategic business initiatives, allows employees to perform their work efficiently and productively, reflects and embodies the values and culture of the company, and is environmentally healthy" (p. 2).

Work space design can enhance employee communication, problem solving and productivity. Work space design that encourages both formal and informal collaboration while respecting employees' needs for privacy is highly valued (Walleisa & Magnolfi, 2003; Nilsson, 2004; Kahler Slater, 2006). Such work space configurations facilitate creativity, knowledge sharing, common understanding and teamwork, as well as the quality, frequency and nature of communication. Studies (Devereaux, Horan & Ferguson, 1997; Kahler Slater, 2006) have also concluded that some permanent physical structures are necessary for employees to feel pride of place and satisfaction in their work environment. Permanence in work space features is rated as highly by employees as visual privacy, size and location

TRUST IN THE WORKPLACE According to the Great Place to Work Institute, "the foundation of every great workplace is trust between employees and management" (para. 2, 2007). Shockley-Zalabak, Ellis and Cesaria (2000) came to the same conclusion when developing a model for measuring organizational trust and its impact on organizational success.

Trust is defined by the Great Place to Work Institute (Lyman, 2003) as "the critical factor that supports effective communication, an ability to collaborate across departments and hierarchies, the willingness to seek fair resolutions to difficult situations, and the overall ability of employees to have confidence in management's vision for the future" (p. 24).

Organizational trust exists on multiple levels: individual, group and institutional (Shockley-Zalabak, et al., 2000). Culturally rooted, trust is defined by shared goals, norms, values and behaviors. Trust is communication-based: Internal and external audiences develop perceptions and opinions about an organization based on messages they hear about the company.

Communication behaviors that build trust include sharing with employees the triumphs and disclosing failures before the media reports them, and providing accurate information and timely feedback (Shockley-Zalabak, et al., 2000; Smith & Mazin, 2004).

Organizational trust is social capital measurable against the corporate bottom line through job satisfaction, productivity and team building.

of offices, and the ability to personalize the work space. Employee participation in designing the work space may ensure greater satisfaction.

Cisco's "Connected Workplace" (2004) is an example of how work space design can enhance efficient use of space, accommodate diverse work styles and reduce perceptions of hierarchy in the workplace. At Cisco, offices designated for management were often vacant (approximately 35 percent of the time), while meeting rooms were in demand. Staff work nontraditional hours, and on-site employees are highly mobile. Their "Connected Workplace" solution includes a wireless environment; a university theme with quads, plazas and common areas; and increased natural lighting. The design offers employees a choice of where to work, and the work environment reflects business needs rather than employee titles. Diverse working styles and requirements are more easily accommodated. Employee satisfaction and collaboration have increased, and real estate and infrastructure costs have been reduced as a result of the design.

MANAGEMENT TRENDS

Owners and managers of small firms have experimented with management practices, such as management by walking around (Smith & Mazin, 2004), and concepts like mapping social networks, open book management and government directives regarding employee communication.

The connectedness between people and the web of knowledge that exists among them describes the manner in which ideas are exchanged and built upon. Social network analysis assumes that work and information flow through a web of informal channels rather than within a hierarchical structure. Essential to social networks is the reciprocity between people, content and the social fabric that connects them. Network analysis, through which collaboration and the exchange of ideas can be optimized, presents a means of improving communication and productivity. The dynamics of employee networks reveal communicative patterns that contribute to efficiency and identify barriers by determining collaborative relationships within an organization as well as weak links. Social network mapping can identify opinion leaders in various knowledge domains and improve the functioning of project teams (Morville, 2002; Cross & Parker, 2004; Krebs, 2005).

Open book management shows some promise for creating a greater connection between communicating business strategy and workforce productivity. According to Case's (1997) research with small to midsize companies that take a more direct approach to continuous performance improvement, "companies do better when employees care not just about quality, efficiency, or any other single performance variable but about the same thing that senior managers are supposed to care about: the success of the business" (p. 118). Open book management consists of "all employees understanding the financial objectives and progress of the organization and being entrusted to manage the business by 'the numbers.' Employees are trusted or empowered to run the business in a way that goes beyond normal employee involvement" (Gray, 2002, p. 3).

Critical to the implementation of open book management systems are the following steps (Case, 1997; Mellor, 1997; Gray, 2002):

1. Develop buy-in throughout the company.
2. Communicate to all parties the importance of understanding the business data.
3. Develop accountability for understanding and ultimately improving performance as evidenced by the business data.
4. Reward employees for successes.
5. Maintain excitement for the process since it is ongoing.

In a review of case studies, Mellor (1997) shows how the open book culture, built on the foundation of open communication with employees, empowers them to identify organizational constraints to business success and increases their loyalty through sharing responsibility.

Zingerman's Delicatessen in Ann Arbor, Michigan, attributes company growth and success to employee communication and open communication practices (Burlingham, 2003). Zingerman's Delicatessen grew from 125 employees in 1994 to 334 people in 2003. The partners introduced their vision for the company in 1994 in the form of a document titled "Zingerman's 2009: A Food Odyssey." The plan was distributed to the company's managers, employees, and customers and drew mixed reviews. The owners introduced a deli council where staff vote on product initiatives and instituted ZingTrain, an entity that provides training for managers and staff as well as external parties. ZingTrain adopted a "step maxim" for great service, handling customer complaints, order accuracy, great finance and the productive resolution of differences, among others. The rules act more as guidelines. ZingTrain expanded its rulebook to a business curriculum. The "University of Zingerman's" is credited with creating a universally understood language through its step maxims, a common culture represented by consistent lettering and cartooning, and an entertaining and informative employee manual.

Dialogue with staff is an imperative, as the implementation of the European Directive on Information and Consultation in early 2005 formally signaled. This directive requires organizations to establish a formal communication consultation with employees. According to the Department of Trade and Industry, the directive gives staff a right to be informed about the business' economic situation, informed and consulted about employment prospects, and about decisions likely to lead to substantial changes in the work organization or contractual relations (Ferrabee, 2005). The directive affects organizations with 150 or more employees in any country that is part of the European Union. "What consultation should look like in practice has been left open to interpretation, with the directive simply calling for 'an exchange of views and establishment of dialogue'" (p. 30). According to Ferrabee, five steps that companies should take in developing a formal consultation process include:

1. Auditing current internal communication processes.
2. Aligning the consultation process with organizational objectives and values.
3. Developing a communication process that incorporates all employees.
4. Using preferred communication vehicles to reach employees.
5. Training managers in the new communication processes.

Small businesses should also anticipate and plan for crises just as large businesses do. The development of a crisis communication plan based on honest and accountable communication practices supports organizational trust and ensures that employees understand their role during times of crisis. Using existing organizational communication tools to share both positive and negative information and alerting staff to their roles in managing a crisis are two concepts key to employee satisfaction during business crises (Gerstein & Tannenbaum, 2005; Millar & Smith, 2002; Traverso, 2001).

EMPLOYEE COMMUNICATION IN SMALL BUSINESSES / To this point, the review of literature has focused on employee communication in large businesses. Not surprisingly, since large businesses are easier to study, these organizations collect and study data regarding their success to share with stakeholders like investors and regulatory entities. Large businesses are less ephemeral, providing a greater opportunity for longitudinal study.

All of the concepts discussed thus far also reflect in the daily operations of small businesses. Developing a greater understanding and appreciation for the practice of employee communication will help SMEs prosper and have long lives—maybe even grow in size (although this is *not* the ultimate goal, since most small business owners are content to remain small). While studying SMEs is not as popular as investigating large businesses, there are studies that provide insight into the current practice of employee communication in SMEs.

In smaller businesses, staff loyalty and responsibility are enhanced by informal relationships, and employee feedback is strongly encouraged. However, to circumvent inconsistencies, policies should assume a written form.

Rainnie (1989) acknowledges that among the challenges of employee communication in small businesses are autocratic management styles, "team spirit" that leads to group think, and common characteristics of entrepreneurship, such as individualism and independence, which are not conducive to healthy, vertical communication.

The management style used by small business owners and managers will influence the success of organizational communication. In a classic work of small business management, researchers (Goss, 1991; Broom, Longenecker, & Moore, 1983) suggest that the more collaborative the work environment, the less conflict and greater employee satisfaction and retention. Sharing power with employees is a delicate balance, since the ultimate responsibility for the business rests with the manager or owner.

In employee communication, small enterprise has an advantage over larger businesses because of its ability to deliver face-to-face communication (Rimler & Humphreys, 1980; Matlay, 1999). In a study of employee satisfaction, Goldfarb Consultants (1999) found that 44 percent of most satisfied employees were in small businesses. Communication between management and staff ranked among the most influential factors correlated to overall job satisfaction.

In a British study of the relationship between employee involvement and small businesses' financial performance, the Policy Studies Institute (1998) reported that small businesses perform better when they involve employees in the business through direct communication and consultation. Smaller businesses can adopt communication practices at relatively low cost, whereas larger businesses must resort to more formal and expensive methods of employee involvement to benefit financially.

A study of the influence of internal and external factors on employee relations practices in small businesses in Ireland (MacMahon, 1996) reported that 67 percent of the small business owners assumed personal responsibility for personnel management. All of the companies exhibited centralized decision making, a simple organizational structure and a tendency to select employees based on their ability to "fit in." Communication practices were described as flexible and informal. Twenty-five percent of the sample reported no formal established method of communication. Structured methods were viewed as a threat to the employment relationship and capable of drawing attention to power inequities that are otherwise unchallenged. However, this lack of "personal distance" between management and employees could potentially result in issues being taken much more personally. Similarly, performance evaluations were viewed as counterproductive. MacMahon (1996) reported that incentive programs that could increase productivity and profitability were hampered by external factors, like competition with larger businesses.

The bottom line: For small to medium-sized businesses, employee communication practices must add value to the business direction for resources to be well spent. Sometimes using a few communication tools well is more effective than using the entire gamut of communication vehicles and overwhelming employees with choices and messages (Holland, 2001).

A number of companies and organizations provide advice on employee communication practices through web sites that cater to small and medium-sized businesses, such as Microsoft's Small Business Center, Business Know How, Workforce Week Management and Small Business School (to name a few). These web sites serve as resources and provide tools for small businesses that include employee handbook templates, policy and procedural manuals, labor law publications, salary scales, business plans and case studies of business success, to list a few.

CONCLUSIONS OF LITERATURE REVIEW / Human resource specialists, consultants and social scientists alike agree that positive employee relations, including effective communication programs and practices, are central to productivity and to subsequent business success.

Connecting organizational communication to the company bottom line and business goal achievement is a key characteristic of organizational cultures that value information sharing and communication.

If a major concern for small business today is pursuing a strategy that creates a sense of purpose and motivation among employees in order to create company value and growth, then a culture of communication founded on sound communication planning to align employees with the business objectives is necessary.

Using an employee communication and personnel management specialist as soon as profits permit is advised based on the assertion that as the size of the company grows so do problems related to employee communication.

The primary aim of this study, linking communication practices with greater productivity and profitability for small businesses, is significantly informed by existing literature of the discipline and practice. The survey results discussed in the following chapters indicate that small to medium-sized companies need to pay greater attention to making the connection between communications that affect employee behaviors and maximize the business goals and the bottom line.

CHAPTER 4 / Findings and Discussion

Small business owners and managers are experts in their industries; many are entrepreneurs who define themselves by the success of their business and the loyalty of their employees—a group of individuals whose productivity is often the measure of the business' success. They know that employees are their greatest asset, yet communications within the business can be taken for granted because, at its foundation, communication is an intangible variable that happens spontaneously and constantly throughout the operation. With so many other aspects of the company to manage, organizational leaders do not have the time to concentrate on perfecting or initiating emerging practices. To use a cliché, when it comes to internal communication, it can be difficult to see the forest for the trees.

"Being too busy to develop new working practices is a problem that affects smaller businesses in particular" (Flexibility, 2007). Small businesses are successful in spite of themselves. With fewer resources at their disposal, SME owners and managers must be creative in solving business challenges. They often engage the expertise of consultants to initiate new processes and improve the business. With this in mind, SME owners also need to engage the expertise of communication professionals (consultants or in-house staff) to assess (audit) and improve internal communication with the ultimate goal of reaching strategic business objectives.

It is apparent from the survey responses of SME owners/managers that they appreciate the contributions that employee communication practices make to the successful operation of their businesses. The lack of measurement and knowledge of emerging strategies may be interpreted as an area for improvement. Small to medium-sized enterprises have the opportunity to use employee communication practices to increase employee engagement and maximize business successes as evidenced by the commentary in the literature review and the results of the survey responses.

Employee loyalty, productivity, engagement and retention are all variables identified as responsible for contributing to business success. Internal organizational communication contributes to these concepts and ultimately the success of SMEs. Formal, planned employee communications can be a hard sell to SME owners and managers because of their entrepreneurial, independent styles and the perception that formal internal communication activities mean an expenditure of resources. But this doesn't have to be the case.

Culture, brand and employee engagement are concepts that die on the boardroom table if not communicated and internalized by employees and management alike. Successful companies, regardless of size, have found a way to effectively and efficiently communicate these concepts to employees, along with the roles employees play in the company's success.

This research project aimed to identify current and emerging employee communication practices and to address the impact of effective internal communication on small businesses.

The primary research questions were:

- What are the common employee communication practices among small businesses?
- What are the emerging employee communication practices among small businesses?
- What is the cost-effectiveness of communication practices in terms of impact on productivity and profitability for small businesses?
- What is the organizational impact (on employee retention, business growth, etc.) of employee communication practices on small businesses?

From the survey results, the following findings are apparent:

- Direct, face-to-face employee communication practices are identified by respondents as the most valuable for building employee engagement and increasing productivity.
- Electronic communication strategies are becoming more valuable to small businesses but remain an emerging practice for most.
- Many small to medium-sized businesses do not have a dedicated budget for communication.
- Many SMEs do not have a strategic communication plan that includes internal communication.
- A large proportion of the businesses surveyed did not measure the effects of employee communication tactics on their profitability.
- Because small to medium-sized businesses do not measure communication effects, there is little direct evidence to connect communication activities to return on investment.

Owner/manager commentary from the in-depth interviews conducted with small businesses elicited the following:

- Positive relationships between owners and managers, defined by communication practices, were credited for employee engagement and productivity.
- Small businesses rely more heavily than larger businesses on face-to-face communication practices due to their small populations and the proximity of their employees to one another.
- Electronic and print communication practices supplement and reinforce the messages and face-to-face communication exchanges.
- The growing pains of expanding in employee population or the addition of multiple locations increase SMEs' need for more formal and planned internal communication practices. This can be frustrating for organizations that want to maintain the "feel" and spontaneity of the small organization. These growing organizations need to plan internal communication more than ever: to ensure that messages are delivered and received in a common manner across the organization, and to identify and confront any barriers to understanding and reaching company goals before they become problems.

WHAT ARE THE COMMON EMPLOYEE COMMUNICATION PRACTICES AMONG SMALL BUSINESSES? / Common employee communication practices for small to medium-sized enterprises include a wide array of tools, from face-to-face methods to printed material to electronic communication. For many SMEs, a combination of practices works best to reach employees and provide opportunities for two-way communication between owners and employees.

Face-to-face, direct communication was the most cited form of communication used by small businesses for communicating with employees. The majority of respondents (86.9 percent) currently use face-to-face communication as a method of employee communication. Another 80.8 percent currently have an open door policy in place, 79.1 percent use management meetings and 76.7 percent use staff meetings. Staff advocates are currently the least used face-to-face communication practice (28.6 percent), followed by employee forums (41.7 percent) and informal gatherings (47.1 percent); however at least 10 percent of respondents plan to use one or more of these practices in the future.

USE OF IN-PERSON PRACTICES

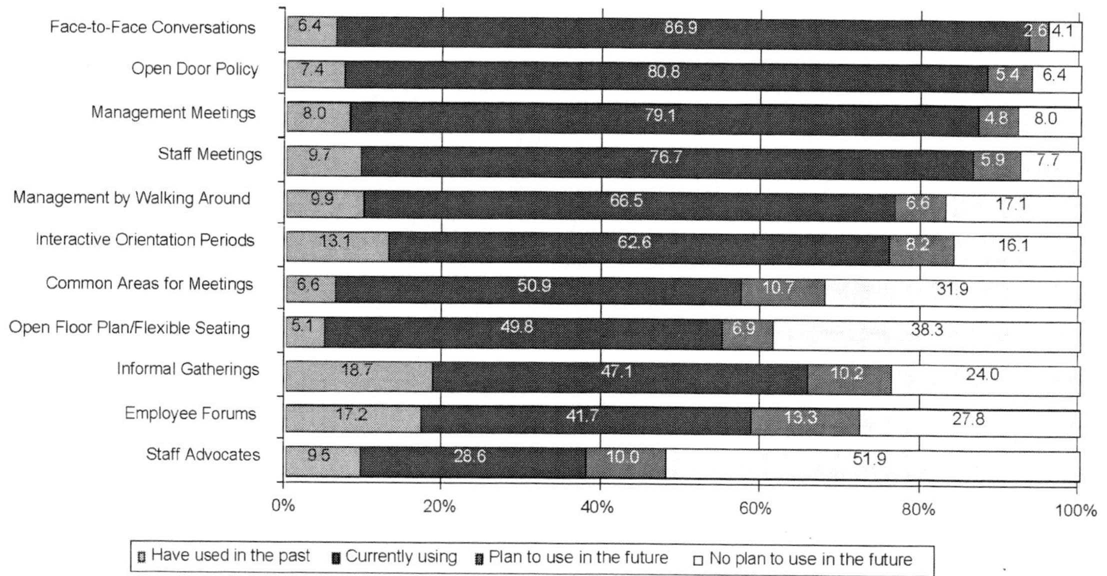

The Fisher Center for Real Estate and Urban Economics (UC Berkeley, 2002) holds inclusive weekly meetings for constructive feedback and social interaction among management and staff. "Fridays at Four" is credited with building strong working relationships, fostering an understanding of individual working styles and providing feedback in a safe, non-recriminating environment. Teamwork and a sense of community are enhanced, and morale and relationships between management and staff are improved.

The use of in-person communication practices by employee population was fairly consistent, with companies with more than 200 employees being more likely than those with fewer employees to use all forms of in-person communication practices, except for informal gatherings (which companies with up to 50 employees are most likely to use) and staff advocates (which companies with 51 to 200 employees are most likely to use).

IN-PERSON USAGE BY NUMBER OF EMPLOYEES

Usage		Number of Employees: Up to 50	51 to 200	More than 200	Total
Interactive Orientation Periods	Number	296	163	147	606
	% Currently Use	54.4%	66.9%	75.5%	62.9%
Face-to-Face Conversations	Number	296	163	147	606
	% Currently Use	84.8%	87.1%	92.5%	87.3%
Management Meetings	Number	296	163	147	606
	% Currently Use	69.6%	84.0%	94.6%	79.5%
Staff Meetings	Number	296	163	147	606
	% Currently Use	70.3%	80.4%	87.1%	77.1%
Employee Forums	Number	296	163	147	606
	% Currently Use	36.1%	44.8%	50.3%	41.9%
Informal Gatherings	Number	296	163	147	606
	% Currently Use	50.0%	43.6%	46.3%	47.4%
Management by Walking Around	Number	296	163	147	606
	% Currently Use	63.2%	68.7%	72.1%	66.8%
Open Door Policy	Number	296	163	147	606
	% Currently Use	76.7%	82.8%	88.4%	81.2%
Staff Advocates	Number	296	163	147	606
	% Currently Use	24.7%	33.1%	32.0%	28.7%
Common Areas for Meetings	Number	296	163	147	606
	% Currently Use	52.7%	49.7%	49.7%	51.2%
Open Floor Plan	Number	296	163	147	606
	% Currently Use	53.0%	49.1%	44.9%	50.0%

In terms of usage by type of company, partnerships are more likely than other types of companies to use all forms of in-person communication, except for management meetings, management by walking around, employee forums and an open door policy (which are more likely to be used by corporations) and staff advocates (which "other" types of companies are most likely to use).

IN-PERSON USAGE BY TYPE OF COMPANY

Usage		Type of Company				
		Proprietorship	Partnership	Corporation	Other	Total
Interactive Orientation Periods	Number	107	97	365	40	609
	% Currently Use	49.5%	69.1%	66.3%	47.5%	62.6%
Face-to-Face Conversations	Number	107	97	365	40	609
	% Currently Use	75.7%	90.7%	89.6%	82.5%	86.9%
Management Meetings	Number	107	97	365	40	609
	% Currently Use	63.6%	82.5%	84.4%	65.0%	79.1%
Staff Meetings	Number	107	97	365	40	609
	% Currently Use	65.4%	85.6%	79.2%	62.5%	76.7%
Employee Forums	Number	107	97	365	40	609
	% Currently Use	34.6%	39.2%	44.9%	37.5%	41.7%
Informal Gatherings	Number	107	97	365	40	609
	% Currently Use	51.4%	53.6%	44.9%	40.0%	47.1%
Management by Walking Around	Number	107	97	365	40	609
	% Currently Use	54.2%	68.0%	70.7%	57.5%	66.5%
Open Door Policy	Number	107	97	365	40	609
	% Currently Use	61.7%	83.5%	86.8%	70.0%	80.8%
Staff Advocates	Number	107	97	365	40	609
	% Currently Use	27.1%	26.8%	29.3%	30.0%	28.6%
Common Area for Meetings	Number	107	97	365	40	609
	% Currently Use	48.6%	68.0%	49.0%	32.5%	50.9%
Open Floor Plan	Number	107	97	365	40	609
	% Currently Use	42.1%	69.1%	49.3%	27.5%	49.8%

For this study, printed communication practices include typical print publications and manuals; hard copy interactive systems, such as suggestion systems, grievance procedures and letters; and management practices that include sharing printed company documents with employees (open book management practices).

The majority of respondents currently use traditional printed employee communication tools, i.e., manuals, handbooks, newspapers, newsletters and magazines. The percentage of respondents currently using printed publications, such as manuals or employee handbooks, as a method of employee communication, was 61.4 percent. The percentage currently using open book management was 41.1 percent. The percentage currently using printed publications, such as newspapers or magazines, was 35.8 percent. The least used print vehicles for employee communication are anonymous suggestion systems (22 percent) and letters mailed to employees' homes (22.5 percent).

USE OF PRINT PRACTICES

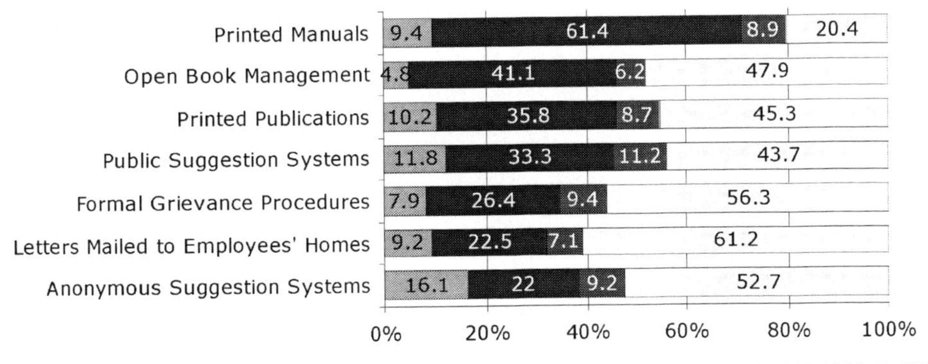

In general, usage of print communication practices increases with the size of an organization. Companies with more than 200 employees are also more likely than those with fewer employees to use all of the print communication practices, with the exception of anonymous and public suggestion systems, which companies with 51 to 200 employees are most likely to use.

PRINT USAGE BY NUMBER OF EMPLOYEES

Usage		Number of Employees			
		Up to 50	51 to 200	More than 200	Total
Formal Grievance Procedures	Number	296	163	147	606
	% Currently Use	14.2%	35.0%	42.2%	26.6%
Anonymous Suggestion Systems	Number	296	163	147	606
	% Currently Use	10.8%	34.4%	31.3%	22.1%
Public Suggestion Systems	Number	296	163	147	606
	% Currently Use	27.4%	42.9%	35.4%	33.5%
Printed Publications	Number	296	163	147	606
	% Currently Use	20.9%	46.0%	55.1%	36.0%
Letters Mailed to Employees' Homes	Number	296	163	147	606
	% Currently Use	11.1%	29.4%	38.1%	22.6%
Open Book Management	Number	296	163	147	606
	% Currently Use	31.8%	47.9%	53.1%	41.3%
Printed Manuals	Number	296	163	147	606
	% Currently Use	47.0%	74.2%	77.6%	61.7%

Companies in the manufacturing sector are more likely than those in other sectors to use public suggestion systems, printed publications, letters mailed to employees' homes and printed manuals. Companies in the health care sector are most likely to use formal grievance procedures, while those in the finance sector are most likely to use open book management. Companies in the construction and health care sector were both most likely (at 43.5 percent) to use anonymous suggestion systems.

PRINT USAGE BY SECTOR

Usage		Sector								
		Profession-al/Scienti-fic/Technical	Manufac-turing	Finance	Infor-mation Services	Retail	Construc-tion	Health Care	Other	Total
Formal Grievance Procedures	Number	232	67	53	52	39	23	23	120	609
	% Currently Use	16.8%	43.3%	30.2%	25.0%	25.6%	21.7%	56.5%	30.0%	26.4%
Anonymous Suggestion Systems	Number	232	67	53	52	39	23	23	120	609
	% Currently Use	15.5%	31.3%	22.6%	15.4%	33.3%	43.5%	43.5%	20.0%	22.0%
Public Suggestion Systems	Number	232	67	53	52	39	23	23	120	609
	% Currently Use	31.5%	53.7%	32.1%	23.1%	35.9%	34.8%	43.5%	27.5%	33.3%
Printed Publications	Number	232	67	53	52	39	23	23	120	609
	% Currently Use	28.4%	49.3%	43.4%	32.7%	30.8%	43.5%	43.5%	39.2%	35.8%
Letters Mailed to Employees' Homes	Number	232	67	53	52	39	23	23	120	609
	% Currently Use	17.7%	38.8%	15.1%	17.3%	28.2%	30.4%	34.8%	22.5%	22.5%
Open Book Manage-ment	Number	232	67	53	52	39	23	23	120	609
	% Currently Use	37.9%	46.3%	58.5%	44.2%	43.6%	47.8%	39.1%	33.3%	41.1%
Printed Manuals	Number	232	67	53	52	39	23	23	120	609
	% Currently Use	55.6%	82.1%	71.7%	51.9%	71.8%	52.2%	73.9%	56.7%	61.4%

According to survey respondents, e-mail is currently the most commonly used electronic communication practice (78.5 percent), followed by portable devices such as cell phones or laptops (75.5 percent) and a company web site (74.5 percent). The least used electronic communication practices are employee blogs (9.4 percent) and telephone hotlines (11.8 percent).

USE OF ELECTRONIC PRACTICES

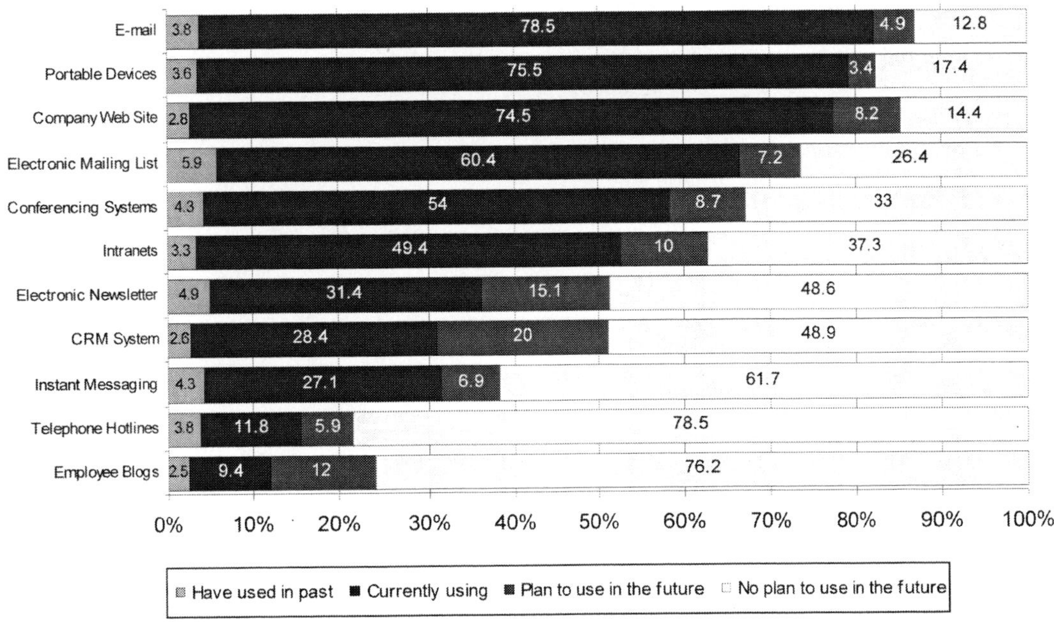

Companies with more than 200 employees are, on the whole, more likely than companies with fewer employees to use all electronic communication practices, with the exception of employee blogs, instant messaging and CRM systems, which companies with 51 to 200 employees are most likely to use.

ELECTRONIC COMMUNICATION USAGE BY NUMBER OF EMPLOYEES

Usage		Number of Employees: Up to 50	51 to 200	More than 200	Total
Electronic Mailing List	Number	296	163	147	606
	% Currently Use	48.0%	66.3%	80.3%	60.7%
Electronic Newsletter	Number	296	163	147	606
	% Currently Use	17.6%	41.1%	49.0%	31.5%
Telephone Hotlines	Number	296	163	147	606
	% Currently Use	7.4%	9.2%	23.8%	11.9%
E-mail	Number	296	163	147	606
	% Currently Use	72.0%	81.6%	89.8%	78.9%
Employee Blogs	Number	296	163	147	606
	% Currently Use	7.1%	13.5%	9.5%	9.4%
Instant Messaging	Number	296	163	147	606
	% Currently Use	25.0%	33.7%	24.5%	27.2%
Intranets	Number	296	163	147	606
	% Currently Use	29.7%	58.9%	79.6%	49.7%
Company Web Site	Number	296	163	147	606
	% Currently Use	65.2%	80.4%	88.4%	74.9%
CRM System	Number	296	163	147	606
	% Currently Use	19.9%	36.8%	36.7%	28.5%
Conferencing Systems	Number	296	163	147	606
	% Currently Use	41.2%	63.8%	70.1%	54.3%
Portable Devices	Number	296	163	147	606
	% Currently Use	67.2%	81.6%	87.1%	75.9%

ATX Forms in Caribou, Maine, holds weekly video conferences they call Idea Labs that link employees to the company's second office 1,700 miles away in Fort Pierce, Florida. The sessions host diverse subject matter and were created to improve communication among staff. The tax-software company, with a staff of 150, also hosts an intranet that houses human resources information and the Idea Labs archives. The company's CEO maintains that the Idea Labs, along with providing a wealth of practical and problem-solving suggestions, create a positive environment, which accounts for an extraordinarily low turnover rate—0 percent for programmers and less than 5 percent for all other staff (Callaway, 2001).

The survey analysis shows more commonalities than differences in the comparison of communication practices across international cultures. Analyzing the common practices by usage and the location of the main office indicates the following commonalities and differences:

- Face-to-face conversations were rated highest by respondents in the U.S., Canada and Europe.
- An open door policy and management meetings were rated the second and third most used in-person communication methods.
- The least used in-person methods were staff advocates and employee forums.

- Organizations based in Canada are more likely than those in Europe and the U.S. to currently use open book management and printed publications. Organizations based in the U.S. are more likely than those in Canada and Europe to currently use letters mailed to employees' homes, anonymous and public suggestion systems, and formal grievance procedures.

EMPLOYEE COMMUNICATION STRATEGIES MAKE A DIFFERENCE

Respondents said the following employee communication strategies made a difference in their businesses:

- Approximately one quarter said that open communication has made a difference.
- Seventeen percent said personal and face-to-face communication has made a difference.
- Those who said meetings have made a difference totaled 16.3 percent.
- Those who said that e-mail, video or telecommunications have really made a difference in their business totaled 12.9 percent.

COMMUNICATION STRATEGY THAT HAS MADE THE BIGGEST DIFFERENCE

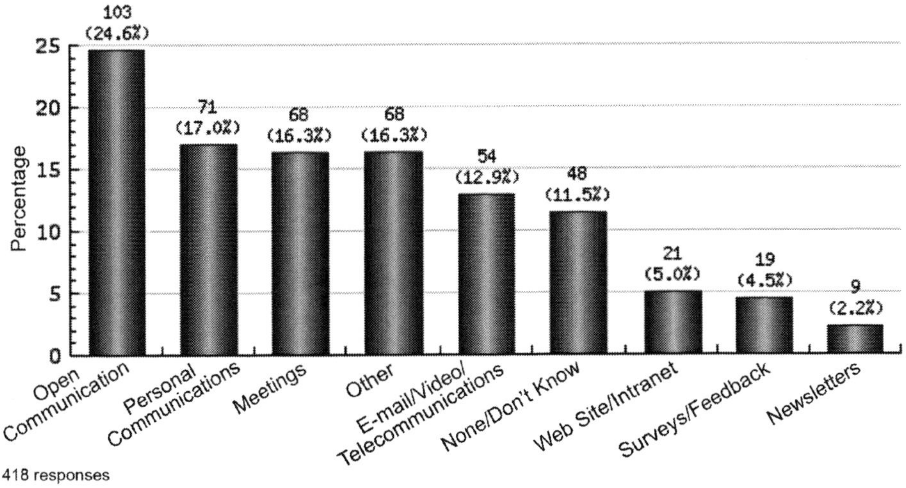

418 responses

Open communication is credited with increasing productivity and morale as well as creating more responsiveness among employees. "Open discussion of internal and client issues in a team environment…makes everyone feel they are 'in this together.' Everyone takes ownership and understands the challenges of a small consulting organization."

Respondents said that face-to-face communication helps "to surface issues, leads to discussion of potential solutions to issues, allows for an exchange of ideas and just boosts morale...employees seek out the opportunities." Face-to-face communication is credited with improving teamwork: "The more we share the work we are doing, the better service we provide to our clients."

Regular meetings between managers and employees provide a forum for the discussion of issues and the exchange of ideas. "Top-down and bottom-up communications allow decisions to be made faster and collectively." Regular meetings are reported to have "a positive impact on business; the employees are the front line and they know where to make changes for the better."

Emerging strategies like e-mail, video and telecommunications are credited with providing more timely and targeted communications. "Weekly e-mail and quarterly company updates keep people connected to the company and each other while assessing our progress to date and what to expect moving forward."

Additionally, other employee communication strategies that respondents raised as valuable included regular new employee orientation sessions and some traditional print communication tools like memos used to remind units of important information. One respondent commented, "Our company is growing so rapidly, it is vital that new employees are introduced to the company, its culture and corporate goals at the start of their employment."

WHAT ARE EMERGING EMPLOYEE COMMUNICATION PRACTICES AMONG SMALL BUSINESSES? / The following table details the most commonly used emerging employee communication practices as reported by survey respondents across the categories of in-person, print and electronic practices. The top five practices included:

- Common areas for meetings (50.9 percent)
- Open floor plan (49.8 percent)
- Intranets (49.4 percent)
- Informal gatherings (47.1 percent)
- Employee forums (41.7 percent)

Interestingly, none of the emerging practices are print communication practices.

Emerging practices that respondents indicated as having a positive impact on productivity included employee forums (70.1 percent), informal gatherings (69.3 percent), instant messaging (68.5 percent), intranets (67.4 percent) and staff advocates (65.5 percent).

In contributions to profitability, emerging practices scores were as follows. The top five practices that have a positive impact on profitability were: employee blogs (56.1 percent), staff advocates (52.3 percent), instant messaging (50.9 percent), intranets (50.5 percent) and employee forums (49.6 percent).

Respondents indicated that emerging practices have the greatest impact on employee behavior (retention and engagement). The top strategies included informal gatherings (80.5 percent), electronic newsletters (75.4 percent), employee forums (75.2 percent), common areas for meetings (71 percent) and instant messaging (70.3 percent).

		% Positive Impact on:		
Practice	% who used	Productivity	Profitability	Employee Behavior
Common Areas for Meetings	50.9	62.6	43.9	71
Open Floor Plan	49.8	61.1	44.6	69.3
Intranets	49.4	67.4	50.5	68.4
Informal Gatherings	47.1	69.3	47.7	80.5
Employee Forums	41.7	70.1	49.6	75.2
Electronic Newsletter	31.4	65.4	49.2	75.4
Staff Advocates	28.6	65.5	52.3	62.1
Instant Messaging	27.1	68.5	50.9	70.3
Telephone Hotline	11.8	51.4	45.8	55.6
Employee Blogs	9.4	54.4	56.1	59.6

E-mail, web sites, intranet sites, blogs and other forms of electronic communication are popular communication tools in the 21st century. From the literature review, it is apparent that large businesses are recognizing the value of these immediate and often virtual interpersonal forms of communication.

Electronic communications (i.e., e-mail) are cited as common employee communication practices, yet many small to medium-sized enterprises have only just begun to explore the variety of communication issues that can be addressed by intranets, virtual meeting environments, blogs and social media (Web 2.0). Other emerging practices for SMEs include some practices that are commonplace for larger businesses, such as employee forums, hotlines, internal branding activities and cultural sensitivities.

Although electronic communication practices are acknowledged by survey respondents as common communication practices on behalf of their organizations, these practices are not rated as highly as other forms of communication. These findings may be evidence that these communication strategies are still emerging for small businesses.

As cited in the literature, the immediacy and interpersonal nature of electronic communications can be a double-edged sword. Employees and customers alike expect timely information and immediate responses to e-mails and other exchanges prompted by intranet sites and public, company web sites. Failure to recognize the importance of the qualities and the commitment that these communication strategies require may be concerns for small businesses whose resources are already stretched thin across other business functions. Yet these electronic media can also be an asset to small businesses for timely distribution of information to all employees regardless of their location.

Electronic media are also being used more frequently as a conduit for more traditional company communication practices, such as the company newsletter and human resource programs like orientations and town hall meetings. In a 2003 survey (Sauer, 2004), only 5 percent of respondents said they received a company e-newsletter. By 2006, 50 percent of companies reported the use of electronic newsletters to reach employees.

Pinnacle Decision Systems Inc., a software company in Middleton, Connecticut, hosts an intranet web site for employees that is designed to inform new hires about policies, procedures and company information (Buchanan, 1999). It also provides a mechanism for new staff to submit orders for business cards, name plates and T-shirts. The web site was introduced following a rapid employee expansion of approximately 40 percent in one year. Dubbed "HQ," and heralded as the conduit for the majority of Pinnacle's routine operations, the site features a brainstorming area for employees' ideas; an open book management page where financial figures are shared with staff; and announcement, classifieds, photo gallery and suggestion sections.

As small businesses grow in size and locations, town hall meetings and employee forums may become more appealing options for maintaining two-way communication. These processes can be facilitated in a virtual environment but are best conducted in person to build employee trust and engagement.

While the survey results show that informal gatherings are not as widely used by SMEs as by larger organizations, such staff events can be used for training and building internal brand values. Since small businesses are just that—small—such events are less costly to provide and have the potential to develop social networks within the company that increase both employee satisfaction and productivity.

The world is becoming a single unified marketplace. The old notion that English is the international language of business is being supplanted in the face of issues of diversity and multiculturalism that large and small companies address on a daily basis. To be competitive in the international marketplace, small businesses should be considering the positive impact of diversity and multiculturalism sensitivity training for employees.

As small businesses grow in size, the ergonomics of the workplace or work space design may become a growing concern as well. Designing work spaces that contribute to productivity and collaboration between employees can improve employee job satisfaction as well as simple productivity and use of resources. SME owners and managers are cautioned to also consider employees' needs for private or quiet space that also contributes to their productivity.

WHAT IS THE COST-EFFECTIVENESS OF COMMUNICATION PRACTICES IN TERMS OF IMPACT ON PRODUCTIVITY AND PROFITABILITY FOR SMALL BUSINESSES? / The respondents indicated that the practices cited previously are used because they are perceived as cost-effective. There is no room for wasting resources in small organizations. A mix of face-to-face, print and electronic practices can meet the needs of a diverse employee population.

COST-EFFECTIVENESS

The survey respondents identified the following employee communication practices as cost-effective:

- **In-person practices:**
  - Face-to-face conversations (92.2 percent)
  - Staff meetings (90.1 percent)
  - Management meetings (89.9 percent)
  - Management by walking around (89.9 percent)
  - Open door policy (89.6 percent)
  - Informal gatherings (89.5 percent)
- **Print practices:**
  - Public suggestions systems (82.7 percent)
  - Open book management (79.6 percent)
  - Printed manuals (77.5 percent)
  - Printed publications (74.8 percent)
- **Electronic practices:**
  - E-mail (94.4 percent)
  - Electronic mailing lists (90.5 percent)
  - Electronic newsletters (89.5 percent)
  - Intranets (89.4 percent)

Respondents whose organizations have more than 200 employees are most likely to have said that most of the methods of in-person communication are somewhat or very cost-effective. Those in companies with 51 to 200 employees are most likely to rate face-to-face conversations as cost-effective. Respondents in companies with 50 or fewer employees are most likely to rate informal gatherings as cost-effective. Those in companies with up to 50 employees and over 200 employees tied in their cost-effectiveness rating for management meetings, both at 96.9 percent.

IN-PERSON COST-EFFECTIVENESS BY NUMBER OF EMPLOYEES

Cost-effectiveness		Number of Employees: Up to 50	51 to 200	More than 200	Total
Interactive Orientation Periods	Number	142	94	99	335
	% Somewhat or Very	94.4%	95.7%	98.0%	95.8%
Face-to-Face Conversations	Number	246	134	124	504
	% Somewhat or Very	96.7%	99.3%	94.4%	96.8%
Management Meetings	Number	195	130	128	453
	% Somewhat or Very	96.9%	92.3%	96.9%	95.6%
Staff Meetings	Number	203	128	118	449
	% Somewhat or Very	93.6%	92.2%	95.8%	93.8%
Employee Forums	Number	99	70	67	236
	% Somewhat or Very	91.9%	90.0%	94.0%	91.9%
Informal Gatherings	Number	145	67	59	271
	% Somewhat or Very	95.2%	94.0%	94.9%	94.8%
Management by Walking Around	Number	179	108	94	381
	% Somewhat or Very	95.5%	95.4%	95.7%	95.5%
Open Door Policy	Number	220	123	117	460
	% Somewhat or Very	95.5%	95.1%	97.4%	95.9%
Staff Advocates	Number	68	46	44	158
	% Somewhat or Very	85.3%	91.3%	93.2%	89.2%
Common Areas for Meetings	Number	146	72	65	283
	% Somewhat or Very	93.2%	93.1%	98.5%	94.3%
Open Floor Plan	Number	148	72	60	280
	% Somewhat or Very	93.9%	95.8%	100.0%	95.7%

With the exception of staff advocates, all practices scored highly in each region, from 88.9 percent to 100 percent.

IN-PERSON COST-EFFECTIVENESS BY LOCATION OF MAIN OFFICE

Cost-effectiveness		Location of Main Office				
		U.S.	Canada	Europe	Other	Total
Interactive Orientation Periods	Number	256	47	13	19	335
	% Somewhat or Very	96.1%	97.9%	92.3%	89.5%	95.8%
Face-to-Face Conversations	Number	380	79	22	23	504
	% Somewhat or Very	96.1%	100.0%	100.0%	95.7%	96.8%
Management Meetings	Number	343	66	20	24	453
	% Somewhat or Very	95.6%	97.0%	95.0%	91.7%	95.6%
Staff Meetings	Number	342	65	18	24	449
	% Somewhat or Very	93.3%	96.9%	94.4%	91.7%	93.8%
Employee Forums	Number	186	30	8	12	236
	% Somewhat or Very	91.9%	96.7%	100.0%	75.0%	91.9%
Informal Gatherings	Number	202	41	13	15	271
	% Somewhat or Very	94.1%	97.6%	100.0%	93.3%	94.8%
Management by Walking Around	Number	299	47	17	18	381
	% Somewhat or Very	95.7%	95.7%	100.0%	88.9%	95.5%
Open Door Policy	Number	349	70	19	22	460
	% Somewhat or Very	95.7%	95.7%	94.7%	100.0%	95.9%
Staff Advocates	Number	133	16	2	7	158
	% Somewhat or Very	0.9	1.0	1.0	0.9	0.9
Common Areas for Meetings	Number	219	39	12	13	283
	% Somewhat or Very	92.7%	100.0%	100.0%	100.0%	94.3%
Open Floor Plan	Number	212	39	14	15	280
	% Somewhat or Very	94.8%	100.0%	100.0%	93.3%	95.7%

Of the respondents who gave cost-effectiveness ratings for their use of print communication practices, open book management is most likely to be seen as somewhat or very cost-effective (94 percent), followed by public suggestion systems (93 percent). The practices least likely to be perceived as cost-effective are anonymous suggestion systems and letters mailed to employees' homes (84 percent each).

PRINT COST-EFFECTIVENESS

Practice	Number	Mean	95% Confidence Interval	
			Lower	Upper
Open Book Management	212	0.94	0.91	0.97
Public Suggestion Systems	181	0.93	0.89	0.97
Printed Manuals	329	0.88	0.85	0.92
Printed Publications	189	0.86	0.81	0.91
Formal Grievance Procedures	118	0.86	0.79	0.92
Anonymous Suggestion Systems	116	0.84	0.78	0.91
Letters Mailed to Employees' Homes	119	0.84	0.77	0.91

Cost-effectiveness ratings for electronic communication practices by the number of employees in an organization were quite mixed. The following practices were rated as most cost-effective by respondents in companies with more than 200 employees: electronic newsletters, employee blogs, intranets, instant messaging, CRM systems and conferencing systems. Those in companies with 51 to 200 employees rated telephone hotlines as most cost-effective, while those in organizations with up to 50 employees rated the following practices most cost-effective: electronic mailing lists, e-mail, the company web site and portable devices.

ELECTRONIC COMMUNICATION COST-EFFECTIVENESS BY NUMBER OF EMPLOYEES

Cost-effectiveness		Number of Employees: Up to 50	51 to 200	More than 200	Total
Electronic Mailing List	Number	137	98	107	342
	% Somewhat or Very	99.3%	94.9%	97.2%	97.4%
Electronic Newsletter	Number	50	65	68	183
	% Somewhat or Very	92.0%	90.8%	97.1%	93.4%
Telephone Hotlines	Number	19	14	24	57
	% Somewhat or Very	84.2%	85.7%	79.2%	82.5%
E-mail	Number	208	129	123	460
	% Somewhat or Very	98.6%	96.9%	98.4%	98.0%
Employee Blogs	Number	19	16	11	46
	% Somewhat or Very	94.7%	87.5%	100.0%	93.5%
Instant Messaging	Number	71	53	26	150
	% Somewhat or Very	95.8%	92.5%	100.0%	95.3%
Intranets	Number	79	93	107	279
	% Somewhat or Very	96.2%	92.5%	100.0%	96.4%
Company Web Site	Number	176	120	114	410
	% Somewhat or Very	98.9%	95.8%	98.2%	97.8%
CRM System	Number	54	57	45	156
	% Somewhat or Very	98.1%	91.2%	100.0%	96.2%
Conferencing Systems	Number	114	95	88	297
	% Somewhat or Very	96.5%	94.7%	100.0%	97.0%
Portable Devices	Number	183	123	109	415
	% Somewhat or Very	97.8%	94.3%	97.2%	96.6%

Cost-effectiveness ratings according to type of company were also quite mixed. Proprietorships were most likely to rate electronic mailing lists, telephone hotlines, e-mail, intranets and the company web site as cost-effective. Corporations were most likely to rate conferencing systems as cost-effective. Partnerships and corporations both gave the highest cost-effectiveness ratings for electronic newsletters, proprietorships and corporations both gave the highest cost-effectiveness ratings for employee blogs, and proprietorships and partnerships both gave the highest cost-effectiveness ratings for instant messaging and CRM systems.

ELECTRONIC COMMUNICATION COST-EFFECTIVENESS BY TYPE OF COMPANY

Cost-effectiveness		Type of Company				
		Proprietorship	Partnership	Corporation	Other	Total
Electronic Mailing List	Number	39	66	215	22	342
	% Somewhat or Very	100.0%	97.0%	97.2%	95.5%	97.4%
Electronic Newsletter	Number	24	30	119	10	183
	% Somewhat or Very	91.7%	93.3%	93.3%	100.0%	93.4%
Telephone Hotlines	Number	8	13	33	3	57
	% Somewhat or Very	87.5%	76.9%	84.8%	66.7%	82.5%
E-mail	Number	65	78	290	27	460
	% Somewhat or Very	98.5%	97.4%	97.9%	100.0%	98.0%
Employee Blogs	Number	8	12	24	2	46
	% Somewhat or Very	100.0%	91.7%	100.0%	0.0%	93.5%
Instant Messaging	Number	28	28	86	8	150
	% Somewhat or Very	96.4%	96.4%	94.2%	100.0%	95.3%
Intranets	Number	32	43	188	16	279
	% Somewhat or Very	96.9%	95.3%	96.3%	100.0%	96.4%
Company Web Site	Number	52	66	267	25	410
	% Somewhat or Very	100.0%	98.5%	97.4%	96.0%	97.8%
CRM System	Number	18	24	106	8	156
	% Somewhat or Very	100.0%	100.0%	94.3%	100.0%	96.2%
Conferencing Systems	Number	34	44	202	17	297
	% Somewhat or Very	97.1%	95.5%	97.0%	100.0%	97.0%
Portable Devices	Number	52	75	264	24	415
	% Somewhat or Very	98.1%	100.0%	95.1%	100.0%	96.6%

By far, face-to-face practices and electronic practices were scored the highest for cost-effectiveness. These practices all rated highly across the categories of productivity, profitability, employee behavior (employee retention and employee engagement) and external communication.

PRODUCTIVITY

All of the face-to-face practices considered by respondents were rated highly in terms of having a positive impact on productivity, from 61.1 percent to 75.6 percent. Face-to-face conversations received the highest ratings, while open floor plans/flexible seating arrangements received the lowest ratings. Staff advocates received the highest rating for having a negative impact on productivity.

IN-PERSON IMPACT ON PRODUCTIVITY

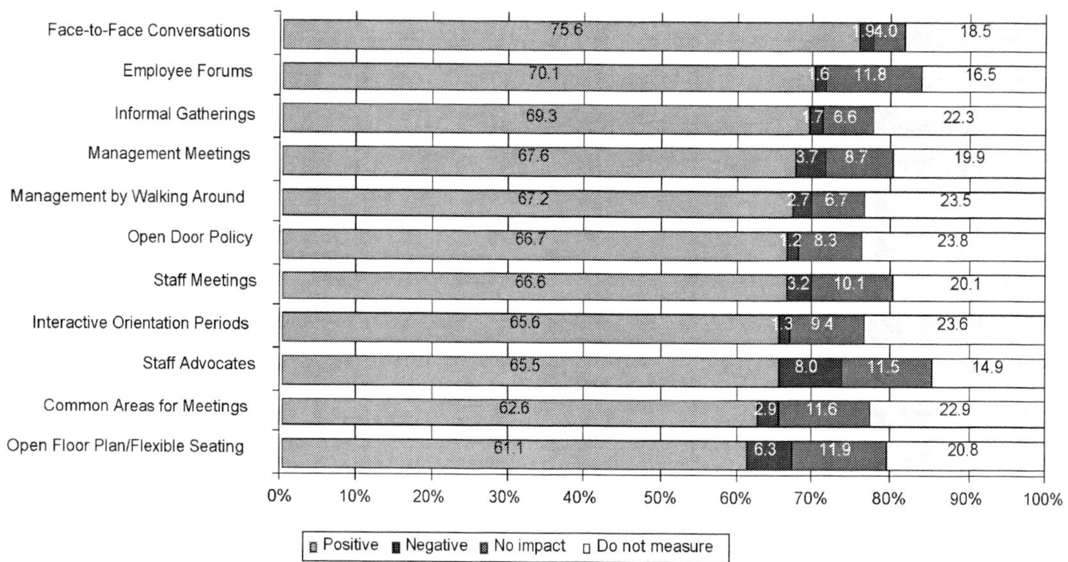

Respondents whose organizations are based in Canada are less likely than those whose companies are based elsewhere to find that in-person communication practices have a positive impact on productivity. Those respondents whose organizations are based in Europe are more likely to say that most in-person communication practices have had a positive impact on profitability.

IN-PERSON IMPACT ON PRODUCTIVITY BY LOCATION OF MAIN OFFICE

Impact on Productivity		Location of Main Office				
		U.S.	Canada	Europe	Other	Total
Interactive Orientation Periods	Number	224	37	12	18	291
	% Positive	87.5%	86.5%	75.0%	72.2%	85.9%
Face-to-Face Conversations	Number	330	61	18	22	431
	% Positive	91.5%	95.1%	100.0%	100.0%	92.8%
Management Meetings	Number	290	58	15	23	386
	% Positive	84.5%	86.2%	73.3%	87.0%	84.5%
Staff Meetings	Number	285	55	12	21	373
	% Positive	82.8%	85.5%	100.0%	76.2%	83.4%
Employee Forums	Number	166	30	6	10	212
	% Positive	85.5%	80.0%	83.3%	70.0%	84.0%
Informal Gatherings	Number	165	34	11	13	223
	% Positive	86.7%	97.1%	100.0%	92.3%	89.2%
Management by Walking Around	Number	246	39	12	13	310
	% Positive	87.0%	87.2%	100.0%	92.3%	87.7%
Open Door Policy	Number	291	52	13	19	375
	% Positive	88.7%	86.5%	84.6%	73.7%	87.5%
Staff Advocates	Number	120	19	1	8	148
	% Positive	79.2%	78.9%	100.0%	37.5%	77.0%
Common Areas for Meetings	Number	187	33	10	9	239
	% Positive	78.1%	87.9%	100.0%	100.0%	81.2%
Open Floor Plan	Number	186	30	12	12	240
	% Positive	76.9%	76.7%	75.0%	83.3%	77.1%

Respondents rated print practices significantly lower than in-person practices in terms of having a positive impact on productivity. Public suggestion systems received the highest ratings, while formal grievance procedures received the lowest ratings.

PRINT IMPACT ON PRODUCTIVITY

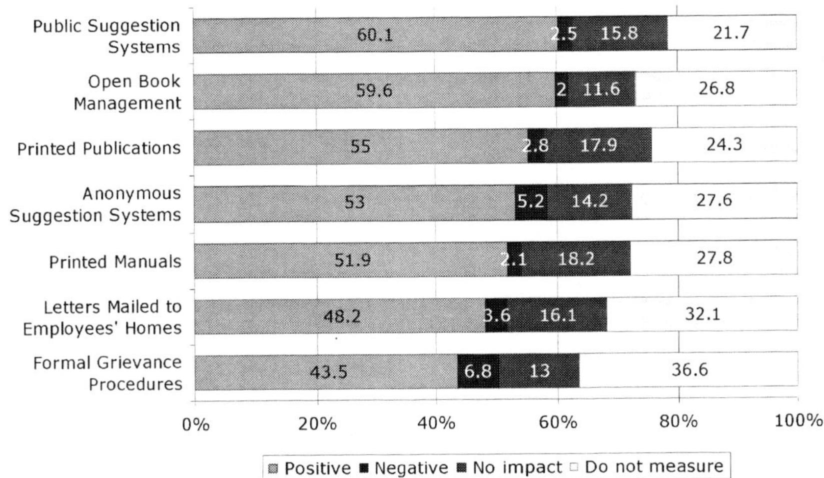

When looking only at those who measured the impact of each print communication practice on productivity, open book management is most likely to have a positive impact (81 percent), followed by public suggestion systems (77 percent). At 69 percent, formal grievance procedures are least likely to have a positive impact on productivity.

PRINT IMPACT ON PRODUCTIVITY AMONG ORGANIZATIONS THAT MEASURE THE IMPACT OF PRINT COMMUNICATION PRACTICES

Practice	Number	Mean	95% Confidence Interval	
			Lower	Upper
Open Book Management	183	0.81	0.76	0.87
Public Suggestion Systems	159	0.77	0.70	0.83
Anonymous Suggestion Systems	97	0.73	0.64	0.82
Printed Publications	165	0.73	0.66	0.80
Printed Manuals	270	0.72	0.66	0.77
Letters Mailed to Employees' Homes	93	0.71	0.62	0.80
Formal Grievance Procedures	102	0.69	0.59	0.78

Over 50 percent of respondents indicated that each electronic practice had a positive impact on productivity. Portable devices received the highest ratings, while telephone hotlines received the lowest ratings.

ELECTRONIC COMMUNICATION IMPACT ON PRODUCTIVITY

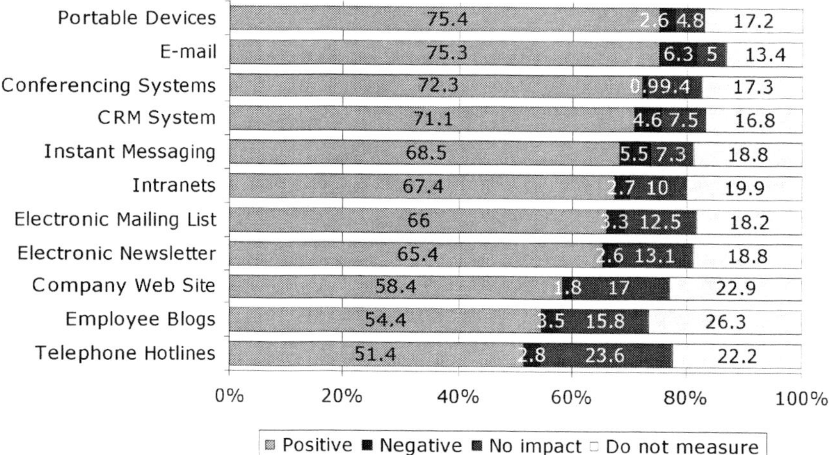

When considering only those respondents who measured the impact of their organization's electronic communication practices on productivity, portable devices were the most likely to have a positive impact (91 percent), followed by conferencing systems (88 percent) and e-mail (87 percent). Telephone hotlines are least likely to have a positive impact on productivity (66 percent).

ELECTRONIC COMMUNICATION IMPACT ON PRODUCTIVITY AMONG ORGANIZATIONS THAT MEASURE THE IMPACT OF ELECTRONIC COMMUNICATION PRACTICES

Practice	Number	Mean	95% Confidence Interval	
			Lower	Upper
Portable Devices	381	0.91	0.88	0.94
Conferencing Systems	272	0.88	0.84	0.91
E-mail	414	0.87	0.84	0.90
CRM System	144	0.85	0.80	0.91
Instant Messaging	134	0.84	0.78	0.91
Intranets	241	0.84	0.80	0.89
Electronic Mailing List	301	0.81	0.76	0.85
Electronic Newsletter	155	0.81	0.74	0.87
Company Web site	350	0.76	0.71	0.80
Employee Blogs	42	0.74	0.60	0.88
Telephone Hotlines	56	0.66	0.53	0.79

PROFITABILITY

Over half of respondents rated each of the following face-to-face practices as having a positive impact on profitability: management meetings, face-to-face conversations, staff advocates and staff meetings. The remainder of the practices received ratings of 43.1 percent to 49.6 percent, with an open door policy receiving the lowest rating.

IN-PERSON IMPACT ON PROFITABILITY

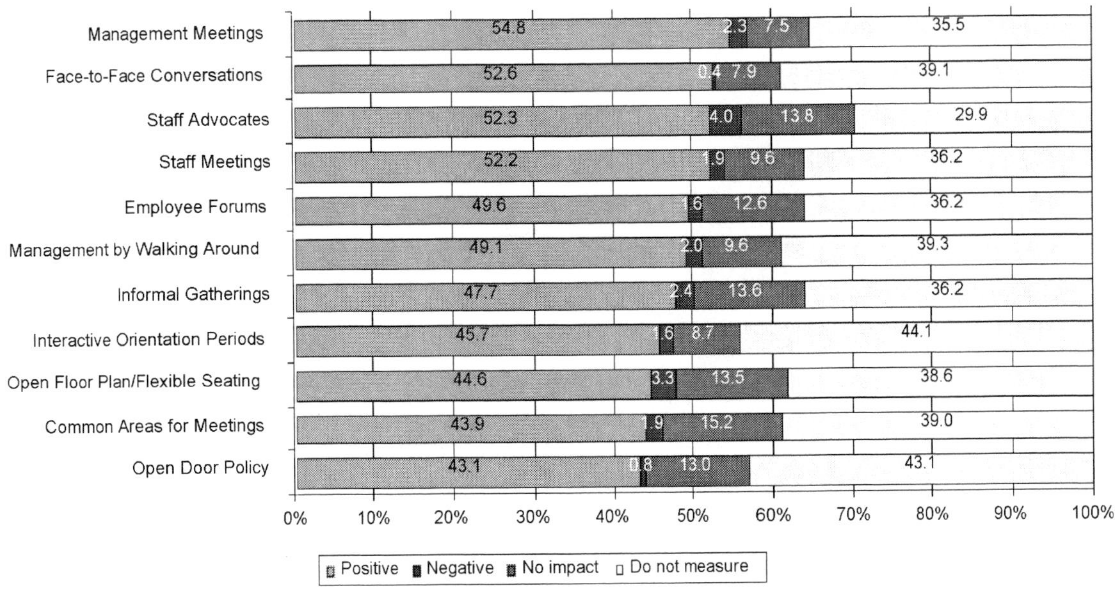

When looking only at those respondents who measured the impact of their in-person communication practices on profitability, face-to-face conversations are most likely to have a positive impact (86 percent). Respondents are also highly likely to say that management meetings have a positive impact (85 percent). More than 70 percent of those who measured the impact of each practice said that the impact was positive.

IN-PERSON IMPACT ON PROFITABILITY AMONG ORGANIZATIONS THAT MEASURE THE IMPACT OF IN-PERSON COMMUNICATION PRACTICES

Practice	Number	Mean	95% Confidence Interval	
			Lower	Upper
Face-to-Face Conversations	322	0.86	0.83	0.90
Management Meetings	311	0.85	0.81	0.89
Staff Meetings	298	0.82	0.77	0.86
Interactive Orientation Periods	213	0.82	0.76	0.87
Management by Walking Around	246	0.81	0.76	0.86
Employee Forums	162	0.78	0.71	0.84
Open Door Policy	280	0.76	0.71	0.81
Informal Gatherings	183	0.75	0.69	0.81
Staff Advocates	122	0.75	0.67	0.82
Open Floor Plan/Flexible Seating	186	0.73	0.66	0.79
Common Areas for Meetings	189	0.72	0.65	0.78

Print practices were not rated highly in terms of having a positive impact on profitability. Public suggestion systems received the highest rating at 48.8 percent, while letters mailed to employees' homes received the lowest rating at 30.7 percent.

PRINT IMPACT ON PROFITABILITY

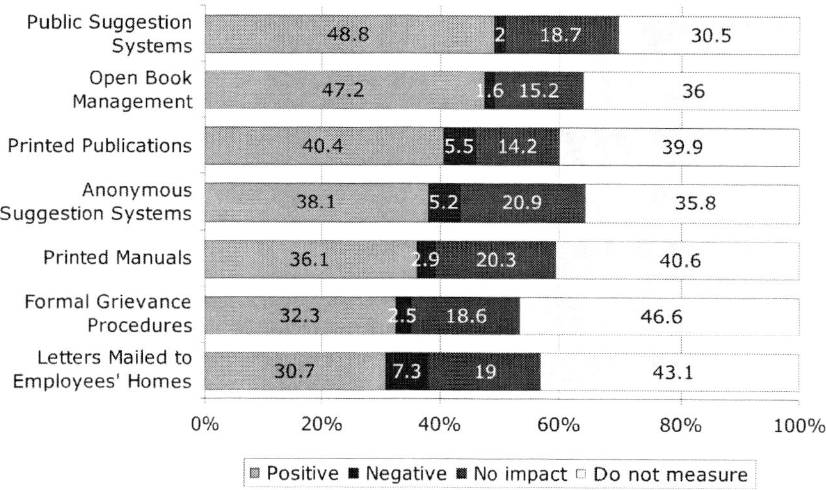

When considering only those who measured the impact of their print communication practices on profitability, open book management is the most likely to have a positive impact (74 percent), followed by public suggestion systems (70 percent). Only 54 percent of those who measured the impact of sending letters to employees' homes said that the impact was positive.

PRINT IMPACT ON PROFITABILITY AMONG ORGANIZATIONS THAT MEASURE THE IMPACT OF PRINT COMMUNICATION PRACTICES

Practice	Number	Mean	95% Confidence Interval	
			Lower	Upper
Open Book Management	160	0.74	0.67	0.81
Public Suggestion Systems	141	0.70	0.63	0.78
Printed Publications	131	0.67	0.59	0.75
Printed Manuals	222	0.61	0.54	0.67
Formal Grievance Procedures	86	0.60	0.50	0.71
Anonymous Suggestion Systems	86	0.59	0.49	0.70
Letters Mailed to Employees' Homes	78	0.54	0.43	0.65

Electronic practices scored fairly well in terms of having a positive impact on profitability. CRM systems were rated highest at 64.2 percent, while telephone hotlines were rated lowest at 45.8 percent.

ELECTRONIC COMMUNICATION IMPACT ON PROFITABILITY

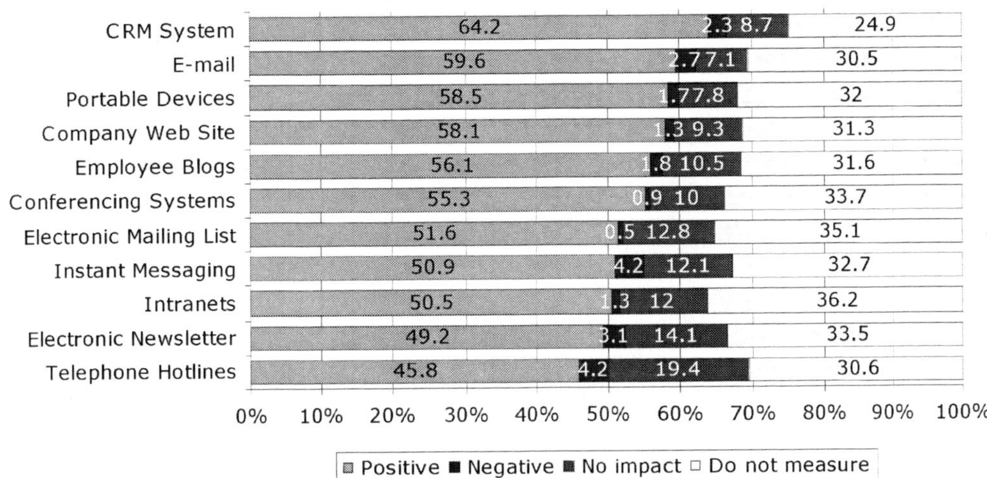

Looking only at those respondents who measured the impact of their organization's electronic communication practices on profitability, portable devices and e-mail are the most likely to have a positive impact (86 percent each). Also, 85 percent of respondents who use CRM systems or company web sites said that they have a positive impact on profitability. Telephone hotlines are least likely to be seen as having a positive impact on profitability (66 percent).

ELECTRONIC COMMUNICATION IMPACT ON PROFITABILITY AMONG ORGANIZATIONS THAT MEASURE THE IMPACT OF ELECTRONIC COMMUNICATION PRACTICES

Practice	Number	Mean	95% Confidence Interval	
			Lower	Upper
Portable Devices	313	0.86	0.82	0.90
E-mail	332	0.86	0.82	0.90
CRM System	130	0.85	0.79	0.92
Company Web Site	312	0.85	0.81	0.89
Conferencing Systems	218	0.83	0.79	0.88
Employee Blogs	39	0.82	0.69	0.95
Electronic Mailing List	239	0.79	0.74	0.85
Intranets	192	0.79	0.73	0.85
Instant Messaging	111	0.76	0.68	0.84
Electronic Newsletter	127	0.74	0.66	0.82
Telephone Hotlines	50	0.66	0.52	0.80

EMPLOYEE BEHAVIOR

Overall, respondents rated face-to-face practices very highly in terms of having a positive impact on employee behavior. Face-to-face conversations received the highest rating, while staff advocates received the lowest rating.

IN-PERSON IMPACT ON EMPLOYEE BEHAVIOR

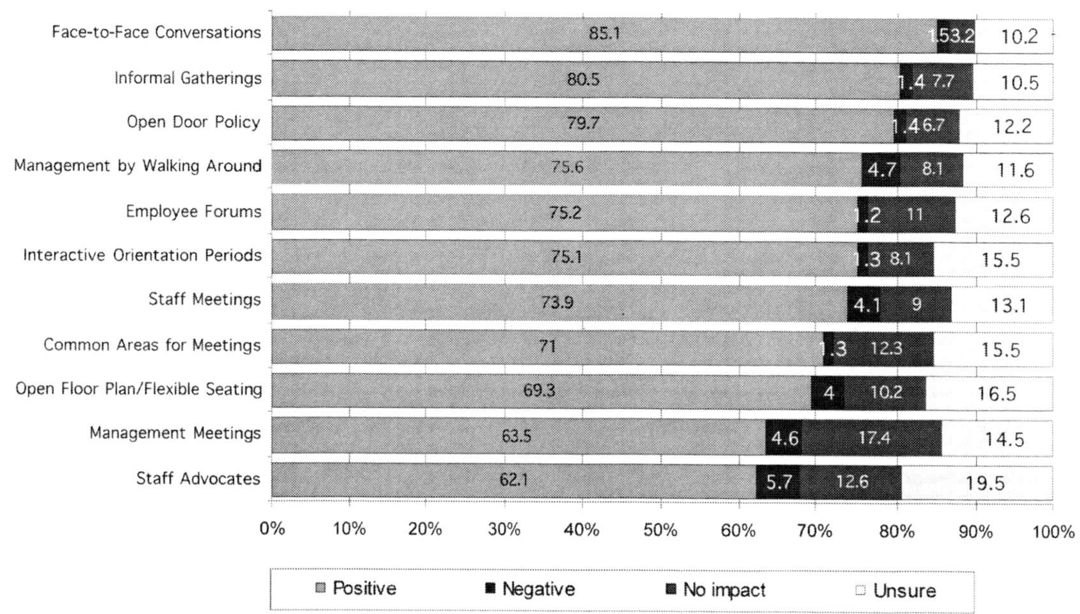

When looking only at those who measured the impact of their in-person communication practices on employee behavior, face-to-face conversations are most likely to have a positive impact (95 percent), followed by an open door policy (91 percent). A large majority of respondents who measured the impact of their practices said that the impact has been positive.

IN-PERSON IMPACT ON EMPLOYEE BEHAVIOR AMONG ORGANIZATIONS THAT MEASURE THE IMPACT OF IN-PERSON COMMUNICATION PRACTICES

Practice	Number	Mean	95% Confidence Interval	
			Lower	Upper
Face-to-Face Conversations	475	0.95	0.93	0.97
Open Door Policy	432	0.91	0.88	0.93
Informal Gatherings	257	0.90	0.86	0.94
Interactive Orientation Periods	322	0.89	0.85	0.92
Employee Forums	222	0.86	0.81	0.91
Management by Walking Around	358	0.85	0.82	0.89
Staff Meetings	406	0.85	0.81	0.88
Common Areas for Meetings	262	0.84	0.79	0.88
Open Floor Plan/Flexible Seating	253	0.83	0.78	0.88
Staff Advocates	140	0.77	0.70	0.84
Management Meetings	412	0.74	0.70	0.79

Over half of respondents found that each print practice had a positive impact on employee behavior. Public suggestion systems received the highest rating, while formal grievance procedures received the lowest rating.

PRINT IMPACT ON EMPLOYEE BEHAVIOR

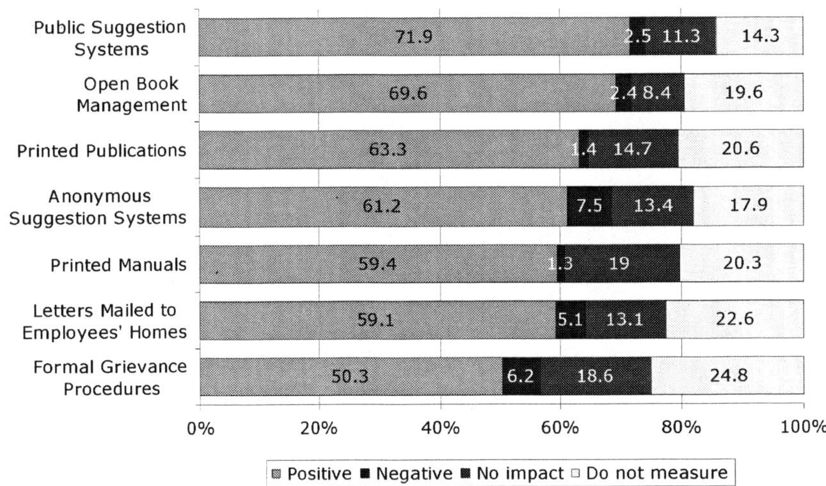

When looking at those who measured the impact of their print communication practices on employee behavior, open book management is the most likely to have a positive impact (87 percent), followed by public suggestion systems (84 percent). Formal grievance procedures are least likely to have a positive impact on employee behavior (67 percent).

PRINT IMPACT ON EMPLOYEE BEHAVIOR AMONG ORGANIZATIONS THAT MEASURE THE IMPACT OF PRINT COMMUNICATION PRACTICES

Practice	Number	Mean	95% Confidence Interval	
			Lower	Upper
Open Book Management	201	0.87	0.82	0.91
Public Suggestion Systems	174	0.84	0.78	0.89
Printed Publications	173	0.80	0.74	0.86
Letters Mailed to Employees' Homes	106	0.76	0.68	0.85
Anonymous Suggestion Systems	110	0.75	0.66	0.83
Printed Manuals	298	0.74	0.70	0.79
Formal Grievance Procedures	121	0.67	0.58	0.75

Electronic practices were scored highly in terms of having a positive impact on employee behavior. Electronic newsletters (at 75.4 percent) scored highest, while the company web site (at 52 percent) scored lowest.

ELECTRONIC COMMUNICATION IMPACT ON EMPLOYEE BEHAVIOR

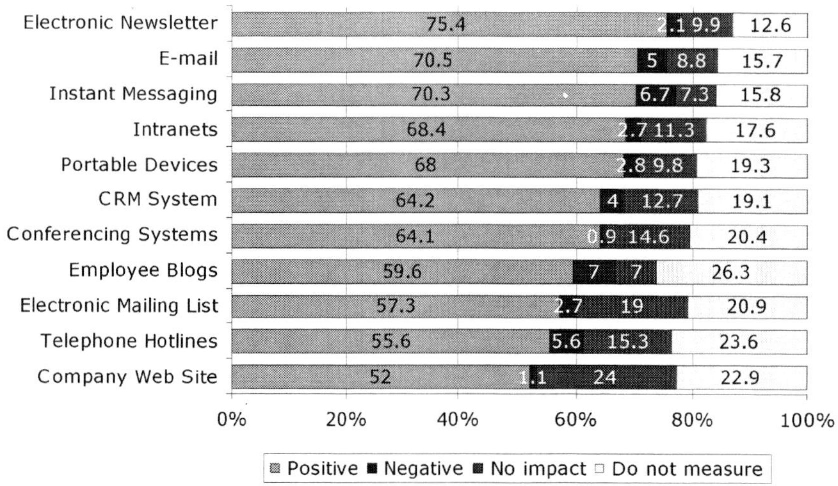

When considering only those respondents who measured the impact of their organization's electronic communication practices on employee behavior, electronic newsletters are most likely to have a positive impact (86 percent), followed by portable devices and e-mail (84 percent each).

ELECTRONIC COMMUNICATION IMPACT ON EMPLOYEE BEHAVIOR AMONG ORGANIZATIONS THAT MEASURE THE IMPACT OF ELECTRONIC COMMUNICATION PRACTICES

Practice	Number	Mean	95% Confidence Interval	
			Lower	Upper
Electronic Newsletter	167	0.86	0.81	0.92
Portable Devices	371	0.84	0.81	0.88
E-mail	403	0.84	0.80	0.87
Instant Messaging	139	0.83	0.77	0.90
Intranets	248	0.83	0.78	0.88
Employee Blogs	42	0.81	0.69	0.93
Conferencing Systems	262	0.81	0.76	0.85
CRM System	140	0.79	0.72	0.86
Telephone Hotlines	55	0.73	0.61	0.85
Electronic Mailing List	291	0.73	0.67	0.78
Company Web Site	350	0.67	0.62	0.72

FACE-TO-FACE COMMUNICATION PRACTICES

The majority of respondents indicated that they use the face-to-face methods cited above because the practices are cost-effective. Since resources are at a premium in small businesses, using those resources to the best advantage of the company and the employees is important. Respondents do not want to develop practices that may cut into productive time for employees or the resources of the company; thus, staff advocates, employee forums and staff meetings are most likely not to be cost-effective, with 9.8 percent of those who use staff advocates rating the concept 1 on a scale of 1 to 3 (1 being least effective; 3 being most effective).

The majority of respondents who use these face-to-face communication practices indicated that the practice has had a positive effect on the productivity in their organization. Face-to-face conversations are most likely to have had a positive impact, followed by employee forums and informal gatherings. The practices most likely to have a negative impact on productivity are staff advocates and implementing an open floor plan.

These face-to-face communication practices open direct lines of exchange between employees and managers. As long as these practices are well managed and continue to focus on company issues and employee satisfaction, managers find them valuable and productive.

Respondents indicated that management meetings had a positive impact on the profitability of their organization, followed by face-to-face conversations. Interestingly, no more than 4 percent of respondents said that using a particular method of face-to-face communication has had a negative impact on the profitability of their organization.

MOST COST-EFFECTIVE FACE-TO-FACE PRACTICES:

- Staff meetings.
- Management meetings.
- Open door policy.
- Management by walking around.
- Interactive orientation periods.
- Common areas for meetings.
- Open floor plan.

MOST LIKELY TO INCREASE PRODUCTIVITY:

- Face-to-face conversations.
- Employee forums.
- Informal gatherings.

MOST LIKELY TO INCREASE PROFITABILITY:

- Management meetings.
- Face-to-face conversations.

MOST LIKELY TO HAVE A POSITIVE EFFECT ON EMPLOYEE BEHAVIOR:

- Face-to-face conversations.
- Informal gatherings.
- Open door policy.

The majority of respondents who use each method of face-to-face communication said that it has had a positive impact on employee behavior. Face-to-face conversations are most likely to have had a positive impact, followed by informal gatherings and an open door policy. The methods most likely to have a negative impact are staff advocates, management by walking around and management meetings.

The face-to-face communication practices identified as having a positive impact on external communication are face-to-face conversations (65.8 percent), staff meetings (58.5 percent) and management meetings (57.1 percent). No more than 4 percent of respondents said that any particular practice has had a negative impact on external relations. Since employees are the greatest ambassadors a company has to influence external publics, these organized and direct practices are valuable.

IN-PERSON IMPACT ON EXTERNAL COMMUNICATIONS

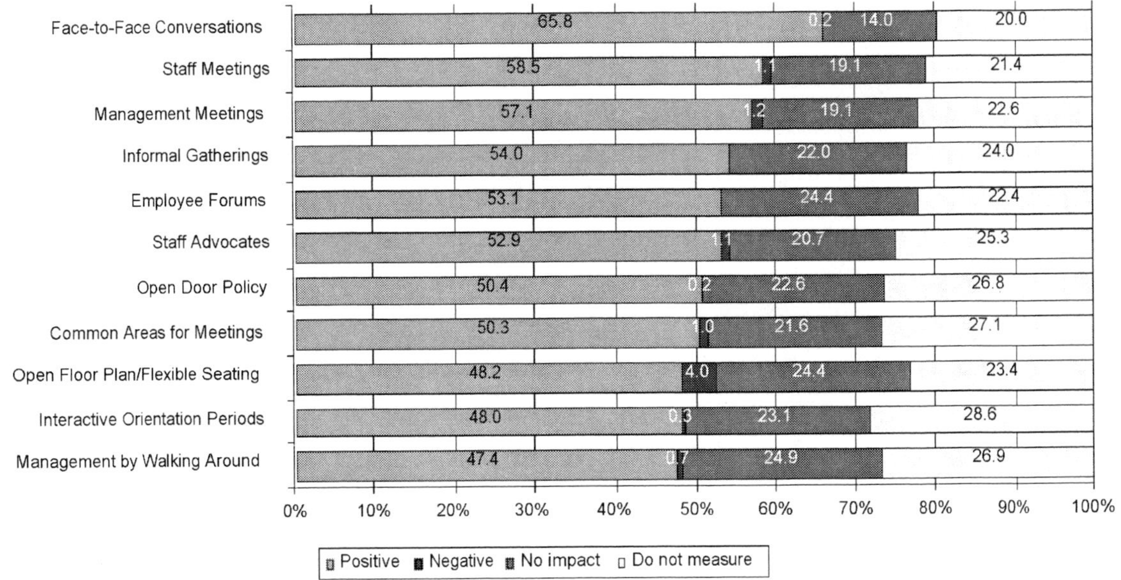

When considering all respondents who currently use each practice, face-to-face conversations were one of the top three in-person communication practices in each category of evaluation. Management meetings also rank high in the areas of cost-effectiveness, positive impact on profitability and positive impact on external communication. Shaded cells show the top practices in each category.

IN-PERSON SUMMARY TABLE

Practice	% Who Used	% At Least Somewhat Cost-effective	% Positive Impact on: Productivity	Profitability	Employee Behavior	External Comm.
Face-to-Face Conversations	86.9	92.2	75.6	52.6	85.1	65.8
Staff Meetings	76.7	90.1	66.6	52.2	73.9	58.5
Informal Gatherings	47.1	89.5	69.3	47.7	80.5	54
Employee Forums	41.7	85.4	70.1	49.6	75.2	53.1
Management Meetings	79.1	89.9	67.6	54.8	63.5	57.1
Open Door Policy	80.8	89.6	66.7	43.1	79.7	50.4
Management by Walking Around	66.5	89.9	67.2	49.1	75.6	47.4
Interactive Orientation Periods	62.6	84.3	65.6	45.7	75.1	48
Common Areas for Meetings	50.9	86.1	62.6	43.9	71	50.3
Staff Advocates	28.6	81	65.5	52.3	62.1	52.9
Open Floor Plan	49.8	88.5	61.1	44.6	69.3	48.2

PRINT COMMUNICATIONS

The majority of respondents who currently use print communications practices said that these methods are cost-effective and indicated this by ratings of 2 or 3 on a scale of 1 to 3. The practices identified as most likely to be cost-effective are public suggestion systems (82.7 percent), open book management (79.6 percent) and printed manuals (77.5 percent). Formal grievance procedures were viewed as least likely to be cost-effective, with only 62.7 percent of those who use them rating them highly.

PRINT COST-EFFECTIVENESS

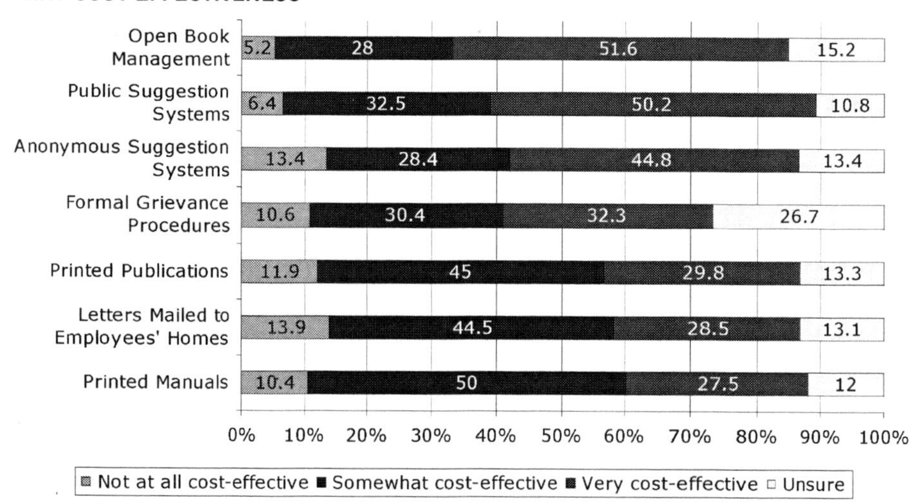

In terms of productivity, the practices most likely to have a positive impact are public suggestion systems and open book management practices. The practices least likely to have a positive effect on an organization's productivity are formal grievance procedures and letters mailed to employees' homes. This rating can be attributed to the lack of interactivity related to letters and the inherent nature of conflict associated with grievance procedures.

Less than half of the respondents who use each print employee communication practice said that using it has had a positive impact on the profitability of their organization. The practices most likely to have a positive impact are public suggestion systems and open book management. The practices most likely to have a negative impact on profitability are letters mailed to employees' homes, printed publications and anonymous suggestion systems. This impression regarding the impact on profitability may be attributed to the fact that these companies do not have a formal measurement system in place for evaluating the impact of these practices on the organization's bottom line through tangible or intangible resources or revenues.

The majority of respondents who currently use each method of print communication said that the practice has had a positive impact on employee behavior. The practices most likely to have a positive impact on employee behavior are public suggestion systems and open book management. These responses speak to the principle noted in the literature review regarding the sharing of company information and employees' need to understand their contributions to the success of the company in meeting its business goals.

No more than 55 percent of respondents whose organizations use particular print communication practice said it has had a positive impact on external communications. Printed publications are most likely to have a positive impact (55 percent), while formal grievance procedures are least likely (26.7 percent). Mailing letters to employees' homes was most likely to have a negative impact (5.1 percent). These findings are not surprising in light of the nature of conflict inherent in formal corporate communications like letters and grievance procedures. These practices do not foster trust or two-way, interactive communication between the management and employees of small companies.

MOST COST-EFFECTIVE PRINT PRACTICES:

- Public suggestion systems.
- Open book management.
- Printed manuals.

MOST LIKELY TO INCREASE PRODUCTIVITY:

- Public suggestion systems.

MOST LIKELY TO INCREASE PROFITABILITY:

- Public suggestion systems.
- Open book management.

MOST LIKELY TO HAVE A POSITIVE EFFECT ON EMPLOYEE BEHAVIOR:

- Open book management.
- Public suggestion systems.

PRINT IMPACT ON EXTERNAL COMMUNICATIONS

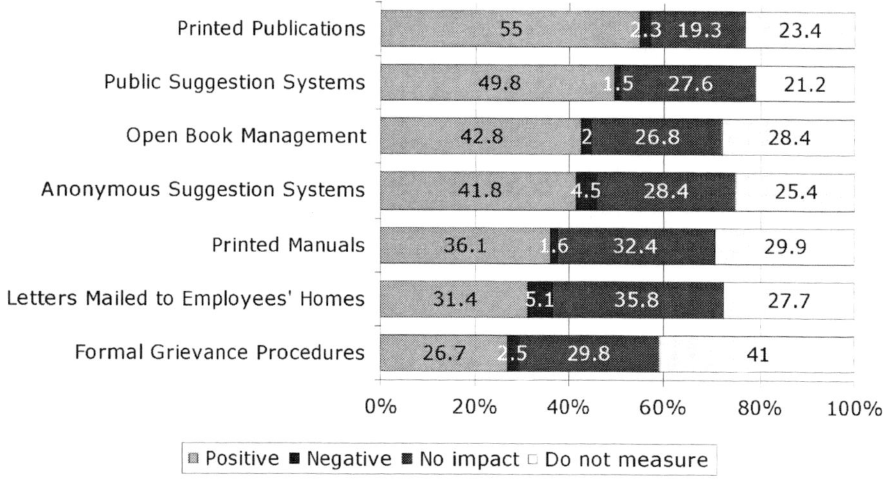

When it came to having a positive impact on organizational success, considering respondents whose organizations use each practice defined as print communication in the study, public suggestion systems, open book management and print publications were the top three practices in this category. Formal grievance procedures and letters mailed to employees' homes are the bottom two practices in all categories except usage, in which letters mailed to employee's homes and anonymous suggestions systems were the bottom categories. The top three print employee communication practices were rated highly for having a positive impact on employee behavior and productivity.

PRINT SUMMARY TABLE

Practice	% Who Used	% At Least Somewhat Cost-effective	% Positive Impact on:			
			Productivity	Profitability	Employee Behavior	External Comm.
Public Suggestion Systems	33.3	82.7	60.1	48.8	71.9	49.8
Open Book Management	41.1	79.6	59.6	47.2	69.6	42.8
Printed Publications	35.8	74.8	55	40.4	63.3	55
Anonymous Suggestion Systems	22	73.2	53	38.1	61.2	41.8
Printed Manuals	61.4	77.5	51.9	36.1	59.4	36.1
Letters Mailed to Employees' Homes	22.5	73	48.2	30.7	59.1	31.4
Formal Grievance Procedures	26.4	62.7	43.5	32.3	50.3	26.7

An open book policy has characterized Anderson & Associates (Anderson, 1999) since its inception out of a home office in 1968 in Virginia. While the company's owner does not attribute profitability directly to the practice, he insists that high levels of trust and loyalty from the engineering firm's 170 employees provide the payoff. Income statements, backlogs, accounts receivable, profitability, revenue and even salaries are posted on the intranet, which also hosts employee photos, a newsletter, a training schedule, policy documents, and drafting and design standards.

With a company roster of 26 employees, Pool Covers Inc. enjoys the distinction of being the largest independent company within its industry. In 1993, the business implemented a participative management program (NCEO, 2002). In 1996, it added an open book policy and an employee shares options program (ESOP) a year later. The ESOP is credited with retaining capital within the business and providing an attractive employee benefits program. Profits on sales increased from 0.4 percent prior to the ESOP to 3 percent following implementation. Financial statements are shared on a monthly basis, and weekly meetings where statement items are discussed in detail are customary. Several incentives are in place, including bonuses for reductions in return visits to clients, installation completions, service orders, sales volume growth and per person shop time. In this way, employees gain a tangible grasp of financial figures. Weekly staff meetings, a steering committee that reviews salaries and pay increases, employee responsibility for warehouse redesign and new truck purchases, employee recognition, and a "book of kudos" ensure an effective communication strategy through active employee participation.

ELECTRONIC COMMUNICATIONS

Respondents indicated that e-mail was considered a cost-effective employee communication practice, with 94.4 percent of respondents giving it the highest rating, followed by electronic mailing lists (90.5 percent). The practice least likely to be considered cost-effective was telephone hotlines (65.3 percent).

ELECTRONIC COMMUNICATION COST-EFFECTIVENESS

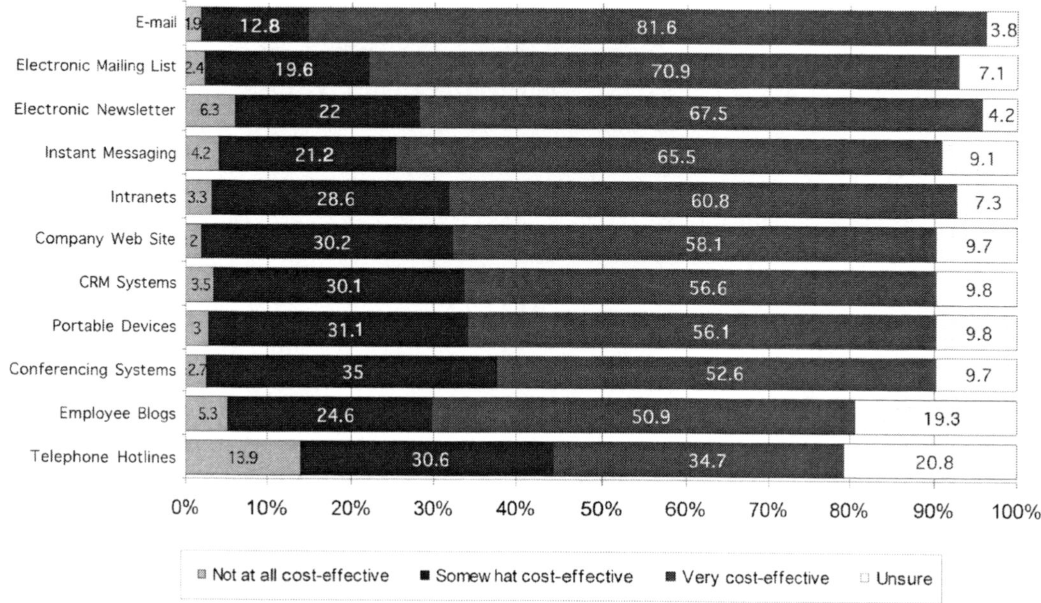

Approximately three quarters of respondents whose organizations use portable devices and e-mail feel that these practices have had a positive impact on productivity. Telephone hotlines were seen as least likely to have a positive impact on productivity, followed by employee blogs.

CRM (customer relationship management) systems were most likely to be seen as having a positive impact on profitability. Telephone hotlines were seen as least likely to have a positive impact, followed by electronic newsletters.

Approximately three quarters of respondents whose organization uses electronic newsletters said that this practice has a positive impact on employee behavior. E-mail and instant messaging are also highly likely to have a positive impact on employee behavior, at 70.5 percent and 70.3 percent, respectively. Company web sites are least likely to have a positive impact on employee behavior (52 percent), followed by telephone hotlines (55.6 percent).

Respondents whose organizations have a company web site are most likely to say that it has a positive impact on external communications (81.5 percent), followed by e-mail (72.2 percent). Intranets are least likely to have a positive impact (38.5 percent), followed by telephone hotlines and instant messaging, 44.4 percent and 45.5 percent, respectively.

ELECTRONIC COMMUNICATION IMPACT ON EXTERNAL COMMUNICATIONS

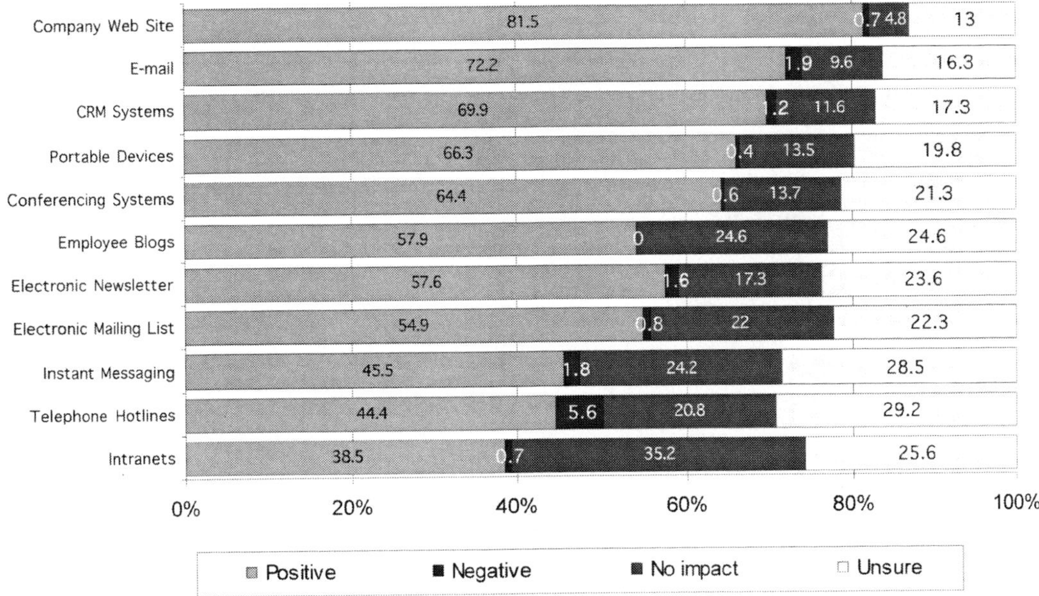

These findings regarding the use of electronic communications by small businesses are contrary to current findings from the literature review regarding the potential impact of electronic communications on productivity and employee engagement. One explanation for this contrast may be that formal electronic communication practices by small businesses are emerging practices that find their roots in the informal communication practices of individuals. Company intranets and public web sites are most effective when the information shared through these tools is timely and accurate. There is no room for error or delay due to lack of personnel to update the information. With human resources spread thin in small businesses, these communication strategies may not be managed as well as in larger businesses.

Considering only those who measured the impact of electronic communication practices on external communication, company web sites are significantly more likely than all other practices to have a positive impact (94 percent). Eighty-six percent of those who measured the impact of e-mail on external relations said the impact was positive, followed by 85 percent of those who measured the impact of CRM systems. Intranets are the least likely to have a positive impact on external communication (52 percent).

ELECTRONIC COMMUNICATION IMPACT ON EXTERNAL COMMUNICATIONS AMONG ORGANIZATIONS THAT MEASURE THE IMPACT OF ELECTRONIC COMMUNICATION PRACTICES

Practice	Number	Mean	95% Confidence Interval	
			Lower	Upper
Company Web Site	395	0.94	0.91	0.96
E-mail	400	0.86	0.83	0.90
CRM System	143	0.85	0.79	0.91
Portable Devices	369	0.83	0.79	0.87
Conferencing Systems	259	0.82	0.77	0.87
Employee Blogs	43	0.77	0.64	0.90
Electronic Newsletters	146	0.75	0.68	0.82
Electronic Mailing List	286	0.71	0.65	0.76
Instant Messaging	118	0.64	0.55	0.72
Telephone Hotlines	51	0.63	0.49	0.76
Intranets	224	0.52	0.45	0.58

MEASURING EMPLOYEE COMMUNICATION

Formally measuring the impact of employee communication practices on return on investment (employee behavior or financial analysis) is not a popular practice among small to medium-sized businesses. Currently, only 36.5 percent of respondents use customer satisfaction surveys as a method of communication research (this measure is not a definitive one to evaluate the effects of internal communication). Those who use employee opinion surveys total 25.3 percent, and 15.4 percent use communication audits.

MOST COST-EFFECTIVE ELECTRONIC PRACTICES:

- E-mail.
- Electronic mailing lists.

MOST LIKELY TO INCREASE PRODUCTIVITY:

- Portable devices.
- E-mail.

MOST LIKELY TO INCREASE PROFITABILITY:

- CRM systems.

MOST LIKELY TO HAVE A POSITIVE EFFECT ON EMPLOYEE BEHAVIOR:

- Electronic newsletters.
- E-mail.
- Instant messaging.

RESEARCH USAGE

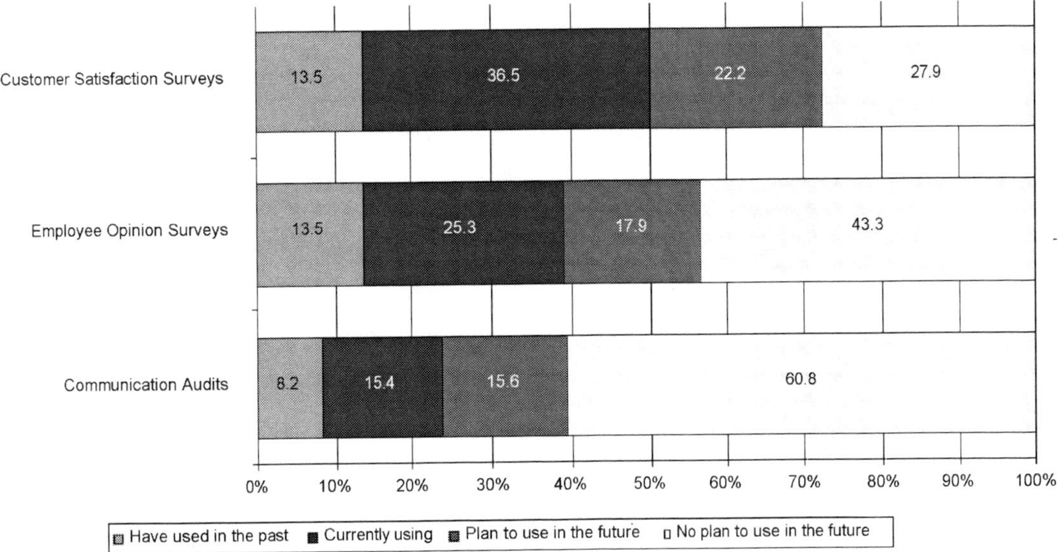

Customer satisfaction surveys, employee opinion surveys and communication audits were considered cost-effective as methods of communication research. More than half of the respondents who use them gave the practices the highest rating. Employee opinion surveys had the highest rating for "not at all cost-effective" (8.4 percent). This finding may be evidence that these organizations are more concerned with the external effects of communications that have a direct bearing on the financial operation of the company. Customer satisfaction is critical to future sales. It should be used to improve employee engagement with the company; thus translating into higher productivity and improved products and services for customers. Employee opinion surveys should be considered as a component of increasing sales.

RESEARCH COST-EFFECTIVENESS

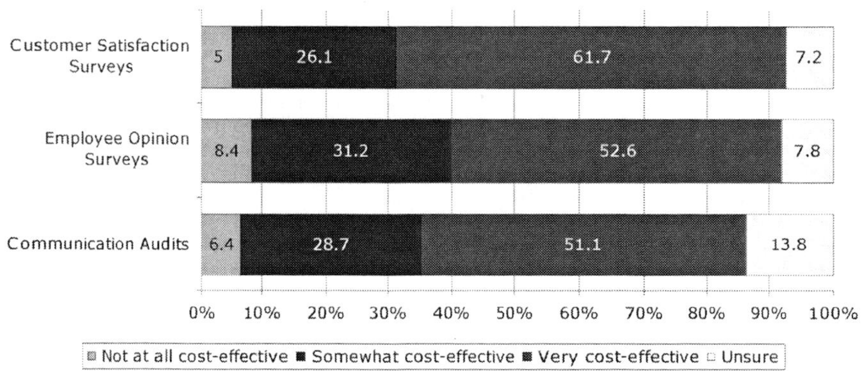

More than three quarters of those who use customer satisfaction surveys as a method of communication research said that this practice has had a positive impact on productivity. Employee opinion surveys are most likely to have a negative impact on productivity (6.5 percent).

RESEARCH IMPACT ON PRODUCTIVITY

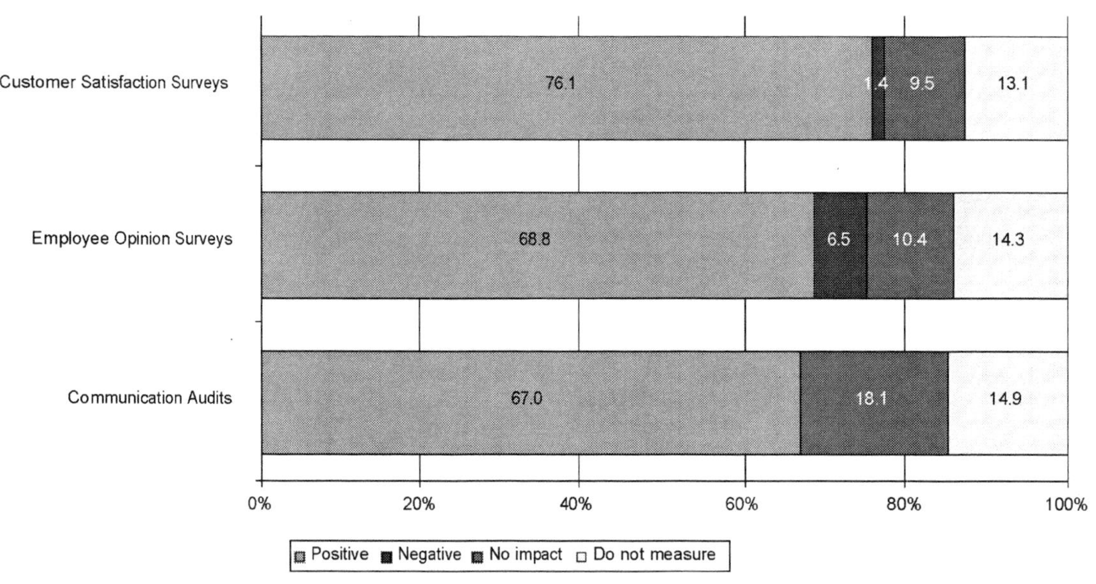

Respondents indicated that customer satisfaction surveys are most likely to have a positive impact on profitability (70.7 percent), while employee opinion surveys are least likely (52.6 percent) to have a positive impact.

RESEARCH IMPACT ON PROFITABILITY

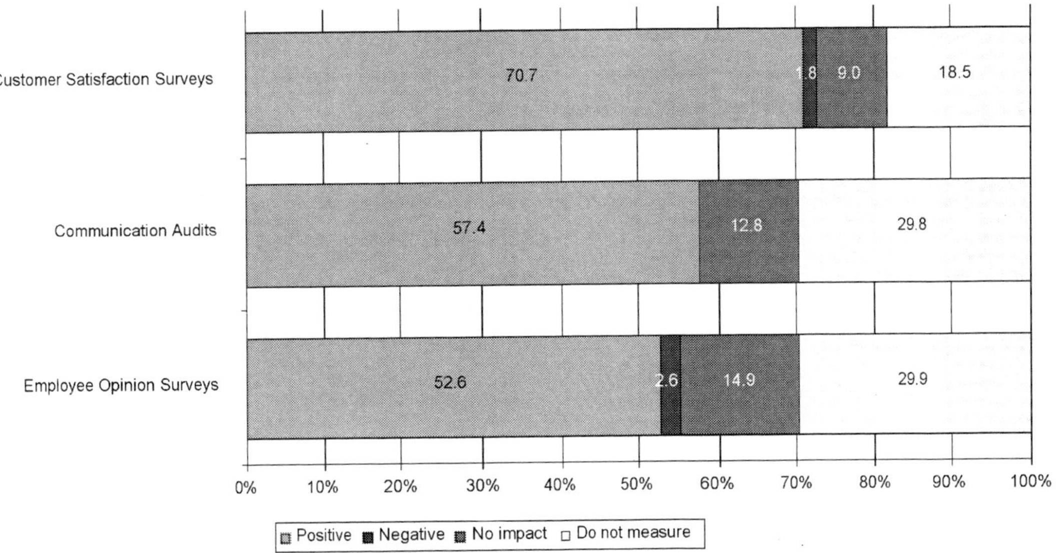

Ironically, more than 70 percent of respondents who use these communication research practices said that these tactics have a positive impact on employee behavior. Employee opinion surveys are most likely to have a negative impact on employee behavior (5.2 percent).

RESEARCH IMPACT ON EMPLOYEE BEHAVIOR

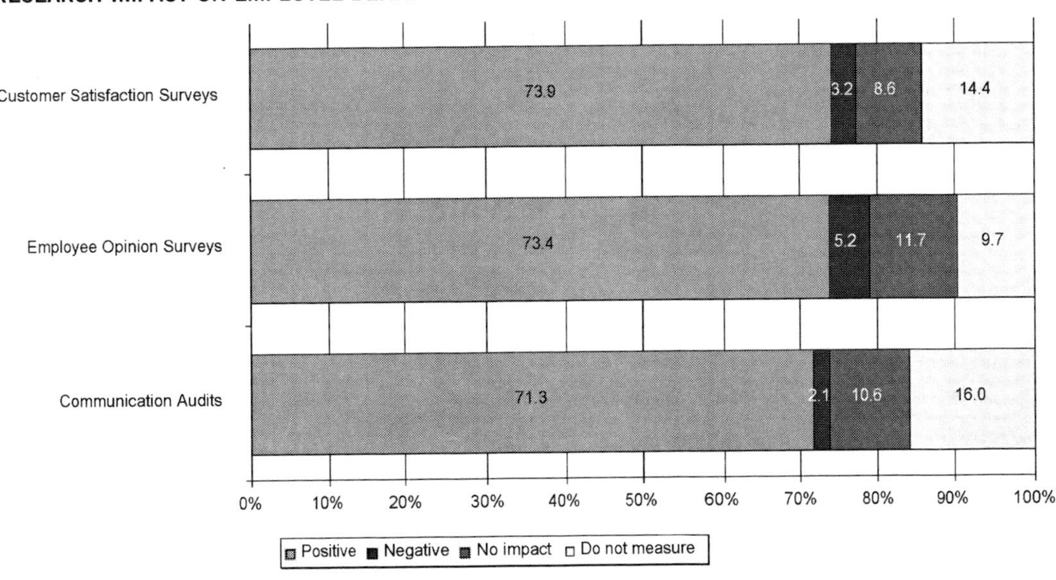

These findings may be evidence that management is not responding to employee opinions; thus, future employee surveys are eliciting additional negative responses in employees who do not feel valued. Customer satisfaction surveys cannot measure employee satisfaction and engagement. Only circumstantial evidence can attribute customer satisfaction to employee behavior. A stronger connection can be made between positive employee behavior and increased customer satisfaction.

Customer satisfaction surveys were perceived to be the most likely to have a positive impact on external communications (82.9 percent), while employee opinion surveys were perceived as the least likely to have a positive impact (47.4 percent). This finding also points to the importance of responding to employee concerns and the impact employees (as ambassadors) have on a company's reputation and image with external publics.

RESEARCH IMPACT ON EXTERNAL COMMUNICATIONS

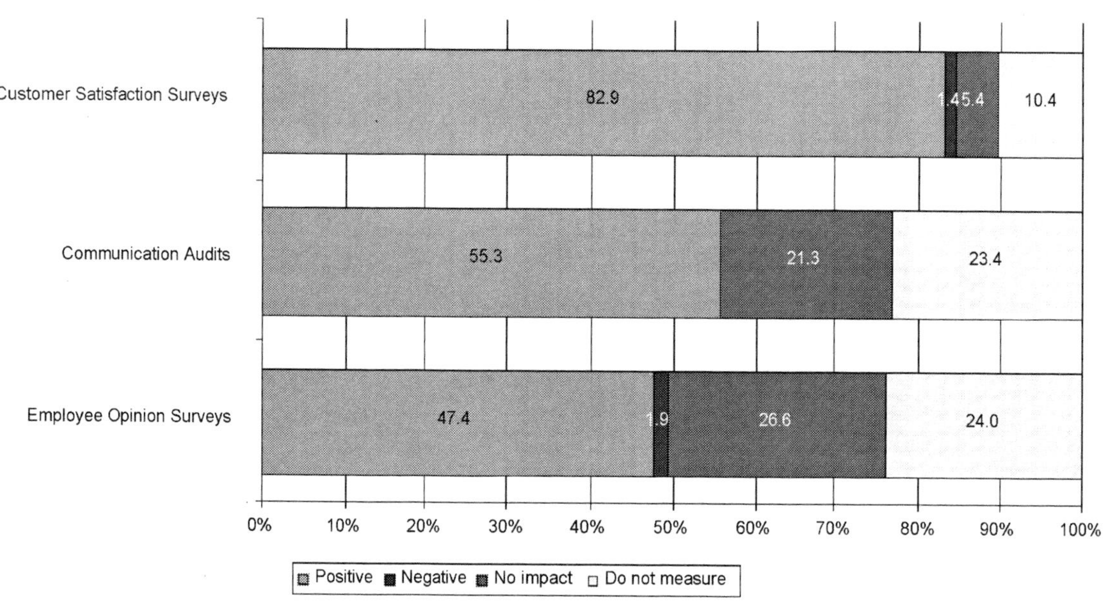

Because customer satisfaction surveys are geared more toward reaching external audiences, these tactics are most likely to be considered cost-effective. Respondents indicated that communication audits are least likely to be considered cost-effective. Employee opinion surveys were least likely to be seen as having a positive impact on profitability and external communication. Respondents indicated that customer satisfaction surveys are likely to have a positive impact on productivity, profitability, employee behavior and external communication, even though formal measurement of these factors is not being conducted by the company. This may be evidence that small businesses would benefit from additional education regarding methods of communication research that benefit both internal and external communication business goals.

Customer satisfaction surveys are popular marketing communication tools and are only tangentially helpful as an assessment of employee communication or employee satisfaction. Literature from the discipline and commentary in the case studies support direct communication with employees and the use of employee opinion surveys and company culture assessments as more effective in identifying employee needs and preferences for improving employee communication and ultimately employee satisfaction and behavior.

RESEARCH SUMMARY TABLE

Practice	% Who Used	% At Least Somewhat Cost-effective	% Positive Impact on: Productivity	Profitability	Employee Behavior	External Comm.
Customer Satisfaction Surveys	36.5	87.8	76.1	70.7	73.9	82.9
Communication Audits	15.4	79.8	67	57.4	71.3	55.3
Employee Opinion Surveys	25.3	83.8	68.8	52.6	73.4	47.4

WHAT IS THE ORGANIZATIONAL IMPACT (ON EMPLOYEE RETENTION, BUSINESS GROWTH, ETC.) OF EMPLOYEE COMMUNICATION PRACTICES IN SMALL BUSINESSES? / In the end, it all comes back to the impact that communication as a business practice has on the company's achievement of its goals and objectives. This study as a whole emphasizes the value of employee communication for small businesses. The findings below reinforce the need for greater attention to formal internal communication process as a potential method of improving business results.

COMMUNICATION AS A BUSINESS FUNCTION

Respondents were asked to indicate how important a number of functions are to their business success by allocating 100 points among each of the eight functions, with more points going to those functions they view as being more important. Business success was defined in terms of personal satisfaction with their enterprise.

Sales and marketing (21.1 points) was the business function that respondents said was most important to their business success. Client services was identified as the second most important function, with an average of 18.1 points. Production was identified as the third most important function; organizational communication ranked fourth in importance. Research and development was identified as the least important business function, with an average of seven points.

IMPORTANCE OF BUSINESS FUNCTIONS

Business Function	Mean	95% Confidence Interval	
		Lower	Upper
Sales and Marketing	21.1	19.8	22.4
Client Services	18.1	16.7	19.5
Production	14.1	12.9	15.3
Communications	12.7	11.8	13.6
Information Technology	9.7	9.0	10.3
Finance	9.2	8.5	9.9
Human Resources	8.1	7.4	8.8
Research and Development	7.0	6.4	7.7

Ironically, the top two business functions are highly reliant upon effective communication for success. It can be argued that production also is highly dependent upon effective interpersonal employee communication, a form of meta-communication within the internal communication discipline that is facilitated by managerial communication. By extension, the HR function has a great impact on employee communication, especially in regards to recruitment, benefits communication and exit interviewing, to name only a few communications of human resources offices. These are critical functions in the process of developing employee engagement, an understanding of employees' roles in reaching company goals and employee loyalty to the company.

COMMUNICATION RESOURCES

Effective communication of any sort—internal or external—cannot occur without some commitment of company resources to support its implementation, growth and development. The percentage of respondents who indicated their business currently has a budget for communication in place totaled 38.1 percent. Those who indicated that their business does not have a communication budget totaled 49.1 percent. The percentage of respondents who were unsure if a communication budget exists was 12.8 percent.

BUDGET FOR COMMUNICATION IN PLACE

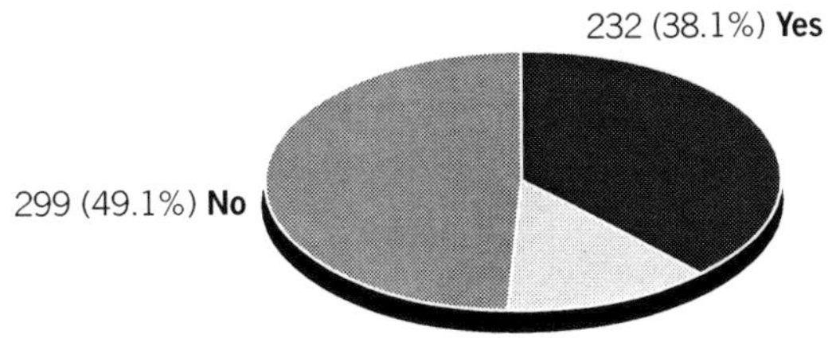

Of those who have a budget for communication, 37.5 percent indicated that less than 5 percent of their business' budget is for communication. The percentage reporting that 5 to 9 percent of the business' budget is dedicated to communication was 15.9 percent. The percentage indicating that 10 to 19 percent of the business' budget was dedicated to communication totaled 28.9 percent. Those who said 20 percent or more was budgeted for communication totaled 17.7 percent. The mean percentage is 10.4 percent, and the median is 6.5 percent.

PERCENTAGE OF BUDGET FOR COMMUNICATION

% of Budget for Communication	Frequency	Percent	Cumulative Percent
Less than 5%	87	37.5	37.5
5% to 9%	37	15.9	53.4
10% to 19%	67	28.9	82.3
20% or more	41	17.7	100.0
Total	232	100.0	

More than half of respondents (56 percent) said that their business does not currently have a strategic communication plan in place; 32.7 percent said that their business does have a plan in place. The remaining 11.3 percent are unsure.

STRATEGIC COMMUNICATION PLAN IN PLACE

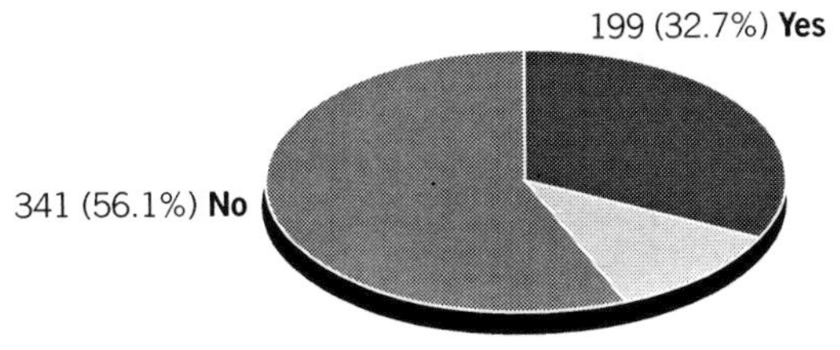

Of those who were able to say how their pre-tax profit margin has changed over the last five years, 42.4 percent said that it increased, 14.1 percent said that it has stayed the same and 9.4 percent said that it has decreased.

HOW HAS YOUR FIRMS PRE-TAX PROFIT MARGIN CHANGED?

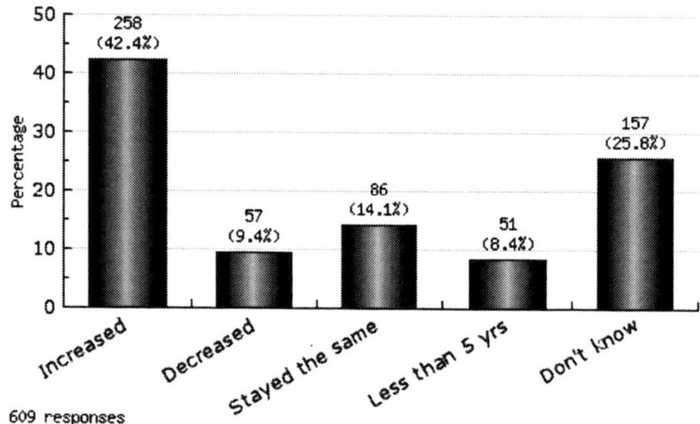

The majority of respondents said that their revenue growth has increased over the past five years (58 percent). Those who said that it has stayed the same totaled 11.5 percent, while 6.9 percent said it has decreased. Those who were unsure totaled 15.4 percent. Those who are part of a company that has been around for less than five years totaled 8.2 percent.

HOW HAS YOUR FIRM'S REVENUE GROWTH CHANGED?

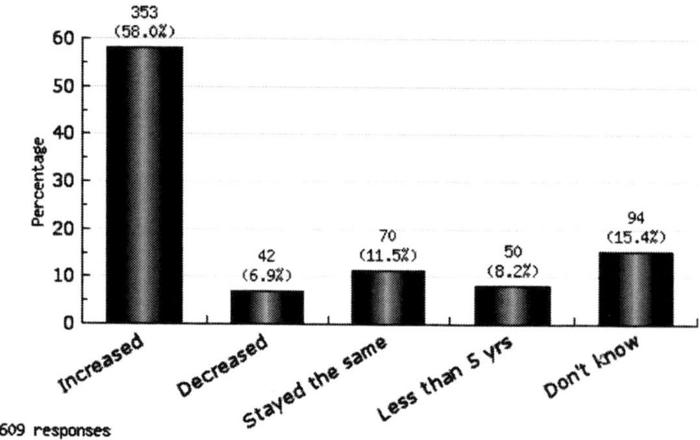

RECOMMENDATIONS FOR SMALL BUSINESSES / After analyzing the literature, the survey results and the commentary by SME owners and managers in the case studies, the following recommendations were developed for small businesses that wish to capitalize on employee communication as a resource for business success:

- Improve direct, two-way communication between management and employees.
- Cultivate a culture that values communication—in all directions within the company.
- Develop career-long communication opportunities.
- Create opportunities for informal communications.
- Connect marketing with internal communications.
- Improve communication research techniques that connect employee communication to the company bottom line.

IMPROVE DIRECT, TWO-WAY COMMUNICATION

As discussed in the survey findings, the literature review and the comments of those interviewed, employee communication encompasses communication encounters from recruitment to daily work activities to the termination of employment. Inherent in this process is the distribution of information as well as the critical function of listening and responding to employee concerns regarding their impact on the company.

Internal communication involves every person in an organization, not just a department manager or corporate communicator. Employee engagement, which contributes significantly to profitability, is directly linked to management's active listening ability. Two-way communication contributes to fewer work stoppages, mutual understanding of the impact of employee behavior on business success and ultimately, higher productivity.

Creating an organizational culture that values open dialogue and feedback in the form of employee suggestions for problem solving and achievement of business goals will create greater employee engagement, loyalty and retention. For some organizations, this type of culture comes naturally without strategically planning its development, while other organizations will need to break many old habits and overcome power barriers to become more focused on two-way communication.

To begin the process of developing open, direct, two-way communication, consider the following recommendations.

Lead by example: Management by walking around and a manager's or owner's willingness to hold meetings with employees to share information through two-way dialogue are two practices that small businesses can use to improve the flow of communication. Once the leaders of an organization start these practices, others will see the benefits and follow. The percentage of survey respondents who indicated that management by walking around had a positive effect on the behavior of their employees was 75.6 percent.

Improve managerial listening skills: Listening is a learned skill. Managers and owners need to learn to listen to employees. The characteristics that make entrepreneurs and managers of small businesses successful (individualism, independence and risk-taking) can make them ineffective communicators. Receiving training in the skill of listening will improve their ability to hear employee comments as solutions to challenges instead of complaints. Listening as part of the two-way flow of information is a behavior that can be learned, and it becomes contagious as groups come to see its value.

Actively demonstrate and develop communication practices: Initially, both employees and managers may find two-way communication difficult. Creating tools that facilitate two-way communication will model valuable communication practices. Some employee communication practices that enable two-way communication include the following:

- Performance evaluations that include a dialogue between supervisor and employee provide an opportunity for rewarding positive behaviors and modifying bad habits.
- Regular staff meetings, with opportunities for employees to offer solutions to problems or barriers, allow them to share in the achievement of business successes.
- Small businesses that are growing in size may find the use of a Balanced Scorecard program helpful in developing communications and evaluating effective business practices.
- Informal meetings between employees and managers allow for discussion of operations in a casual forum.
- A suggestion system (either public or anonymous) is an ongoing means for collecting employee concerns and suggestions for improving the company as a whole. Research from the survey suggests that employees like to remain anonymous in their communication with management, but progressive organizations are creating cultures that eliminate the need for anonymity.
- For medium-sized businesses, steering committees or employee forums are means for developing organized systems of two-way communication.

Plan internal communication activities: A thoughtful, strategic plan is the best way to implement and evaluate communications.

- Set goals—involve employees and leadership in the process.
- Ensure that differences are acknowledged when identifying audiences.

- Choose effective media and tactics to communicate with different audiences—include training and cultural support.
- Budget for communication practices.
- Develop a plan of action that includes evaluation measures.
- Execute the plan and use evaluation data to improve two-way communication practices.

CULTIVATE A CULTURE THAT VALUES COMMUNICATION

Hand in hand with developing and implementing two-way communication is the cultivation of an organizational culture that values communication, dialogue between managers and employees, and interpersonal communication among employees that builds teamwork and engagement. An organizational culture that is built on trust, mutual respect, and two-way communication will yield loyal and engaged employees.

Share company information with employees to improve their understanding of their role in achieving business goals: The practice of open book management is an example of communication that contributes to employee engagement and, ultimately, business success. Sharing sensitive financial information can be difficult for some managers or owners who have kept those figures to themselves.

Communicating the financial status of a company requires a planned, strategic approach to achieve positive results. This type of communication requires strong cultural and administrative support from company leadership. Open book management is based on the following principles:

- Sharing all relevant financial information with employees.
- Training employees so they understand the financial information.
- Giving employees responsibility for the numbers under their control.
- Giving employees a financial stake in how the company performs.
- Communicating financial information to assist in dissemination, comprehension, tracking and building employee engagement.

When communicating financial information in an open book environment, company leadership should consider connecting numbers to real-life experiences, building "a line of sight" from daily work to the big goals and making the financial data engaging for employees so that they understand it.

Reinforce the culture through the addition of new communication media: As new communication tools become available, consider how these tools can be used to complement current employee communication practices. New communication tools may improve the use of company resources. For example, the use of e-mail and intranets has been proven to increase the speed of conducting business as well as reduce the use of physical resources:

- Blogs (Weblogs) have become popular in cutting through layers in an organization and giving employees and management a voice.
- Intranets that allow employee interaction through forums, collaboration platforms, etc., reinforce two-way communication.
- Work space design that makes use of open floor plans or flexible seating arrangements has been shown to encourage informal, open communication.
- Ensuring that employees know their roles in times of crises or emergencies ensures trusted communication.
- Provide gender and cultural sensitivity training to embrace differences in the workplace and provide innovative strategies for overcoming barriers to communication.
- Improve two-way communication and innovation in the business by recognizing the value of social networks.
- Offer access to technology-based communication tools to all employees. Organizations with traveling or remote employees or multiple locations should consider more inclusive means of communication.

Recognize language and multiculturalism in the workplace: The workplace continues to grow more diverse. Managers and owners must be aware and open to the diverse communication styles and needs of the workforce; this includes multicultural issues as well as gender differences. Organizations that employ people from diverse backgrounds should use proactive practices to make two-way communication easier, including:

- Orientation, ESL training, interpreters and mentors for new employees.
- Cultural awareness and language training for existing employees.
- Conflict resolution training for all employees.
- Celebrating differences to create a culture of tolerance and patience.
- Written and oral communications translated by bilingual employees—although not every person is an expert on their culture.
- An understanding of the communication preferences by gender and cultural backgrounds.
- Attention to nonverbal communication cues.

DEVELOP CAREER-LONG COMMUNICATION OPPORTUNITIES / At various stages of an employee's development, different types of communication are needed. Evidence from the survey results as well as from the literature review and case commentaries shows that the orientation of new employees is a critical time for establishing an understanding of an employee's fit with the company and the organization's culture overall. As employees progress through an organization, they can develop communication skills and practices that reinforce the culture and corporate strategy. The recent start of the Baby Boom exodus from the paid workforce highlights the need for knowledge transfer to maintain corporate memory. Two-way, open communication can facilitate this process.

Orientation is where it all begins: Survey results show a rise in the popularity of interactive orientation periods and ongoing orientation sessions to refresh employees about organizational strategies. Orientation programs are most often the responsibility of HR. Extending the purpose of orientation to keeping all employees up to date on the state of the company requires professional communicators to assist in the development of this system. Organizational development and training professionals may also help in this process. Understanding the expectations of younger generations of employees is necessary for meeting their communication preferences in the development of a two-way flow of information.

Orientation sessions for new employees provide a forum to establish norms and expectations—including cultural ideals and communication practices. Employers surveyed said that orientation works:

- Sixty-five percent of businesses find that interactive orientations have a positive effect on productivity.
- Forty-five percent note a positive impact on profitability.
- Seventy-five percent see a positive impact on employee behavior.
- Forty-eight percent measured a positive impact on external communications.

Many orientations in small organizations include an employee handbook and a tour that ends at the employee's workstation to "get them working right away." This practice represents a missed opportunity to write on a blank slate offered by an enthusiastic, unbiased new employee. A small investment of resources at this time maximizes employee engagement and reduces turnover (both of which are directly related to profitability).

Small businesses can improve orientation programs by delegating a coach or mentor to help new employees learn about the company and their job. Also, developing interpersonal connections within the organization should be a first priority, second to the printed documents that employees can read to reinforce the messages from peers and supervisors. Using this relationship-based model requires that mentors and managers are trained and knowledgeable in regards to company policies and practices.

Ongoing communication and skill development: Ongoing engagement of employees includes communication of corporate strategy and measurement of progress. On average, 95 percent of a company's employees are unaware of or do not understand its strategy (Kaplan & Norton, 2005). In addition to improving two-way communication, organizations can connect with employees in a number of ways throughout their career with the company.

Many organizations are creating their own branded training programs (even though some of the modules may be provided by outside contractors). These organizations brand their training to give it a distinct presence in the company. Training is used to drive culture by reinforcing values, creating language and interacting with others. Some current training practices include:

- Lectures
- Small group discussions
- Seminars
- Conferences
- Case analyses
- Programmed instruction
- Committee work
- Role-play simulations

The company intranet is also being used to provide training opportunities for employees. Through participation in trade and professional organizations, as well as local and regional chambers of commerce, small businesses can link to training opportunities through web technologies.

Performance evaluations provide two-way communication: More than an opportunity to review an employee's performance at meeting their job responsibilities, regular performance evaluations are best used to develop and monitor employee progress toward career advancement in the company and achievements toward company goals. These regular sessions allow managers and employees to discuss and plan employee contributions to the strategic business goals. Used in tandem with an open book approach to sharing company financial information, performance evaluations provide the connection that leads to greater employee engagement and loyalty.

Plan for knowledge transfer: Employees are the greatest intangible asset of any organization, regardless of size. Without employees, work does not get done, customers are not cultivated, and products and services are not delivered. As employees mature from new recruits to senior members of the company, their knowledge about the company and the culture (the way we do things around here) grows exponentially.

As employees prepare to retire or leave the company for greater career advancement, a system must be in place to transfer the knowledge and skills of one generation of employees to the next in order to provide continuity:

- Knowledge transfer planning can reduce employee training costs and redundancy errors as employees mature with the company.
- Using a mentor or coaching model that is initiated during the orientation of new employees is one way of connecting new employees with more seasoned employees. This coaching relationship should be an ongoing one that grows as employees progress through their life span with the organization.
- Formalized systems, such as job shadowing, new employee training sessions, and process mapping are currently used to ensure that process and organizational cultural concerns are maintained.

CREATE OPPORTUNITIES FOR INFORMAL COMMUNICATION

Results in this study show that face-to-face conversations are used by almost every company; are cost-effective; and have a positive effect on employee behavior, productivity and customer interactions. This is especially important when departments are divided physically, by shifts, or by work and when interdepartmental collaboration is required for success. Creating opportunities for open, face-to-face interaction reinforces communication efforts across the company as a whole.

Collaboration happens naturally through social networks in companies. Encouraging those networks and other interaction throughout a workday creates opportunities for conversations to happen naturally.

Suggestions for encouraging informal communications that lead to greater employee engagement and employee-driven solutions (productivity) include:

- Holding a number of short stand-up meetings or team huddles. These can be another alternative to monthly meetings or may be used in conjunction with regular staff meetings.
- Applying the concept of management by walking around, whereby managers or owners can create opportunities for conversations with employees, be active participants and promote open communication.
- Using the principles of open book management, owners and managers equip employees with the knowledge and skills to engage in informal dialogue about company goals and strategies.
- Encouraging employees and managers to share a meal together—"let's do lunch"—to learn about one another and their goals in the workplace.

- Participating in or hosting a local or regional chamber of commerce social gathering also allows employees and managers to meet informally with one another as well as serve as ambassadors of the company with visitors from the business community.
- Holding regularly scheduled informal meetings offers opportunities for employees to meet, collaborate and interact. It is important to find activities or events of common interest so as not to exclude people. These events should avoid strong business content to allow for natural collaboration. They could be as simple as a first Friday after work reception.
- Encouraging volunteerism activities or community service activities among employees is another way of developing these informal connections, i.e., a team of employees might participate in a local walk-a-thon, help build a local playground or contribute their talents to a charity like Habitat for Humanity.
- Celebrating company milestones to acknowledge the contributions of employees in business successes.
- Using work space design as a strategy for allowing informal communication opportunities to develop between staff and leadership. Work space design strategies may include creating conversation areas and common areas that all employees eventually frequent throughout the day.

CONNECT MARKETING WITH INTERNAL COMMUNICATION

Employees are the face of a company. They should be the first to know about marketing campaigns. Not only can they serve as a focus group for testing marketing strategies and advertising campaigns, but they are also more likely to support and talk about company marketing campaigns if these strategies are shared with them in advance. This way, they become greater brand ambassadors for the company. Research from the literature review shows that companies are using internal communication to build brand value, improve the customer experience and communicate value propositions with customers.

Some suggestions for marketing-driven internal communications include:

- Internal brand launches.
- Staff training events that feature marketing as content.
- Training on brand values during orientation.
- Brainstorming sessions with all employees during planning processes.
- International marketing consultation with employees from different countries.

- Employee blogs designed for internal and external consumption.
- A rich intranet and web site where employees see the connection between marketing messages and business strategies.

IMPROVE COMMUNICATION RESEARCH TECHNIQUES THAT CONNECT EMPLOYEE COMMUNICATION TO THE COMPANY BOTTOM LINE

Small businesses should consider means to measure the effectiveness of internal communication. Some inexpensive measures that would benefit small businesses in evaluating and developing greater employee engagement and employee loyalty include pulse surveys on specific issues, employee exit interviews, simple suggestion systems and company culture surveys (either developed internally or externally).

Like all forms of organizational research and planning, employee surveys are useless unless management takes action on employee suggestions to improve the organization. Neglecting employee input, especially once solicited, leaves employees feeling like a cog in the machine, not like valued, productive members of the organization.

Holding regular unit meetings or company town hall meetings and following up with employees on their suggestions for improving company processes can aid in measurement and evaluation.

Finding ways to show internal communication results through employee engagement and retention (which are proven to contribute to profitability) is essential to demonstrating that communication supports both strategic and financial goals of the organization. Building on the success of small achievements will increase the credibility of internal communication as well as its support of corporate strategy and the achievement of the corporate vision. This will require creativity and strategic planning. A strategic choice of tactics to maximize return and measure results will be critical to demonstrating the value of internal communication.

One opportunity for medium-sized businesses to maximize the effectiveness of internal communication is to create a position specifically responsible for company communication that works with human resources and marketing communication to coordinate employee communication. Such a position would be best aligned with the executive management of the organization.

CHAPTER 5 / Assessing and Planning Employee Communication

INTRODUCTION / Many research studies (including those cited in this report) deal in generalities. A poll of employee communication preferences of small companies may seem like a panacea to the questions: What do employees want? What are employees' preferred communication practices? But the most popular practices may not be the most effective for your organization.

Every small company and its population of employees are different. An international survey of employee preferences allows us to talk in generalities about communication practices, but the specifics that make each company culture unique are the characteristics that drive successful communication programs.

Every company communicates with its employees—some better than others. Some have come to their present state through evolution or trial and error, while others have systematically developed an effective communication program that effectively aligns internal communication plans with organizational goals and objectives. It is never too late or too early to evaluate the status of employee communication.

WHO WILL TAKE THE LEAD? / Along with the recommendations from this study, one must recognize that small business owners/managers are busy people who are often strapped with the bulk of the management responsibilities, including organizational communication. As noted in the study, employee communication planning and implementation may be a responsibility of the business owner/manager, it may be delegated to a specific department head (i.e., human resources or marketing), or it may be shared by a management team including HR and marketing. *This is the first decision to be made before embarking on the plan that follows.*

WHAT ARE THE GOALS AND OBJECTIVES? / To cite from the study:

> Employee communication is the process of exchanging information and creating understanding and behaviors among employees that reinforce the organization's vision, values and culture, enabling employees to communicate the company's message to external audiences.
>
> Effective employee communication consists of the right information and the right message delivered in a clear manner; it is two-way and essential to the health and productivity of a business (Smith & Mazin, 2004; McAleese & Hargie, 2004).
>
> The greatest benefit from effective employee communication is a knowledgeable workforce that is satisfied and productive, which leads to positive interactions with customers, investors and the community.

Aligning internal communication plans with organizational goals and objectives is a key step in developing and strengthening business performance. Internal communication plans also need to acknowledge and fit into the company's culture.

Articulating the goals and objectives of employee communication activities is important to developing the process and choosing appropriate communication practices. Employee communication goals and objectives should reinforce strategic business goals and support the direction of the company as a whole. Here are some examples:

- Improve direct, two-way communication between management and employees.
- Cultivate a culture that values communication—in all directions within the company.
- Inform and educate employees about advancement opportunities.
- Create opportunities for informal communications.
- Keep employees informed about issues that affect their work at the company and in the industry.
- Keep employees informed about changes to policies and procedures that affect their work.
- Create a community of employees within the company.
- Educate employees about the business strategy of the company, their role in meeting company goals and the benefits they gain in contributing to the success of the company.
- Provide a two-way communication channel that encourages employees to contribute to meeting strategic business goals.
- Encourage management to engage in two-way communication practices that create a productive company culture.

Employees need to know about the company, the industry and their customers, as well as their specific job functions. Employees also need to feel that they are valued and are part of a community within the company. Different communication practices are better suited for meeting these different goals and objectives.

HOW DO YOUR CURRENT EMPLOYEE COMMUNICATION PRACTICES MEASURE UP? / Using the specific objectives defined for employee communication, it is necessary to review the current practices the company uses to communicate with employees—from companywide to department to team practices—from hire to retire. This process is called a communication audit. The purpose of a communication audit is to assess the strengths and weaknesses of internal communication practices and ultimately align the messages and practices with the strategy of the company and the needs of the employees. A thorough communication audit will aid in developing open, two-way communication and will identify barriers or constraints to open communication across the company. A communication audit may be done in-house by the person or team responsible for the employee communication function or may be contracted to an outside communication firm.

The advantages of performing this function in-house are cost savings and allowing the employee communication team or leader to get familiar with past communication practices and strategies. The disadvantage of performing this function in-house is that the team or leader may not be objective in the evaluation because they are too close to the process.

The advantages of hiring an outside firm to conduct the communication audit are the objective analysis and additional expertise in the practice of communication (knowledge of best practices in the field). The disadvantage is the expense to the company.

The following is an overview of the communication audit process:

- Review the goals and objectives of the employee communication program in light of the current business model and strategic business plan.
- Analyze the content of current communication practices (face-to-face, print, electronic, multimedia, formal and informal) to determine whether objectives are being met and ensure that company messages, brand and strategies are being delivered consistently. This analysis should include the strengths and weaknesses of each communication practice (content, accuracy, image and cost-effectiveness). To assess the effectiveness of face-to-face communication with managers and peers, focus groups or a pulse survey may be conducted, or a member of the audit team may attend department meetings.
- Conduct an employee survey to assess the employees' use of and opinions about each communication practice. In this survey, employees may be asked about the face-to-face commu-

nication they have with their immediate supervisor as well as peer employees. Also allow employees to suggest communication practices that are not currently used by the company. Use the employee survey to seek employee feedback on the quality of company communications: What is the company's biggest communication weakness? Is there a communication tool the company isn't using but should be? Where do you go to find information about company policies, news about the company, etc.? What communication tools do you rely on most frequently and least frequently?

- Focus groups may also be conducted with key employee groups in order to meet their specific needs, as these may be different from the needs of the employee community as a whole. (For example, night shift employees may have a greater need for information than day shift employees simply because the human resources office is not open to answer questions during their work hours. Additional communication practices may be necessary to meet these gaps in two-way communications.)

With this assessment in hand, current communication practices may either be modified to meet the stated objectives or eliminated, and new practices that better meet company objectives and employee preferences may be initiated. For example, new media practices like intranets and blogs may be more cost-effective and easier to implement than traditional practices like newsletters and printed manuals. They also provide a more direct link to audiences. On the other hand, traditional practices may be perceived as trusted and preferred by employees and should be retained for sensitive information delivery. Communication audits and employee surveys should be conducted on a regular basis to keep pace with the communication needs of employees.

Communication practices should be used strategically, in line with a strategic plan. Part of that planning should include regular evaluation of the company's communication practices. Just as employees and managers meet regularly to discuss team and individual performance, communication practices should also be reviewed for effectiveness. This process of evaluation allows for two-way communication and feedback regarding the use of these practices. Soliciting employee opinions regarding communication practices boosts morale. As the employee population grows and changes, employee communication preferences will also grow and evolve. In addition, during times of organizational change, more communication with employees may be necessary to keep them apprised of the effects of change on the organization and their lives.

Communicate about the process and the results. If you are going to ask employees for their input, you should be willing to share a summary of the evaluation with them. This continues to let them know the impact they have on the company. After all, without employees, what would your company be?

EMPLOYEE COMMUNICATION SURVEY: SAMPLE QUESTIONS

These are generic questions. They may be modified for the different communication tools the company uses.

Face-to-Face Communication

- How would you rate the quality of company meetings?

  ❑ High ❑ Average ❑ Below average ❑ Poor

- How valuable is the information shared at company meetings?

  ❑ Very ❑ Somewhat ❑ Not at all

- Are company meetings held at the appropriate frequency throughout the year?

  ❑ Yes ❑ No

- Do you have an opportunity to provide feedback during the company meeting?

  ❑ Yes ❑ No

- How can we improve company meetings?

____

____

____

- If technology (videoconferencing or teleconferencing) is used, how effective is it?

  ❑ Very ❑ Somewhat ❑ Not at all

Print Publications

- What kind of information do you expect to find in the company newsletter?

___

___

___

- What kind of information would you like to see in the company newsletter?

___

___

___

- How useful do you find the company newsletter?

  ❑ Very ❑ Somewhat ❑ Not at all

- How often do you read the company newsletter?

  ❑ Every issue ❑ Occasionally ❑ Never

- What is your favorite section of the company newsletter?

___

- Is the newsletter published on a regular schedule?

  ❑ Yes ❑ No

- Is the frequency of the newsletter appropriate?

  ❑ Yes ❑ No

Electronic Media

- How many company e-mails do you receive each week?

____

- How many company e-mails are you unable to read?

____

- Which e-mails do you avoid reading on a regular basis?

____

- Why?

____

____

____

- How often do you read e-mails from your manager/owner?

  ❑ Always ❑ Sometimes ❑ Never

- What kind of information is most useful to receive through e-mail?

____

____

____

- What kind of information would you prefer not to receive through e-mail?

____

____

____

- How often do you use the company intranet?

  ❑ Every day ❑ Occasionally ❑ Never

- What sections of the company intranet do you use most often?

____

____

____

- How often do you read the company e-newsletter?

  ❑ Every issue ❑ Occasionally ❑ Never

- What section of the company e-newsletter do you read most often?

____

- Do you print out the company e-newsletter? ❑ Yes ❑ No
- How often? ❑ Every issue ❑ Occasionally ❑ Never
- Is the frequency of the company e-newsletter appropriate?

  ❑ Yes ❑ No

Overall Employee Communications

- What is the company's biggest communication weakness?

___

___

___

- Is there a communication tool the company isn't using but should be?

❑ Yes ❑ No

- If so, what is it?

___

___

- Where do you go to find information about company policies, news about the company, etc.?

___

___

___

- What communication tools do you rely on most frequently?

___

___

- Why?

___

___

- What communication tools do you rely on least frequently?

____

____

____

- Why?

____

____

____

SELECTING COMMUNICATION PRACTICES / Successful employee communication programs include a mix of communication practices. Communication practices should be selected based on employee preference/usage (social presence), cost-effectiveness, strength of media (media richness) and strategic business goals. Social presence refers to the sociability of the practice—its warmth, sensitivity and ease of use. Media richness refers to the density of the information; interactivity, responsiveness and immediacy as well as the formal use of language are issues associated with media richness. The choice of communication media also sends a message regarding the importance of the information and the employees.

FACE-TO-FACE COMMUNICATIONS

Face-to-face communication practices have a higher degree of social presence and media richness than other forms of communication because of the opportunities for immediate feedback and fine-tuning of the message through questions and answers as well as facial expressions. Employees know that the owner's or manager's time is valuable. By using face-to-face communication, owners/managers are showing the employees that they are important to the company and that the message they are communicating is important to the direction of the company.

Face-to-face communication is effective for communicating important and sensitive information, raising collective awareness and creating learning opportunities. Face-to-face communication—from a companywide meeting to managers meeting in small groups with employees—requires that the manager be prepared to answer questions and engage in discussion with employees.

As seen in the study findings, face-to-face communication between management and employees is a critical component of any employee communication program. Employees trust their immediate supervisor for information about their performance as well as direction for meeting strategic business goals as a team. Employees benefit from hearing company news from the company leadership. They evaluate the credibility of the information and participate with questions and commentary. For businesses with multiple locations, teleconferencing or videoconferences can suffice for face-to-face communication opportunities. For businesses that work in shifts around the clock, multiple face-to-face meetings can be held to allow each group of employees to participate in this process. Town hall meetings may be held to share information with all employees at one time to reduce the risk of misinterpretation.

Evaluating face-to-face communications, like team meetings, can be tricky. Managers may feel they are being evaluated on their performance, instead of on the practice as a tool for company communication. Evaluating face-to-face communication may be accomplished through a survey of employees or by having a member of the audit team attend a few meetings conducted by different managers. A survey of employees should include questions regarding the effectiveness of meetings and the usefulness of the information they receive. Managers should also be included in the process; ask them about how well meetings are run. Meeting evaluations should address the value of the content, the operation of the meeting, and the overall strengths and weaknesses of holding meetings.

To improve two-way communication, encourage managers to increase the use of management by walking around so employees can ask questions in a less formal setting. Managers may also encourage employees to send them questions and comments to be used for improving later meetings.

PRINT PUBLICATIONS

Print publications provide a portable source of information. Short forms like newsletters can be easy to use, adding to their social presence. Print publications, like an employee manual or guide, can be full of information; these are qualities of media richness. Regardless of how sophisticated electronic technology gets, there will always be a place for print publications in employee communication programs.

Print publications—newsletters, manuals, brochures, handbooks, posters and correspondence—are effective at sharing in-depth information and company stories as well as reinforcing the company culture, mission and strategic business direction. Print communication can reinforce concepts and raise awareness of issues in the workplace as well as communicate policies and procedures. Newsletters and periodical publications allow the company to keep employees up to date on news and information about the company and human interest stories about employees. Depending on the frequency of the publication, these can be used for sharing timely information and for providing information that employees can refer back to time and again. Handbooks and manuals (orientation materials) have a longer shelf life and are typically updated only as necessary, i.e., as policies and procedures change. Company letters take time to construct but are valuable tools for sharing sensitive information with employees.

To improve the degree of interactivity and responsiveness of print publications, these practices need to include a form of feedback, like a suggestion or follow-up system that provides employees a means for two-way communication.

When evaluating print publications, collect a representative sample of the past issues of the publication for review; four or five should suffice. Consider the following as the evaluation:

- The goals and objectives of employee communication.
- The goals being met by this publication.
- The publication schedule and circulation.
- The strengths and weaknesses of the publication.
- How employees use the publication.
- Whether employees use the publication.

In the employee communication survey included in the communication audit, consider asking questions like: What types of information do you expect to find in this publication?

ELECTRONIC MEDIA

Electronic media—e-mail, intranets, company web sites, blogs, electronic meetings and e-newsletters—are quickly becoming popular in employee communication programs. Electronic media can be easy to use, but they lack the warmth and sensitivity associated with high social presence. Electronic media score highly on media richness because these practices are dense with information and can be equipped with two-way feedback systems that provide an opportunity for information clarification and improvement.

Electronic media can communicate time-sensitive information in an immediate and unified way across the company. Company intranets can provide a self-serve location for employees to learn about everything from career opportunities to human resources policies and the latest company news. Content from the print newsletter can be transmitted in electronic form to employees. Questions from hotlines and employee suggestion systems can be collected and shared through a frequently asked question section on the company intranet. And through the use of e-mail, members of the company can share short and long messages regarding daily practices as well as industry news.

Electronic media can simulate face-to-face communication through real-time Internet technology or even the informal chat room format. These practices may benefit companies with multiple locations and the need to share information immediately while providing a two-way communication environment. Social presence is reduced; however, since employees do not have the opportunity to see the speaker or hear the inflection of his or her voice.

While electronic media appear to be able to simulate many face-to-face and print practices, many employees today are experiencing "information overload" because so much information is being delivered through e-mail. Employees have a difficult time evaluating which messages are important. E-newsletters save on physical resources but are less thoroughly read because of this information overload.

When evaluating electronic publications (e-newsletters, online employee manuals, e-mail correspondence), collect a representative sample of the past issues of the publication for review; four or five should suffice. Consider the following as the evaluation:

- The goals and objectives of employee communication.
- The goals being met by this publication.
- The publication schedule and circulation.
- The strengths and weaknesses of the publication.
- How employees use the publication.
- Whether employees use the publication.

For company e-mails, consider "information overload" when evaluating employees' use of e-mail and the amount they read. An evaluation of e-mails should include a collection of a month's worth of company e-mails. Consider the following:

- The quality of information.
- The usefulness of information.
- The rate of use (opening) by employees.

Are e-mails properly titled in the subject line? Do e-mails include one subject, or are many buried under one subject heading? Simply improving the use of the subject line and keeping e-mails simple and limited to one subject will improve employee use of company e-mails.

CONCLUDING COMMENTS / As repeated throughout this section and the study as a whole, there is no one-size-fits-all solution for employee communication in small companies. Employee communication programs work best when a variety of media are used to communicate with employees. Assessing employee preferences and current employee communication practices will improve employee satisfaction as well as employees' understanding of their role in the success of the company.

Refer to "Recommendations for Small Firms" (p. 89) for specific best practices cited from the study. The following case studies also provide insight into successful practices for small businesses.

CHAPTER 6 / Small Business Communication Practices Case Studies

BACK IN MOTION / Back in Motion is a full-service rehabilitation, disability management and vocational services company in British Columbia, Canada. Back in Motion has two primary locations (in Richmond and Surrey) and several smaller sites that provide select services. The two primary sites each provide state-of-the-art gym and rehabilitation facilities, offices, physical examination and assessment rooms, work simulation facilities, and offices.

According to Ken Hemphill, one of the managing directors, the company was started by a multidisciplinary group of four health care professionals and an administrative specialist in 1993. The company's ownership and senior executive team represent the disciplines of psychology, vocational rehabilitation, physical therapy and finance. In 2006, the company reported its size as 57 employees. Back in Motion was honored as one of the 30 "Best Workplaces" in Canada in 2005 by Great Place to Work® Institute Canada.

THE CULTURE

The organizational culture of Back in Motion is based on teamwork and achieving goals through open communication and respect for staff and clients. Staff describe it as productive and professional, fun and friendly. The staff represents a number of disciplines, including physicians, occupational therapists, psychologists, registered clinical counselors, physical therapists, kinesiologists and vocational rehabilitation counselors. This team of professionals appreciates the needs of both employers and workers as they support clients' progress toward returning to the workforce and independence.

Communication is a vital part of the culture. In a health care environment, communication between staff and management is just as important as the communication between staff and clients. Sensitivity to the needs and expectations of the client and the business are paramount for reaching goals at all levels.

The culture of openness and respect is evidenced through the company's use of communication to reach business goals and develop new services to grow the business. Staff are valued for their contributions to strategic planning initiatives and operations plans. Communication flows two-way as management engages staff in planning, and the staff raise issues to improve the operation of the company.

COMMUNICATION STRATEGIES

The management team shares the responsibility for internal or employee communication. Marketing and business development are responsible for external communication. The internal communication mix for Back in Motion includes formal and informal strategies, depending on the nature of the messages.

Human resources issues tend to be handled on a formal and planned basis. Orientations, performance evaluations and career development initiatives are a few examples. It is important that all staff are provided with uniform information in a highly regulated sector like health care. Career development opportunities are provided for staff as a means to recognize their valuable professional contributions and continue to improve the services that the firm has to offer clients. Attending to staff needs for career development also allows the firm to remain competitive and to retain employees who might otherwise leave for opportunities at other businesses.

The most important ongoing communication practice is face-to-face communication. Even with the multiple locations, Hemphill emphasizes the importance of sharing information with staff and managers in person. "When we were small, just five people, face-to-face was enough. As we have grown in size and number of locations, communication by necessity has become more formal. But we still prefer to communicate face-to-face." This is accomplished through monthly operational meetings and less formal discussions with staff on a daily basis about company expectations, the company mission and vision, and the staff's role in reaching company goals.

Print and electronic communications are used to supplement the face-to-face communication opportunities. Summaries from meetings are shared with staff who are unable to attend. Print publications are used more for external communication.

E-mail provides uniform messages and reaches everyone in all locations at one time. But the quality of communication in e-mail is shallow. In this fast-paced environment, e-mail can easily be overlooked.

The monthly operational business meetings held at one of the two primary sites are the best means for two-way communication when the goal is to share information with all employees at once. Of course, direct unit manager communication with staff is critical to the success of the company.

Back in Motion is committed to maintaining its well-balanced organizational culture. Orientation includes a discussion about the organizational culture. The company conducted an internal corporate culture survey for two years; in 2005 and 2006 they chose to participate in the Great Place to Work® Institute Canada "Best Workplaces" survey. This external objective assessment of many company characteristics that define organizational culture allows the company to benchmark its progress against other companies, plan improvements, evaluate communication effectiveness and celebrate successes.

Holistic internal communication practices contribute in significant ways to the growth of the company. An open atmosphere in which people feel free to communicate and contribute to the success of the business results in high quality programs and a place where employees want to be every day.

KAHLER SLATER ARCHITECTS INC. / Kahler Slater Architects Inc. is a creative, interdisciplinary design firm with clients around the world. The firm has four locations: Milwaukee, Madison and Green Bay, Wisconsin; and Burlington, North Carolina. "We work with our clients to create a holistic experience that encompasses all realms of an organization—perception, people, products, services and place." The company has been recognized for three years in a row (2004–2006) by the Great Place to Work Institute® as a Great Place to Work in the U.S. One hundred fifty employees comprise this creative community of architects, marketers, researchers, graphic designers, branding specialists and consultants. The firm will celebrate 100 years of business in 2008.

THE CULTURE

According to Kelly Gaglione, principal, director of client services and communications strategist, Kahler Slater has a unique, creative culture that is friendly, collaborative, nonhierarchical and driven by the passions of the firm members. Referring to the company web site, the company is described as "a close-knit group that works hard and plays hard. Our work inspires us, and our play invigorates us."

The concept of collaboration and teamwork extends well past the nature of the design work to the structure of the company itself. Three CEOs share the executive leadership of the firm. According to Gaglione, this was a deliberate decision on the part of the leadership when the firm was reorganizing. The CEOs—or "3EOs"—share the responsibility of company leadership. Each has a specific portfolio of responsibilities. Communication—internal and external—is the one facet of organizational leadership for which each of the CEOs is responsible. Communication and leadership are inseparable.

Employees embrace the company vision. Because collaboration and teamwork are keys to the success of design work and the company at large, buy-in on decisions is highly valued. Employees enjoy a great deal of autonomy in this process as evidenced by the flexible work schedules.

COMMUNICATION STRATEGIES

Communication is part of everyone's job—from the CEOs to the principals and team leaders. In this culture, formal and informal internal communication practices are used.

To keep employees up to date on company business, a number of regular meetings are held—all-staff meetings, team meetings, and principal and owner meetings. During the monthly all-staff meeting, locations are linked by either video or audio conferencing. These meetings are expressly for celebrating success and project advancement, i.e., progress reports and news of the firm. The meeting agenda is driven by the employees and the projects of the firm; special discussion topics may be suggested by anyone in the firm. Every team holds weekly meetings to keep projects on track and people connected to one another. Through the use of these face-to-face meetings, information flow is cyclical and builds a community of understanding: What is discussed in a team meeting may become the basis of a special topic discussion at a monthly meeting. The direction articulated at a principals meeting will be addressed in monthly meetings and further discussed at the team level as projects progress.

The firm holds an annual staff retreat at which the leadership delivers the "state of the firm." This retreat provides a forum for addressing the firm's vision and direction, special topics and employee camaraderie. "The 3EOs go all out to make the event fun and educational. Their presentation is themed: One year they came dressed as ship captains to discuss our course and direction; another year it was mountain climbers."

Interaction between members of the firm is also encouraged through the physical design of the work space at Kahler Slater. "As architects and designers, our research and work focus on the place—workplace design that contributes to employee communication and employee satisfaction. We live that everyday." When the firm remodeled the office space, "we turned the office inside out." Since collaboration is key to the culture, an open office work environment was created with lower partitions between individual offices, the development of team collaboration spaces (TCS)—conference areas that invite interaction from the firm as a whole—and open areas—pin-up spaces where staff may share their work and request critiques from everyone in the office. Even the CEOs have open offices (cubes).

Electronic communication practices are an expectation for facilitating immediate, real-time information. The company intranet is used for formal communication like policies and procedures typically found in an employee manual. E-mails are an expected form of communication and are used most frequently to keep the members at the four office locations connected on a minute-by-minute basis.

Traditions have been modified in the age of electronic communication. According to Gaglione, the firm has a tradition of announcing new commissions by the ringing of a large antique ship's bell that is located in the Milwaukee office. To share this protocol with the other three offices, an e-mail titled "the ringing of the bell" is sent concurrently with the traditional announcement. A teleconference call may also be set up so that the members across the firm's four locations can share in the celebration and hear the bell.

Print communication is used on a limited basis for official information like OSHA regulations and confidential information like compensation reviews.

Informal social gatherings are also encouraged on an irregular basis. These events are sponsored and organized by staff. Dubbed "Fridays at Four," these social gatherings offer an opportunity to network with other employees and share creative ideas, snacks and refreshments. Held on-site in a creative café room with white boards and comfortable furniture, these gatherings are a chance for staff to brainstorm and unwind.

The success of internal communication for Kahler Slater is a combination of these methods. Daily formal communication is facilitated by e-mail, but face-to-face meetings and interactions are best for developing greater understanding and managing two-way universal responses. Face-to-face communication is an expectation in a small firm. It is unavoidable in close spaces and in an environment where offices share projects and corporate strategy. It is the best way to share and develop understanding of everything from team projects to the corporate vision.

Like many small businesses, Kahler Slater does not formally evaluate its internal communication programs. But as Gaglione notes, internal communication gets evaluated through the Great Place to Work Institute® employee survey each year. Communication is the basis for developing a culture in which employees want to work and play...a place to develop their passions.

JOHN G. HOFLAND LTD. / John G. Hofland Ltd., a family-owned floral business located in Mississauga, Ontario, has been in operation since 1956. Over the years, Hofland has evolved into one of Canada's largest full-service floral wholesalers. They maintain two warehouse facilities, a retail store and office, and a fleet of 15 delivery vehicles. The company has two physical locations. Five employees work from the remote warehouse, about 6 kilometers from the main location where approximately 115 employees work.

As a full-service floral wholesaler, John G. Hofland operates across North America, offering a wide selection of unique flowers and greens imported from around the world. Hofland also carries a selection of complimentary giftware.

"Providing World Class selection of the highest quality products backed by unmatched service" is Hofland's driving business philosophy. They attribute their loyal customer base to their pursuit of this philosophy, which also drives company operations.

In 2006, John G. Hofland Ltd. was recognized by the Great Place to Work Institute® as one of the Best Places to Work in Canada.

THE CULTURE

According to Debbie Montanera-Bojda, human resources manager at John G. Hofland Ltd., the culture at Hofland is casual, fast-paced and team-spirited. "Employees are willing to help one another. We are a seasonal business, which means we have weeks throughout the year that are extremely busy and extremely fast-paced."

COMMUNICATION STRATEGIES

The president of the company is responsible for internal communication and for the corporate updates and smaller brainstorming sessions the company uses to engage employees in planning and problem-solving. The president encourages open communication.

Hofland relies on a mix of formal, planned employee communications and informal employee communication practices. Informal communication is more frequently used and is characterized by an "open door policy" where employees are encouraged to speak freely and voice opinions or concerns to company management.

According to Montanera-Bojda, the best way to learn about problems or inefficiencies is to speak to the employees. They know what will work best in their jobs and may have suggestions for improvement. At Hofland, major business decisions are discussed with employees. Decisions are first discussed at quarterly corporate update meetings where the president discusses business results or strategic plans. Later, smaller discussion groups are formed to brainstorm ideas, discuss concerns or offer suggestions. An example of an issue that was addressed through brainstorming sessions included streamlining procedures to improve productivity. Also, when the company was feeling the stress of "outgrowing their current warehouse," brainstorming sessions were held to discuss the implications of moving to a new location or splitting the business and the impact these issues would have on the cash-and-carry customers.

Face-to-face communication is encouraged because questions can be thoroughly answered and additional questions can be fielded in a dialog. Other forms of communication the company uses to keep employees informed and engaged in the operation of the business include monthly printed newsletters, the quarterly corporate update meetings, meetings with supervisors/managers, postings throughout the facility, e-mail and attachments to pay slips.

These more formal communication strategies are used to make announcements and provide business results; news of upcoming events; changes to benefits, health and safety news; and other information that affects everyone in the company.

Supervisor and manager meetings, coupled with the president's message in the corporate address, encourage two-way communication. According to Montanera-Bojda, "We encourage employee feedback, suggestions and opinions. It is what keeps our employees engaged."

Communication practices may change depending on the situation at hand, the immediacy of the information, and the impact it has on the business and employees. For example, a reminder about benefits coverage can be communicated through the newsletter and postings because this information is straightforward and does not require a reply from the employees. Situations in which feedback is requested from employees will require more face-to-face communications.

Communication practices contribute to knowledgeable and engaged employees. "When employees feel like they matter to the company and that their job is important to the company's success, then they will work harder, as a team, for a common goal."

Hofland does not formally evaluate its employee communication practices at this time. Participation in the Great Places to Work® employee survey provides information that can be used to assess communication as one of many business components that contribute to a successful company.

BADGER MINING CORPORATION / Badger Mining Corporation, headquartered in Berlin, Wisconsin, is a privately held, family-owned international corporation that produces silica sand for industrial use. Plant operations are located in Fairwater and Taylor, Wisconsin; Pahrump, Nevada; and Poland. The C.A. Chier Resource Center is located in Berlin, Wisconsin. Badger Mining Corporation employs 183 associates, including advisory associates, leaders, coaches and associates.

The company traces its history to the early 1900s. In recent years, their work within the industry and as a company has been recognized with numerous awards. In 1997 and 1999, BMC was awarded the Business Friend of the Environment Award from the Wisconsin Environmental Working Group. In 1999, the company was also awarded the John Brogan Award for Outstanding Environmental Achievement. In 2006, BMC received two national safety awards: the Sentinels of Safety Program Safety Trophy for its outstanding safety records by the Mine Safety and Health Administration and the National Mining Association, and the Safety Achievement Award from the U.S. Department of Labor's Mine Safety and Health Administration and the Industrial Minerals Association—North America. In 2006, Badger Mining Company was honored nationally as the number one "Best Small Company to Work for in America" by the Great Place to Work® Institute.

THE CULTURE

High-quality communication practices are part and parcel of BMC's mission "to become the quality leader in the industrial minerals industry with a team of people committed to excellence and a passion for satisfying [their] customers." Company growth is steady and driven by the highest quality standards.

According to Mellisa Stafford, training and staffing associate, BMC's culture is one of employee empowerment fostered by organizational trust. This is exemplified by the use of self-directed work teams that identify, evaluate and develop opportunities for the company. BMC is committed to environmental responsibility, safety, health and integrity, while providing a rewarding and enjoyable place to work. Employees share in the success of the company through a 20 percent profit sharing program.

BMC uses a flat organizational structure, which fosters greater connections between leadership and associates. According to Stafford, employee empowerment and trust are the results of open communication and caring within the organization. Leadership cares about employee opinions and encourages employees to contribute to problem solving. Leadership gives associates the power to do their work and trusts that associates will use their best judgment and practices. Consequently, associates know they are valued, and they are passionate about the work they do.

COMMUNICATION STRATEGIES

Communication is key at Badger Mining Corporation. Stafford credits employee communication that begins with orientation and progresses with associates throughout their careers as one of many practices that connect associates in a meaningful way to the operations of the company. Along with typical orientation programming that introduces associates to company policies and procedures, BMC engages associates in numerous evaluation and feedback opportunities, at which time associates provide feedback about how the company is doing. Within the first 30 days of employment, associates participate in a progress assessment, which is just the first of many times that associates will have the opportunity to be evaluated and—more important—will have the opportunity to evaluate the company. According to Stafford, the company makes a point of acting on the suggestions of associates, because they have insights into the daily operation of the company.

Internal communication is a shared process depending on the information being delivered. Communication within the company is responsibility-driven. For example, benefits information is communicated by human resources; a team of customer relations and public relations associates are responsible for the quarterly company newsletter, "Badger Banner"; the safety team is responsible for communicating safety issues; and the executive leadership is responsible for sharing financial information and strategic direction.

Face-to-face communication opportunities are critical to internal communication success. Team meetings are held twice a year, and every associate attends. These meetings cover everything from benefits to safety information to financial summaries to the strategic direction of the company.

As a mining company, safety is very important. Monthly safety meetings are held at each location, coupled with the annual companywide, day-long safety refresher meeting. Safety teams keep safety in the forefront at each location as well.

The company uses a number of print and electronic practices to reinforce the face-to-face practices. The newsletter is distributed to associates at all U.S. locations. Some information regarding benefits and HR issues is still sent to employees' homes because this is where the decision making about benefits takes place. Announcements are posted in the company plants to alert associates to opportunities. Through the company intranet, associates can access information about each plant facility as well as the employee manual. Company e-mails are used to broadcast information to all employees.

The company also uses an open book management approach; complete financial information (income statements, balance sheets, etc.) is shared with all employees monthly so they are always aware of the financial status of the company. "The associates truly work with a common goal because they understand the mission and values of the company. They know that the success they have in their job translates to the success of the company."

While Badger Mining Corporation is only beginning to measure the impact of its internal communication practices, they know from anecdotal qualitative data that employee satisfaction is high. In the past, the company conducted occasional culture surveys that supported the anecdotal data. In 2006, the company began participating in the Great Place to Work® Institute survey and plans to continue to use the results of this survey to evaluate employee communications and other strategic business practices.

According to Stafford, communication is something that is embedded in the culture of Badger Mining Corporation. It is impossible to separate it from the organization and the people who care about the place like a family.

VIACK* / VIACK is the company behind the VIA3 Assured Collaboration Service, a fully secure online collaboration solution. VIA3 enables business and government professionals to meet with colleagues and clients anywhere, working together and sharing information as easily and effectively as if they were in the same conference room. The advantages of the software for clients are savings in downtime, travel and administrative expenses; enhanced productivity; and more responsive service. VIACK Corporation was founded in 1999 and has offices located in Washington, D.C., Arizona and Washington state.

THE CULTURE

VIACK is both functionally and geographically divided. The offices are located in different places due to the location of the talent and the client base. For example, because the engineering talent is located in Redmond, Washington, much of the R&D staff is located there. Because VIACK is a supplier to the government sector, they have a sales office in Washington, D.C. In addition, their corporate office is located in Scottsdale, Arizona. Amazingly, even with the different locations, VIACK still feels like a small, family-owned business with a very open culture.

COMMUNICATION STRATEGIES

VIACK credits the company culture to their own software. They use their online collaborative tool, which they market, for communicating within the company. Rather than a telephone, employees use the collaboration tool with a webcam and a headset. The collaboration tool enables staff to see 14 people on the screen with audio and instant messaging capabilities. Typically, employees gather in a main area, and they can communicate with staff in all of the different locations.

In addition to technology, there is a real openness in the attitude of top management. Management frequently stops in and sees employees at the different locations. Face-to-face communication is still used a great deal at VIACK. Especially during challenging times, management ensures that they are accessible. For example, the CEO will go to the engineering facility when there are difficulties getting new products out. These face-to-face communication strategies make sure the staff feels valued and supported. This also encourages staff to express opinions to management.

Overall, VIACK is a flat organization without a lot of structure. Using an open door policy and delegating broad areas of responsibilities, the staff works together in an environment of mutual respect. VIACK used to have an anonymous suggestion system, but it is no longer used because people now feel comfortable asking the CEO hard questions.

*This case study was contributed by Insightrix.

BONFIRE COMMUNICATIONS* / Bonfire Communications is located in San Francisco and was founded in 2001. By combining strategic and organizational consulting with interactive design, branding and marketing, Bonfire created what they call the "Bonfire Magic"—a communication approach that is greater than the sum of its parts. The initiative is unique and successful. Using multidisciplinary teams, the company has worked on implementing supply chain processes, large enterprise technologies, branding initiatives, reorganizations and mergers for companies around the world. It has created new ways of bringing new visions to life, building programs that inspire participation and action from employees, customers and the marketplace.

THE CULTURE

The culture can best be described through Bonfire's philosophy—results-oriented but fun. The 27 employees are an energetic, business-savvy and passionate team of professionals committed to making a positive impact in the world. With a fast and efficient working style, the staff collaborates with clients and teammates to develop straightforward, creative solutions to complex business challenges. All the while, their work is infused with an appreciation for everyday life and laughter. In addition, Bonfire can be described as a learning organization. The collaborative working style lets everyone know what everyone else is working on. The key is to leverage skills.

COMMUNICATION STRATEGIES

The company is in growth mode; therefore, management must make sure that employees are connected daily in terms of operational procedures and culture. Understanding business processes as the company grows has been an issue, and making sure the staff has the appropriate forms and required training has been challenging. During the past few years of growth, Bonfire has documented new and emerging business processes within the firm and shared them with staff to assist in keeping them connected. Bonfire developed an employee/operations manual and is working on a company manifesto for a cultural orientation. The manifesto defines the company for contractors and clients.

As the company has grown, it has developed more tools to support internal dialog, including the intranet and the internal employee blog. Bonfire also uses an open floor layout. The directors have offices with walls and doors but no ceilings. This allows directors to have enclosed space for writing and making calls with clients, without being cut off from the rest of the staff. The managers are located next to creative services, which facilitates the creative process. The managers are also close to the directors to offer them support. This arrangement has contributed to improved communication.

Bonfire uses open book management. The business is driven by targets. Overall, employees understand targeted company revenue, profit and project profitability. Bonfire also uses a combined bonus pool. If revenue and profit goals are reached for the year, every person gets a bonus that is 10 percent of their salary.

*This case study was contributed by Insightrix.

TRI OCEAN ENGINEERING LTD.* / Tri Ocean Engineering Ltd. is a consulting engineering firm that provides comprehensive engineering, procurement and project management services to the production, drilling and processing sectors of the petroleum industry worldwide. The company has expertise in fit-for-purpose designs for onshore, arctic and offshore facilities. Tri Ocean was established in Calgary, Alberta, as an employee-owned, fully Canadian company. The senior technical personnel have extensive onshore and offshore production and drilling experience. Tri Ocean's services include the preparation of feasibility studies, preliminary designs and cost estimates; design criteria; detailed drawings and specifications; equipment specifications; and operating manuals. These design services are complemented by providing procurement, construction supervision, start-up assistance, and project operation and management. In total, there are approximately 400 employees at Tri Ocean. The parent company of Tri Ocean is ASRC Energy Services.

THE CULTURE

Tri Ocean Engineering is a project team-based organization. The culture is one of measuring results, collaboration and working toward a common goal.

COMMUNICATION STRATEGIES

Communication between the two companies, ASRC and Tri Ocean, is currently conducted by intranet, telephone and e-mail. The challenge is having both organizations get the same message out to their staff.

Internally, Tri Ocean has a newsletter—with an electronic and a print version, each of which has slightly different content. The online newsletter comes from management and deals with new work the company has coming in, jobs landed through the bidding process and other stories of interest. The print newsletter, following IABC recommendations, is circulated quarterly and distributed to all employees.

Tri Ocean utilizes face-to-face communications quite a bit. The president coordinates messages to the staff through town hall meetings. These meetings are opportunities for the president to communicate directly with the staff, and they occur toward the end of the workday. Employees can socialize with management after the town hall meeting. These meetings happen every second month. In addition, managers meet with their staff every week.

*This case study was contributed by Insightrix.

ENCORE CAPITAL GROUP INC.* / Encore Capital Group Inc. used to be a company of less than 500 employees. As a result of a joint venture, the organization quickly expanded to just over 1,000 employees. This case study illustrates the changes and challenges a small business goes through when it expands to the next level. The company has three sites that offer many communication challenges.

THE CULTURE

Prior to the expansion, Encore Capital Group had a family feel. To some degree, this feeling still remains. However, due to the larger organizational structure, the organization has had to become more formal. Encore is trying to keep a small company feeling in a bigger organization. Employees still need to make decisions quickly using a small organization approach.

COMMUNICATION STRATEGIES

Face-to-face communication is key to Encore. The CEO frequently goes on road shows. At these road shows, the CEO talks about success stories. After the road show, follow-up communications, such as e-mails and newsletters, reinforce the message. Encore also holds monthly town hall meetings at which employees can ask questions of senior management. Management by walking around is also conducted.

Encore has skip level meetings in which employees can bypass their managers and go to different levels to get answers to their questions. This opens the eyes of management to employee issues. These meetings are held on an ad hoc basis and when red flag issues arise.

Encore uses an open floor plan. The offices are in an open cubicle format. The key is collaboration at Encore, and the open floor plan supports this. Sometimes it can be noisy, but the benefit is that it breaks down barriers between staff. One thing that can be a struggle is the desire for more structure from some of the new employees. But the open floor plan can also be appealing. People need to fit the organization, and the people Encore is looking for (team-oriented and collaborative) like the open floor plans.

Encore had a newsletter but stopped using it a few years ago. It was a burden to put the information together when the company was smaller (prior to the acquisition). However, Encore is now considering bringing the newsletter back.

Today, Encore relies more on the Internet. The electronic newsletter, which is still utilized at Encore, is used as a follow-up to the town hall meeting to apprise those who missed the meeting of the highlights. The company intranet is being enhanced. It was easier to manage when Encore was smaller, but now that the company is bigger, everyone wants to put something on it. Currently, there are too many entry points, and a logical structure is lacking. The intranet is being simplified to become a two-way vehicle, rather than an archive of information.

Encore uses open book management. The staff at Encore is results-oriented so they need to know where they are in financial terms at any time. One lesson the company has learned is that goals must be tangible and achievable. Encore uses dashboards to release the results on a regular basis. All business units have a dashboard that they monitor, which includes their targets and their results. The targets are based on company targets and then broken down into the different divisions.

Encore conducts employee engagement surveys, from which management learns a great deal about the organization. Management relies on these surveys to determine annual benchmarks. The survey drives communication and includes benchmarks from the Great Place to Work Institute. These electronic surveys are used to identify gaps between Encore and other companies. The response rate from the survey is between 80 percent and the low 90s. Encore schedules times during the weekday when people can complete the survey.

Although Encore does not have a formal suggestion system, employees are expected to come up with ideas.

Communication strategies have changed as the size of the organization has changed. Encore must determine the messages it wants to communicate and the key objectives that employees should meet through internal communication practices. The CEO road shows, town halls, e-mails to the workforce and round tables (monthly meetings that include a group of nominated employees) have been key. The emphasis is on bottom-up communication.

*This case study was contributed by Insightrix.

REFERENCES

Allen, G. (1989, September). Employee loyalty: Dead or just different? *Communication World, 6*(9), 17–19.

Anderson, K. (1999, September). By the (open) book. *Inc., 21*(13), 33–34.

Anton, F. R. (1980). *Worker participation: Prescription for industrial change.* Calgary, Alberta, Canada: Detselig Enterprises Limited.

Bado, J. (2002). *Four steps to building better business people.* The National Center for Employee Ownership. Retrieved from *www.nceo.org/library/obm_bado.html.*

Balderson, W. D. (2000). *Canadian entrepreneurship and small business management.* Toronto: McGraw Hill.

Barrier, M. (1995, February). Creating a violence-free company culture. *Nation's Business, 83*(2), 18–24.

Beckman, M. D., **Good**, W. S. & **Wyckham**, R. G. (1982). Human resources strategy. *Small business management: Concepts and cases.* Toronto: John Wiley & Sons, pp. 351–373.

Bedi, H. (1996, April). Insider feedback: A useful asset. *Asian Business, 32*(4), 44.

Benico Ltd. (2005). *Coping with language barriers in benefits communications.* Retrieved from *insurancenewsletters.com/newsletters/cahu/jun04/language.htm.*

Bolton, J.E. (1971). *Small firms: Report of the committee of inquiry on small firms.* London: HMSO.

Broom, H.N., **Longenecker**, J. G., & **Moore**, C. W. (1983). *Small-business management.* Cincinnati, Ohio, U.S.: South-Western Publishing.

Buchanan, L. (1999, November). Best of the small business Web. *Inc., 21*(17), 62–111.

Burlingham, B. (2003, January). The coolest small company in America. *Inc., 25*(1), 64–71.

Burstiner, I. (1998). *The small business handbook.* London: Simon & Schuster.

(2002). Communicating with remote workers. *The Business Communicator, 3*(3), 6–8.

(2006). Will social media affect who leads internal communication? *The Business Communicator, 7*(7), p. 1–2.

Callaway, E. (2001). Caribou peekaboo. *Inc., 23*(14), 150.

Carland, J. & **Carland**, J. (1990). *Small business management: Tools for success.* Boston: PWS-Kent.

Case, J. (1997, March/April). Opening the books. *Harvard Business Review, 75*(2), 118–127.

Cisco Information Technology. (2004, December 13). *Cisco connected workplace.* Retrieved from *www.cisco.com/web/about/ciscoitatwork/case_studies/real_estate_d12.html.*

Cross, R. & **Parker**, A. (2004). *The hidden power of social networks: Understanding how work really gets done in organizations.* Boston: Harvard Business School Press.

Department of Trade and Industry. (2006, August 31). *Statistical press release.* Retrieved from *www.dtistats.net/smes/sme/smestats2005-ukspr.pdf.*

Edelman, R. (2004). *New frontiers in employee communications: Current practices and future trends.* Retrieved from *www.edelman.com/image/insights/content/Edelman_Employee_Communications_Trend_Report.pdf.*

Edelman Change and Employee Engagement Group. (2006). *New frontiers in employee communications 2006.* Retrieved from *www.edelman.com/image/insights/content/NewFrontiers2006_Finalpaper.pdf.*

European Commission. (2007). *The new SME definition: User guide and model declaration.* Enterprise and Industry Publications. Retrieved from *ec.europa.eu/enterprise/enterprise_policy/sme_definition/sme_user_guide.pdf.*

Evatt, D.S., **Ruiz**, C. & **Triplett**, J.F. (2005). *Thinking big, staying small: Communication practices of small organizations.* San Francisco: IABC.

Ferguson Devereaux, S., **Horan**, H. & **Ferguson**, A. M. (1997). Indicators of permanence in workspace features: Perceived importance and relationship to workspace satisfaction. *Canadian Journal of Communication, 22*(1), 1–16.

Ferrabee, D. (2005, January). Developing an employee consultation process. *Strategic Communication Management, 9*(1), 30–33.

Fleishman-Hillard International Communications. (2002). *Review of current employee communications practices.* St. Louis, Missouri, U.S.: Fleishman-Hillard.

Flexibility Ltd. (2007). *Flexible work and small businesses.* Retrieved from *www.flexibility.co.uk/flexwork/general/SMEs.htm.*

Gay, C., **Mahony**, M. & **Graves**, J. (2005). *Best practices in employee communication: A study of global challenges and approaches.* San Francisco: IABC.

Gerstein, I. & **Tannenbaum**, B.A. (2005, March). The talking cure. *CMA Management, 79* (1), 18–19.

Goldfarb Consultants. (1999, October). Study on workplace satisfaction in private, public sectors. Toronto: Goldfarb.

Goss, D. (1991). *Small business and society.* New York City: Routledge.

Gray, R. (2002, March). At a glance…open-book management. *The Business Communicator, 2*(9), 3.

Gray, R. (2006, December). To blog or not to blog. *The Business Communicator, 7*(7), 3.

Gray, R. & **Robertson**, L. (2005, July/August). Effective internal communication starts at the top. *Communication World, 22*(4), 26–28.

Great Place to Work Institute. (2006). *Best small & medium companies to work for in America 2006.* Retrieved from *www.greatplacetowork.com/best/list-sme-2006.htm.*

Great Place to Work Institute. (2007). *The Great Place to Work Institute.* Retrieved from *www.greatplacetowork.com/gptw/index.php.*

Grunig, J.E. (1992). *Excellence in public relations and communication management.* Hillsdale, New Jersey, U.S.: Lawrence Erlbaum Associates.

Hammonds, K. H. (2005, August). Why we hate HR. *Fast Company, 97*, 40–47.

Happold, T. (2005). *Workspace design.* U.K.: DBA.

Holland, R.J. (2001, March/April). Slowdown: What to communicate before your fortunes turn. *Journal of Employee Communication Management*, 44–49.

Holmes, S. & **Gibson**, B. (2001). *Definition of small business: Final report.* Kingston, Australia: Small Business Coalition. Retrieved from *www.smallbusiness.org.au/sbc/publications/sbc004.pdf.*

Industry Canada. (2007a). *Industry Canada.* Retrieved from *www.ic.gc.ca.*

Industry Canada. (2007b). *Small business research and policy: Key small business statistics—January 2007.* Retrieved from *strategis.ic.gc.ca/epic/site/sbrp-rppe.nsf/en/rd02097e.html.*

Insightlink Communications. (2004, January). *The state of employee satisfaction.* Retrieved from *www.insightlink.com/State_of_employee_satisfaction.html.*

Kahler Slater Architects Inc. (2006). *What makes a great workplace? Learning from best place to work companies* (White Paper). Milwaukee, Wisconsin, U.S.: Kahler Slater Architects Inc.

Kandath, K. P., **Oetzel**, J., **Rogers**, E. M., & **Mayer-Guell**, A. M. (2003). *Communication behavior of virtual workforces.* San Francisco: IABC.

Kapel, C. & **Thompson**, M. (2005, January 17). Effective communications link employees to business, customers. *Canadian HR Reporter, 18*(1), 12.

Kaplan, R. S. & **Norton**, D.P. (2005, October). The office of strategy management. *Harvard Business Review, 83*(10), 72–80.

Kilby, N. (2004, June 24). Power to the people. *Marketing Week, 27*(26), 47–48.

Komando, K. (2005). *Why your small business needs an intranet.* Retrieved from *www.microsoft.com/smallbusiness/resources/technology/communications/why_your_small_business_needs_an_intranet.mspx.*

Krebs, V. (2005). *An introduction to social network analysis.* Retrieved from *www.orgnet.com/sna.html.*

Krotz, J. L. (2005). Turn annual reviews into continuous feedback. Retrieved from *www.microsoft.com/smallbusiness/resources/management/employee_relations/turn_annual_reviews_into_continuous_feedback.mspx.*

Larkin, S. & **Larkin**, T.J. (1994). *Communicating change: Winning employee support for new business goals.* New York City: McGraw-Hill.

Lawson, M. (2004, August/September). Getting staff feedback on messages. *Strategic Communication Management, 8*(5), 6–7.

Leininger, J. (2004, January/February). The key to retention: Committed employees. *China Business Review, 31*(1), 16–17, 38–39.

Locke, E.A. (1976). The nature and causes of job satisfaction. In M.D. Dunnette, (Ed.), *Handbook of industrial and organizational psychology* (pp. 1297–1346). Chicago: Rand McNally.

Lyman, A. (2003, November/December). Building trust in the workplace. *Strategic HR Review, 3*(1), 24–27.

Lyon, D. (2001, November). Staff satisfaction: One of the keys to a successful practice. *Journal of Financial Planning, 14*(11), 46–50.

MacMahon, J. (1996). Employee relations in small firms in Ireland: An exploratory study of small manufacturing firms. *Employee Relations, 18*(5), 66–80.

Marlow, S. (1997). The employment environment and smaller firms. *International School of Entrepreneurial Behavior and Research, 3*(3), 143–148.

Massey, C. (2004). Employee practices in New Zealand SMEs. *Employee Relations, 26*(1), 94–105.

Matlay, H. (1999). Employee relations in small firms: A micro-business perspective. *Employee Relations, 21*(3), 285–295.

May, B. E., **Lau**, R. S. M. & **Johnson**, S. K. (1999, December). A longitudinal study of quality of work life and business performance. *South Dakota Business Review, 58*(2), 1–7.

McAleese, D. & **Hargie**, O. (2004, November). Five guiding principles of culture management: A synthesis of best practice. *Journal of Communication Management, 9*(2), 155–170.

McCown, N. (2005). *Investigating the influence of an organization's corporate leader on employee communication.* New York: Conference Papers, International Communication Association 2005 Annual Meeting, pp. 1–30.

Mellor, V. (1997, August/September). Communicating in an open book environment. *Strategic Communication Management, 1*(5), 22–27.

Millar, D. & **Smith**, L.L. (2002). *Crisis management and communication: How to gain and maintain control* (2nd ed.). San Francisco: IABC.

Morville, P. (2002, February 21). *Social network analysis.* Retrieved from *www.semanticstudios.com/publications/semantics/000006.php.*

Murgolo-Poore, M. & **Pitt**, L. (2001). Intranets and employee communication: PR behind the firewall. *Journal of Communication Management, 5*(3), 231–241.

National Center for Employee Ownership. (2002). *Open-book management at Pool Covers, Inc.* Retrieved from *www.nceo.org/library/obm_poolcovers.html.*

National Federation of Independent Business. (2000). *Small business policy guide.* Washington, D.C.: NFIB Education Foundation.

Nilsson, M. (2004, December). The creativity imperative. *Future of work agenda.* Retrieved from *www.thefutureofwork.net.*

Office of Advocacy. (2006, June). *Small business frequently asked questions.* Retrieved from *www.sba.gov/advo/stats/sbfaq.pdf.*

Owens, D. M. (2005, September). Multilingual workforces: How can employers help employees who speak different languages work in harmony? *HR Magazine, 50*(9), 125–128.

Pincus, J. D. (1994, May). Top dog meets excellence. *Communication World, 11*(5), 26–29.

Policy Studies Institute. (1998, October). Direct communication with employees boosts small firms' financial performance. *PSI.* Retrieved from *www.psi.org.uk/news/pressrelease.asp?news_item_id=39.*

Rainnie, A. (1989). *Industrial relations in small firms: Small isn't beautiful.* New York City: Routledge.

Reichheld, F. F. (2001, October). Satisfaction: The false path to employee loyalty. *Harvard Management Update, 6*(3), 3–4.

Rimler, G. W. & **Humphreys**, N. J. (1980). *Small business: Developing the winning management team.* New York City: Amacom.

Robinson, D., **Perryman**, S. & **Hayday**, S. (2004, April). *The drivers of employee engagement.* IES Report 408. Institute for Employment Studies: University of Sussex, Brighton, U.K.

Roxe, L. A. (1979). *Personnel management for the smaller company: A hands-on manual.* New York City: Amacom.

Sanders, J. (2004) *Beware of gender stereotypes in the workplace.* Retrieved from *www.janesanders.com/articles/article_beware.html.*

Schaefer, P. (2005). *Flex work arrangements: Employer solutions to common problems.* Attard Communications. Retrieved from *www.businessknowhow.com/manage/flex-work.htm.* (2002, February/March). Enhancing employee communication via the intranet. *Strategic Communication Management, 6*(2), 3.

Shockley-Zalabak, P., **Ellis**, K., & **Cesaria**, R. (2000). *Measuring organizational trust.* San Francisco: IABC.

SHRM. (2004, November). *What makes employees happy?* The Society for Human Resource Management Press Room. Retrieved from *www.shrm.org/press/.*

Shuler, B. (1998). Creating an environment for feedback. *Strategic Communication Management, 3*(1), 26–29.

Siegel, W. L. (1978). *People management for small business.* New York City: John Wiley & Sons.

Sinickas, A. D. (2005). The role of intranets and other e-channels in employee communication preference. *Journal of Website Promotion, 1*(1), 31–51.

Smith, S. & **Mazin**, R. (2004). *The HR answer book: An indispensable guide for managers and human resource professionals.* New York City: Amacom.

Srinivas, H. (2005). *Online technology and networking: Some gender perspectives.* The Global Development Research Center. Retrieved from *www.gdrc.org/gender/ait-paper.html.* (2007). Statistics Canada. Retrieved from *www.Statcan.ca.*

Therkelsen, D. J. & **Fiebich**, C. L. (2003, November). The supervisor: The linchpin of employee relations. *Journal of Communication Management, 8*(2), 120–129.

Traverso, D.K. (2001). *The small business owner's guide to a good night's sleep.* New York City: Bloomberg Press.

University of California, Berkeley. (2002). *Workplace success stories—best practices 2002 (Fridays at four).* Retrieved from *www.hrweb.berkeley.edu/seads/success/fridays.htm.*

Usry, M. L. & **White**, M. (Winter-Spring, 2000). Multicultural awareness in small businesses: Learning from the big guys. *Business Forum, 25*(1/2), 10–13.

Vanfossen, B. (1996). *Gender differences in communication.* Towson University, Maryland, U.S.: Institute for Teaching and Research on Women.

Vogt, P. (2004, March/April). Awareness to action: Connecting employees to the bottom line. *Communication World, 21*(2), 22–26.

Walleisa, J. & **Magnolfi**, J. (2003). *Encouraging collaboration through workspace design.* Boston: Harvard Design School.

Watson Wyatt Worldwide. (2003). *Connecting organizational communication to financial performance: 2003/2004 communication ROI study.* Washington, D.C.: Watson Wyatt Worldwide.

Whiteley, A., **Cheung**, S. & **Zhang**, S.Q. (2000). *Human resource strategies in China.* Singapore: World Scientific.

Whitworth, B. & **Riccomini**, B. (2005, March/April). Management communication: Unlocking higher employee performance. *Communication World, 22*(2), 18–22.

Wilkinson, A. (1999). Employment relations in SMEs. *Employee Relations, 21*(3), 206–217.

Williams, L. & **Dong**, Q. (1999). *Key elements of effective supervisor/employee communication.* San Francisco: IABC Research Foundation.

Yates, K. (December 2003/January 2004). Linking communication to profits. *Strategic Communication Management, 8*(1), 8.

BIOGRAPHIES

Tamara Gillis, Ed.D., ABC, performed research and analysis and wrote the final report for this research project. She is associate professor and immediate past chairman of the department of communications at Elizabethtown College in Pennsylvania. Her research interests include change management, civic involvement, organizational design and the impact of new media. She also serves as a communications consultant with Cooper Wright LLC. In her career, she has led communication programs for higher education institutions, associations and a health care corporation. She has served as faculty in Swaziland, Namibia, and the Semester at Sea program. The IABC Research Foundation honored her with the 2004 Foundation Lifetime Friend Award. In 2001–02 she chaired the IABC Research Foundation. She has held leadership positions at the district and international levels of IABC. The author of numerous articles and book chapters, she is coauthor of a text on community media in Africa and the editor and a contributing author to *The IABC Handbook of Organizational Communication* (Jossey-Bass, 2006). She holds a doctorate from the University of Pittsburgh.

INSIGHTRIX RESEARCH TEAM

Corrin Harper is president of Insightrix Research Inc. She is also a sessional lecturer with the College of Commerce, University of Saskatchewan, teaching courses in personnel management and organizational behavior. She holds a bachelor's degree in commerce and an MBA from the University of Saskatchewan.

Jackie Keele is a senior project manager for Insightrix Research Inc. Prior to joining Insightrix, Jackie worked at Saskatchewan Blue Cross analyzing business requirements and providing recommendations on system applications to senior management and end users. She earned her bachelor of arts in psychology from the University of Saskatchewan and computer systems technology from Saskatchewan Institute of Applied Science and Technology.

Jessica Schnell is director of research services for Insightrix Research Inc. She has training in a variety of areas of statistical analysis. Prior to joining Insightrix, Jessica completed her undergraduate degree from the University of Regina with a combined major in mathematics and statistics.

Alexandra Campbell is a data analyst with Insightrix Research Inc.

The Insightrix Research team gathered the data for this research project.

APPENDIX A / Survey Details

The survey data was compiled by Insightrix®.

What is your position with this company?

- In regards to their position within their company, 28.9 percent of respondents are owners, 27.4 percent are managers, 22.5 percent are senior managers and 17.2 percent are employees.

FIGURE 1 – POSITION WITHIN COMPANY

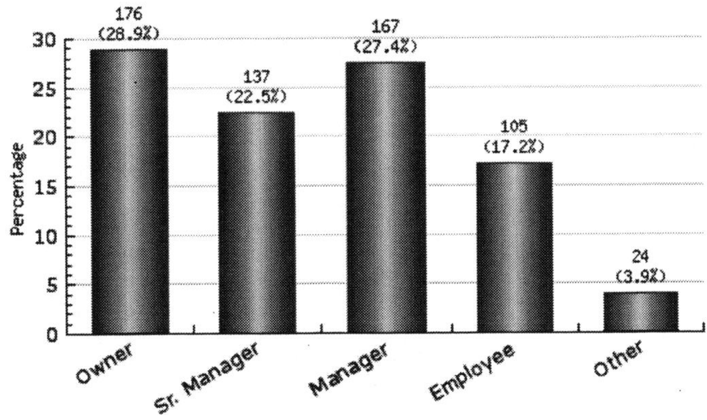

Entries under "Other":

(5) Director

(2) Partner

(2) Supervisor

(1) "One-Man Band"

(1) Account executive

(1) PR manager

(1) Recruiter

(1) Consultant

(1) Contractor

(1) Director of marketing and public relations

(1) HR administrator

(1) Lecturer

(1) Administrator

(1) Assistant director

(1) Account manager and director of new business

Does one of your primary responsibilities include managing communication for your organization?

- The percentage of respondents responsible for managing communication for their organization is 81.8 percent, while 18.2 percent do not have this responsibility.

FIGURE 2 – RESPONSIBLE FOR MANAGING COMMUNICATION

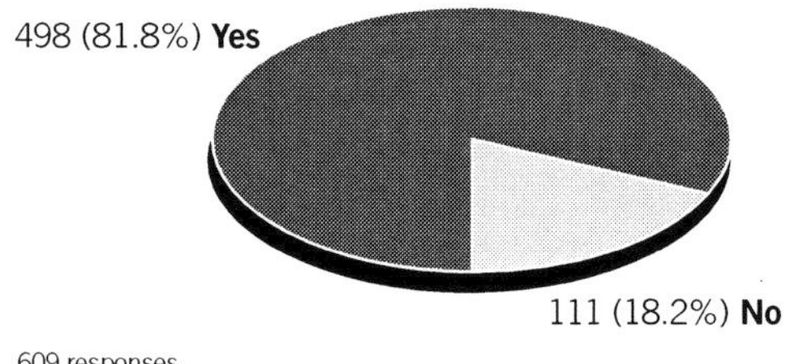

609 responses

- Respondents who indicated that their position within the company is "employee" are least likely to be responsible for managing communication (50.5 percent).

TABLE 1 – RESPONSIBILITY FOR MANAGING COMMUNICATION BY POSITION WITHIN COMPANY

What is your position with this company?			Are you responsible for managing communication for this organization? Yes	No	Total
	Owner	Count	171	5	176
		%	97.2%	2.8%	100.0%
	Senior Manager	Count	122	15	137
		%	89.1%	10.9%	100.0%
	Manager	Count	133	34	167
		%	79.6%	20.4%	100.0%
	Employee	Count	53	52	105
		%	50.5%	49.5%	100.0%
	Other	Count	19	5	24
		%	79.2%	20.8%	100.0%
Total		Count	498	111	609
		%	81.8%	18.2%	100.0%

Including owners, what is the average number of full-time *and* part-time employees in the entire company?

- Overall, 48.8 percent of respondents indicated that their entire company has 50 employees or fewer. Another 26.9 percent said their company has 51 to 200 employees, and 24.3 percent said there were more than 200 employees in their company.

TABLE 2 – NUMBER OF EMPLOYEES

Number of Employees	Frequency	Percent	Cumulative Percent
Up to 50	296	48.8	48.8
51 to 200	163	26.9	75.7
More than 200	147	24.3	100.0
Total	606	100.0	

What sector best describes your organization?

- The percentage of respondents who work in the professional, scientific and technical services sector is 38.1 percent. Another 11 percent work in the manufacturing and food processing sector, 8.7 percent work in finance and insurance, and 8.5 percent work in the information sector.

TABLE 3 – SECTOR

Sector	Total number	% of Responses	Cumulative %
Professional, Scientific and Technical Services	232	38.1	38.1
Manufacturing and Food Processing	67	11.0	49.1
Finance and Insurance	53	8.7	57.8
Information	52	8.5	66.3
Retail Trade	39	6.4	72.7
Construction	23	3.8	76.5
Health Care	23	3.8	80.3
Hospitality and Food Services	18	3	83.3
Transportation and Warehousing	16	2.6	85.9
Wholesale Trade	14	2.3	88.2
Real Estate and Rental and Leasing	13	2.1	90.3
Educational Services	12	2	92.3
Arts, Entertainment and Recreation	11	1.8	94.1
Agriculture, Forestry, Fishing, Hunting	9	1.5	95.6
Other	8	1.3	96.9
Utilities	6	1	97.9
Administrative and Support	6	1	98.9
Mining	5	0.8	99.7
Waste Management and Remedial Services	2	0.3	100
Total	**609**	**100**	

Entries under "Other":

(1) Agency

(1) Franchisor—custom home building

(1) Health and pension benefits

(1) Integrated marketing

(1) Pet food

(1) Repair service

What type of company is your organization?

- The percentage of those who indicated that their company is a corporation was 59.9 percent. Another 17.6 percent said their company is a proprietorship, while 15.9 percent work for a partnership and 1.3 percent (8 respondents) for a cooperative.

FIGURE 3 – TYPE OF COMPANY

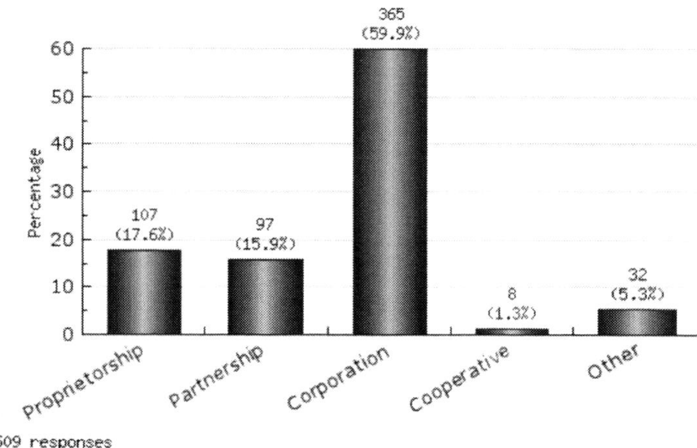

Entries under "Other":

(12) Limited liability company	(1) ESOP
(2) Not employed	(1) Individual enterprise
(2) Privately owned	(2) Sole proprietor
(1) N/A	(2) Subsidiary
(1) Private limited	(1) Social service agency
(1) S-Corporation	(1) Affiliate
(1) Trust	(1) Consulting agency
(1) University	(1) Division company

(1) Multiple companies. One is a proprietorship; one is a corporation.

IS THE CEO FEMALE OR MALE?

- Approximately three quarters of respondents said that their CEO is male, while 22.7 percent said their CEO is female.

FIGURE 4 – GENDER OF CEO

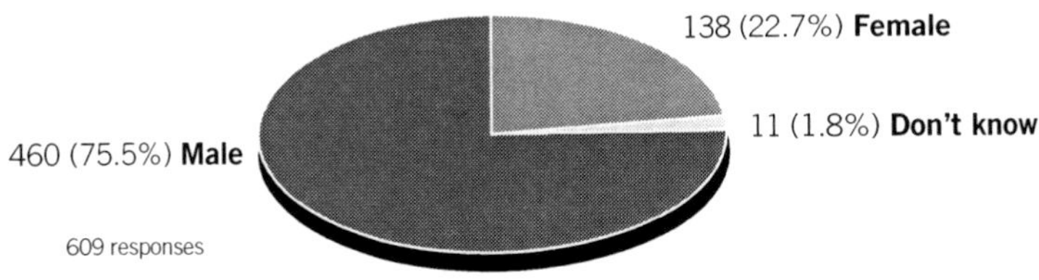

In what area is your *main* office located?

- Approximately three quarters of respondents indicated that their main office is located in the U.S. Another 14.6 percent said their main office is in Canada, while 4.3 percent said Europe and 1.6 percent said Asia. Eight respondents said their main office is in Mexico, six respondents said Australia, three respondents said South America and one respondent said Africa.

FIGURE 5 – LOCATION OF MAIN OFFICE

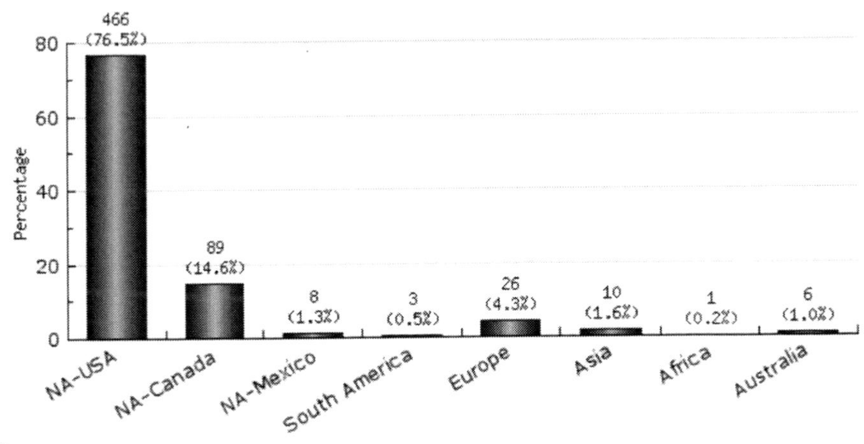

In how many different sites does your firm have offices, plants or stores, including the main office?

- The percentage of respondents who said that their firm has offices, plants or stores, including the main office, in only one site was 39.7 percent. Those with two sites totaled 16.8 percent, while 30.8 percent have three to 10 sites, and 10.4 percent have 11 to 50 sites. Only 2.3 percent of respondents indicated that their firm has more than 50 sites.

TABLE 4 – NUMBER OF SITES

Number of sites	Frequency	Percent	Cumulative Percent
1	237	39.7	39.7
2	100	16.8	56.4
3 to 10	184	30.8	87.3
11 to 50	62	10.4	97.7
More than 50	14	2.3	100.0
Total	597	100.0	

IN-PERSON COMMUNICATION / These communication methods typically involve the verbal relay and exchange of information where all parties are physically present.

Please indicate the level of current or intended use for the following in-person communication practices.

- The percentage of respondents who currently use face-to-face communication as a method of in-person communication was 86.9 percent. Another 80.8 percent currently have an open door policy in place, while 79.1 percent use management meetings and 76.7 percent use staff meetings as methods of in-person communication. Staff advocates are currently the least used in-person communication practice (28.6 percent), followed by employee forums (41.7 percent) and informal gatherings (47.1 percent); however, at least 10 percent of respondents plan to use one or more of these practices in the future.

FIGURE 6 – IN-PERSON USAGE

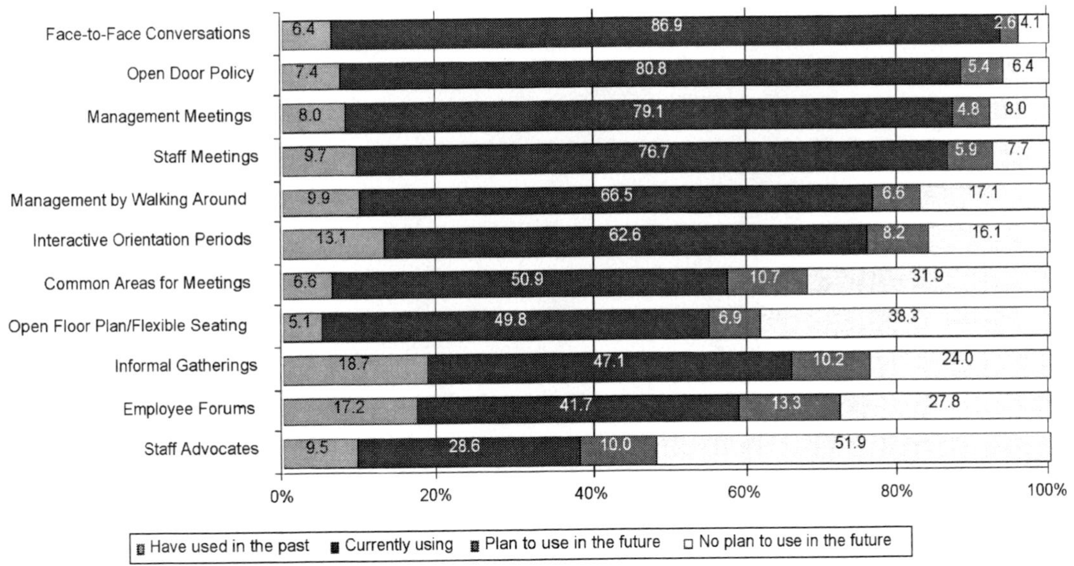

- Organizations based in the U.S. are most likely to use management by walking around, staff advocates and common areas for meetings. Companies based in Canada are most likely to use face-to-face conversations. Organizations based in Europe are most likely to use informal gatherings and an open floor plan. Companies based in areas outside of North America and Europe are most likely to use interactive orientation periods, management meetings, staff meetings, employee forums and an open door policy.

TABLE 5 – IN-PERSON USAGE BY LOCATION OF MAIN OFFICE

Usage		Location of Main Office				
		U.S.	Canada	Europe	Other	Total
Interactive Orientation Periods	Number	466	89	26	28	609
	% Currently Use	62.7%	58.4%	57.7%	78.6%	62.6%
Face-to-Face Conversations	Number	466	89	26	28	609
	% Currently Use	86.3%	91.0%	84.6%	85.7%	86.9%
Management Meetings	Number	466	89	26	28	609
	% Currently Use	78.1%	80.9%	80.8%	89.3%	79.1%
Staff Meetings	Number	466	89	26	28	609
	% Currently Use	76.2%	77.5%	73.1%	85.7%	76.7%
Employee Forums	Number	466	89	26	28	609
	% Currently Use	43.1%	36.0%	30.8%	46.4%	41.7%
Informal Gatherings	Number	466	89	26	28	609
	% Currently Use	45.9%	48.3%	57.7%	53.6%	47.1%
Management by Walking Around	Number	466	89	26	28	609
	% Currently Use	68.9%	55.1%	65.4%	64.3%	66.5%
Open Door Policy	Number	466	89	26	28	609
	% Currently Use	80.7%	82.0%	73.1%	85.7%	80.8%
Staff Advocates	Number	466	89	26	28	609
	% Currently Use	30.7%	22.5%	7.7%	32.1%	28.6%
Common Areas for Meetings	Number	466	89	26	28	609
	% Currently Use	51.9%	47.2%	50.0%	46.4%	50.9%
Open Floor Plan	Number	466	89	26	28	609
	% Currently Use	50.0%	43.8%	57.7%	57.1%	49.8%

- Organizations with male CEOs are more likely than those with female CEOs to currently use all methods of in-person communication, except for informal gatherings and common areas for meetings.

TABLE 6 – IN-PERSON USAGE BY CEO GENDER

Usage		Gender of CEO		
		Male	Female	Total
Interactive Orientation Periods	Number	460	138	598
	% Currently Use	66.5%	51.4%	63.0%
Face-to-Face Conversations	Number	460	138	598
	% Currently Use	90.0%	76.8%	87.0%
Management Meetings	Number	460	138	598
	% Currently Use	83.0%	68.1%	79.6%
Staff Meetings	Number	460	138	598
	% Currently Use	80.4%	65.9%	77.1%
Employee Forums	Number	460	138	598
	% Currently Use	44.6%	34.1%	42.1%
Informal Gatherings	Number	460	138	598
	% Currently Use	45.4%	52.9%	47.2%
Management by Walking Around	Number	460	138	598
	% Currently Use	68.9%	59.4%	66.7%
Open Door Policy	Number	460	138	598
	% Currently Use	84.3%	69.6%	80.9%
Staff Advocates	Number	460	138	598
	% Currently Use	30.4%	22.5%	28.6%
Common Areas for Meetings	Number	460	138	598
	% Currently Use	51.3%	51.4%	51.3%
Open Floor Plan	Number	460	138	598
	% Currently Use	51.3%	44.2%	49.7%

- Companies with more than 200 employees are more likely than those with fewer employees to use all of the methods of in-person communication, except for informal gatherings and an open floor plan, which companies with up to 50 employees are most likely to use, and staff advocates, which companies with 51 to 200 employees are most likely to use.

TABLE 7 – IN-PERSON USAGE BY NUMBER OF EMPLOYEES

Usage		Number of Employees			
		Up to 50	51 to 200	More than 200	Total
Interactive Orientation Periods	Number	296	163	147	606
	% Currently Use	54.4%	66.9%	75.5%	62.9%
Face-to-Face Conversations	Number	296	163	147	606
	% Currently Use	84.8%	87.1%	92.5%	87.3%
Management Meetings	Number	296	163	147	606
	% Currently Use	69.6%	84.0%	94.6%	79.5%
Staff Meetings	Number	296	163	147	606
	% Currently Use	70.3%	80.4%	87.1%	77.1%
Employee Forums	Number	296	163	147	606
	% Currently Use	36.1%	44.8%	50.3%	41.9%
Informal Gatherings	Number	296	163	147	606
	% Currently Use	50.0%	43.6%	46.3%	47.4%
Management by Walking Around	Number	296	163	147	606
	% Currently Use	63.2%	68.7%	72.1%	66.8%
Open Door Policy	Number	296	163	147	606
	% Currently Use	76.7%	82.8%	88.4%	81.2%
Staff Advocates	Number	296	163	147	606
	% Currently Use	24.7%	33.1%	32.0%	28.7%
Common Areas for Meetings	Number	296	163	147	606
	% Currently Use	52.7%	49.7%	49.7%	51.2%
Open Floor Plan	Number	296	163	147	606
	% Currently Use	53.0%	49.1%	44.9%	50.0%

- Partnerships are more likely than other types of companies to use all methods of in-person communication except for management meetings, employee forums, management by walking around, an open door policy and staff advocates, which corporations are most likely to use.

TABLE 8 – IN-PERSON USAGE BY TYPE OF COMPANY

Usage		Type of Company				
		Proprietorship	Partnership	Corporation	Other	Total
Interactive Orientation Periods	Number	107	97	365	40	609
	% Currently Use	49.5%	69.1%	66.3%	47.5%	62.6%
Face-to-Face Conversations	Number	107	97	365	40	609
	% Currently Use	75.7%	90.7%	89.6%	82.5%	86.9%
Management Meetings	Number	107	97	365	40	609
	% Currently Use	63.6%	82.5%	84.4%	65.0%	79.1%
Staff Meetings	Number	107	97	365	40	609
	% Currently Use	65.4%	85.6%	79.2%	62.5%	76.7%
Employee Forums	Number	107	97	365	40	609
	% Currently Use	34.6%	39.2%	44.9%	37.5%	41.7%
Informal Gatherings	Number	107	97	365	40	609
	% Currently Use	51.4%	53.6%	44.9%	40.0%	47.1%
Management by Walking Around	Number	107	97	365	40	609
	% Currently Use	54.2%	68.0%	70.7%	57.5%	66.5%
Open Door Policy	Number	107	97	365	40	609
	% Currently Use	61.7%	83.5%	86.8%	70.0%	80.8%
Staff Advocates	Number	107	97	365	40	609
	% Currently Use	27.1%	26.8%	29.3%	30.0%	28.6%
Common Area for Meetings	Number	107	97	365	40	609
	% Currently Use	48.6%	68.0%	49.0%	32.5%	50.9%
Open Floor Plan	Number	107	97	365	40	609
	% Currently Use	42.1%	69.1%	49.3%	27.5%	49.8%

Are you using any other in-person communication strategies in your organization? If so, briefly describe the practice below.

- Eighty-one respondents (13.3 percent) indicated other in-person communication strategies that they use in their organization. Of those, the most common type of communication mentioned was meetings where various levels of employees are present. Other commonly mentioned strategies were personal or social communication with employees and in-person training or review sessions.

Please rate the following practices on a scale of 1 to 3 where "1" is *not at all cost-effective*, "2" is *somewhat cost-effective* and "3" is *very cost-effective*. Cost-effectiveness refers to those practices that were worth the cost of implementing:

- The majority of respondents who use each method said that it is very cost-effective. The practice that respondents are most likely to have said is very cost-effective is face-to-face conversations, with 73.9 percent giving a rating of 3 out of 3. Another 70.3 percent said that having an open door policy is very cost-effective, and 66.7 percent said that management by walking around is very cost-effective. Staff advocates are the most likely to be not at all cost-effective, with 9.8 percent of those who use them giving a rating of 1 out of 3.

FIGURE 7 – IN-PERSON COST-EFFECTIVENESS

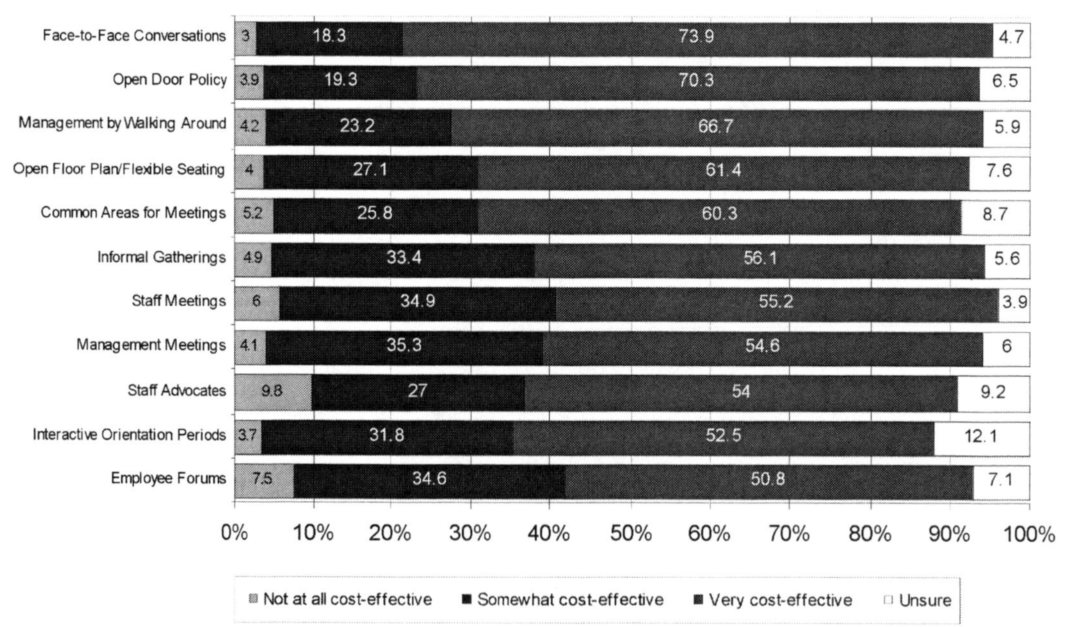

- Considering only those respondents who gave a cost-effectiveness rating for their in-person communication practices, at least 89 percent of respondents found each practice to be cost-effective. Looking at the 95 percent confidence intervals, if the lower limit for one strategy is higher than the upper limit for another (i.e., they do not overlap), then we can conclude that the difference is significant. For example, face-to-face conversations are significantly more cost-effective than staff advocates.

TABLE 9 – IN-PERSON COST-EFFECTIVENESS

Practice	Number	% Somewhat or Very	95% Confidence Interval	
			Lower	Upper
Face-to-Face Conversations	504	0.97	0.95	0.98
Open Door Policy	460	0.96	0.94	0.98
Interactive Orientation Periods	335	0.96	0.94	0.98
Open Floor Plan/Flexible Seating	280	0.96	0.93	0.98
Management Meetings	453	0.96	0.94	0.97
Management by Walking Around	381	0.96	0.93	0.98
Informal Gatherings	271	0.95	0.92	0.97
Common Areas for Meetings	283	0.94	0.92	0.97
Staff Meetings	449	0.94	0.92	0.96
Employee Forums	236	0.92	0.88	0.95
Staff Advocates	158	0.89	0.84	0.94

- Respondents whose organizations have more than 200 employees are most likely to have said that most of the methods of in-person communication are somewhat or very cost-effective. Those in companies with 51 to 200 employees are most likely to rate face-to-face conversations as cost-effective. Respondents in companies with 50 or fewer employees are most likely to rate informal gatherings as cost-effective. Those in companies with up to 50 employees and over 200 employees tied in their cost-effectiveness rating for management meetings, both at 96.9 percent.

TABLE 10 – IN-PERSON COST-EFFECTIVENESS BY NUMBER OF EMPLOYEES

Cost-effectiveness		Number of Employees			
		Up to 50	51 to 200	More than 200	Total
Interactive Orientation Periods	Number	142	94	99	335
	% Somewhat or Very	94.4%	95.7%	98.0%	95.8%
Face-to-Face Conversations	Number	246	134	124	504
	% Somewhat or Very	96.7%	99.3%	94.4%	96.8%
Management Meetings	Number	195	130	128	453
	% Somewhat or Very	96.9%	92.3%	96.9%	95.6%
Staff Meetings	Number	203	128	118	449
	% Somewhat or Very	93.6%	92.2%	95.8%	93.8%
Employee Forums	Number	99	70	67	236
	% Somewhat or Very	91.9%	90.0%	94.0%	91.9%
Informal Gatherings	Number	145	67	59	271
	% Somewhat or Very	95.2%	94.0%	94.9%	94.8%
Management by Walking Around	Number	179	108	94	381
	% Somewhat or Very	95.5%	95.4%	95.7%	95.5%
Open Door Policy	Number	220	123	117	460
	% Somewhat or Very	95.5%	95.1%	97.4%	95.9%
Staff Advocates	Number	68	46	44	158
	% Somewhat or Very	85.3%	91.3%	93.2%	89.2%
Common Areas for Meetings	Number	146	72	65	283
	% Somewhat or Very	93.2%	93.1%	98.5%	94.3%
Open Floor Plan	Number	148	72	60	280
	% Somewhat or Very	93.9%	95.8%	100.0%	95.7%

- Respondents from companies based in Europe and Canada are more likely than those based in other countries to have said that most in-person communication practices are somewhat or very cost-effective.

TABLE 11 – IN-PERSON COST-EFFECTIVENESS BY LOCATION OF MAIN OFFICE

Cost-effectiveness		Location of Main Office				
		U.S.	Canada	Europe	Other	Total
Interactive Orientation Periods	Number	256	47	13	19	335
	% Somewhat or Very	96.1%	97.9%	92.3%	89.5%	95.8%
Face-to-Face Conversations	Number	380	79	22	23	504
	% Somewhat or Very	96.1%	100.0%	100.0%	95.7%	96.8%
Management Meetings	Number	343	66	20	24	453
	% Somewhat or Very	95.6%	97.0%	95.0%	91.7%	95.6%
Staff Meetings	Number	342	65	18	24	449
	% Somewhat or Very	93.3%	96.9%	94.4%	91.7%	93.8%
Employee Forums	Number	186	30	8	12	236
	% Somewhat or Very	91.9%	96.7%	100.0%	75.0%	91.9%
Informal Gatherings	Number	202	41	13	15	271
	% Somewhat or Very	94.1%	97.6%	100.0%	93.3%	94.8%
Management by Walking Around	Number	299	47	17	18	381
	% Somewhat or Very	95.7%	95.7%	100.0%	88.9%	95.5%
Open Door Policy	Number	349	70	19	22	460
	% Somewhat or Very	95.7%	95.7%	94.7%	100.0%	95.9%
Staff Advocates	Number	133	16	2	7	158
	% Somewhat or Very	0.9	1.0	1.0	0.9	0.9
Common Areas for Meetings	Number	219	39	12	13	283
	% Somewhat or Very	92.7%	100.0%	100.0%	100.0%	94.3%
Open Floor Plan	Number	212	39	14	15	280
	% Somewhat or Very	94.8%	100.0%	100.0%	93.3%	95.7%

Please indicate whether the following practices had a positive or negative impact on the productivity of your organization.

- The majority of respondents who use each in-person communication practice said that it has had a positive effect on the productivity of their organization. Face-to-face conversations are most likely to have had a positive impact (75.6 percent), followed by employee forums (70.1 percent) and informal gatherings (69.3 percent). The practices most likely to have a negative impact on productivity are staff advocates (8 percent) and implementing an open floor plan (6.3 percent).

FIGURE 8 – IN-PERSON IMPACT ON PRODUCTIVITY

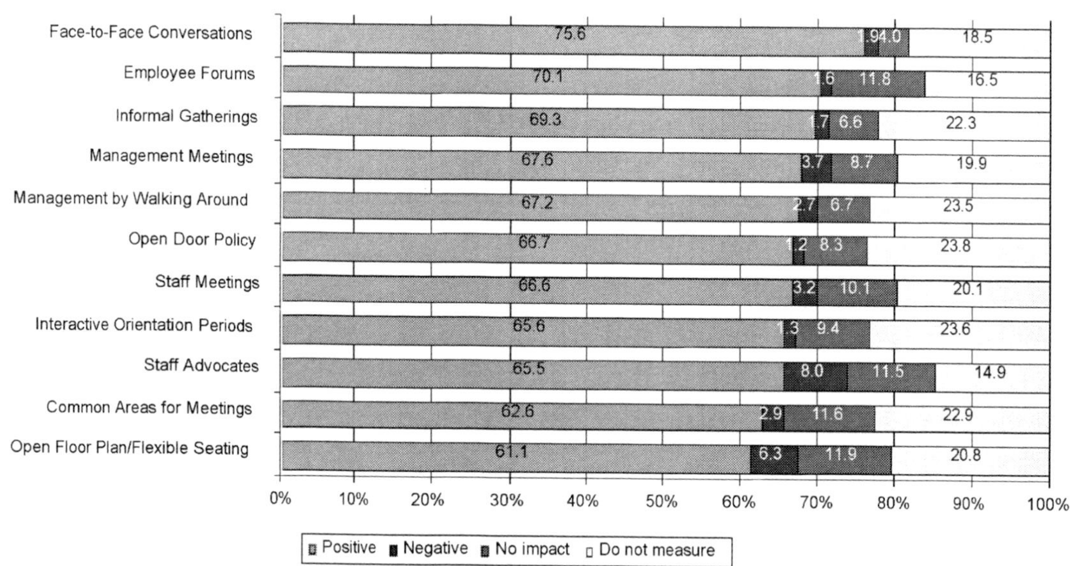

- More than three quarters of those who measured the impact of their in-person communication practices on the productivity of their organization indicated that the impact of each was positive. Again, face-to-face conversations were most likely to have a positive impact, while staff advocates were least likely.

TABLE 12 – IN-PERSON IMPACT ON PRODUCTIVITY AMONG ORGANIZATIONS THAT MEASURED THE IMPACT OF IN-PERSON COMMUNICATION PRACTICES

			95% Confidence Interval	
Practice	Number	Mean	Lower	Upper
Face-to-Face Conversations	431	0.93	0.90	0.95
Informal Gatherings	223	0.89	0.85	0.93
Management by Walking Around	310	0.88	0.84	0.91
Open Door Policy	375	0.87	0.84	0.91
Interactive Orientation Periods	291	0.86	0.82	0.90
Management Meetings	386	0.84	0.81	0.88
Employee Forums	212	0.84	0.79	0.89
Staff Meetings	373	0.83	0.80	0.87
Common Areas for Meetings	239	0.81	0.76	0.86
Open Floor Plan/Flexible Seating	240	0.77	0.72	0.82
Staff Advocates	148	0.77	0.70	0.84

- Respondents whose organizations are based in Europe are most likely to say that face-to-face conversations, staff meetings, informal gatherings, management by walking around, staff advocates and common areas for meetings have had a positive impact on productivity. Those in organizations based in the U.S. are most likely to indicate that interactive orientation periods, employee forums and an open door policy and have had a positive impact on productivity. Respondents in companies based outside of North America and Europe were most likely to say that management meetings and an open floor plan have had a positive impact on productivity.

TABLE 13 – IN-PERSON IMPACT ON PRODUCTIVITY BY LOCATION OF MAIN OFFICE

Impact on Productivity		Location of Main Office				
		U.S.	Canada	Europe	Other	Total
Interactive Orientation Periods	Number	224	37	12	18	291
	% Positive	87.5%	86.5%	75.0%	72.2%	85.9%
Face-to-Face Conversations	Number	330	61	18	22	431
	% Positive	91.5%	95.1%	100.0%	100.0%	92.8%
Management Meetings	Number	290	58	15	23	386
	% Positive	84.5%	86.2%	73.3%	87.0%	84.5%
Staff Meetings	Number	285	55	12	21	373
	% Positive	82.8%	85.5%	100.0%	76.2%	83.4%
Employee Forums	Number	166	30	6	10	212
	% Positive	85.5%	80.0%	83.3%	70.0%	84.0%
Informal Gatherings	Number	165	34	11	13	223
	% Positive	86.7%	97.1%	100.0%	92.3%	89.2%
Management by Walking Around	Number	246	39	12	13	310
	% Positive	87.0%	87.2%	100.0%	92.3%	87.7%
Open Door Policy	Number	291	52	13	19	375
	% Positive	88.7%	86.5%	84.6%	73.7%	87.5%
Staff Advocates	Number	120	19	1	8	148
	% Positive	79.2%	78.9%	100.0%	37.5%	77.0%
Common Areas for Meetings	Number	187	33	10	9	239
	% Positive	78.1%	87.9%	100.0%	100.0%	81.2%
Open Floor Plan	Number	186	30	12	12	240
	% Positive	76.9%	76.7%	75.0%	83.3%	77.1%

Please indicate whether the following practices had a positive or negative impact on the profitability in your organization.

- Respondents said that management meetings had a positive impact on the profitability of their organization (54.8 percent), followed by face-to-face conversations (52.6 percent). Interestingly, no more than 4 percent of respondents said that using a particular method of in-person communication has had a negative impact on the profitability of their organization.

FIGURE 9 – IN-PERSON IMPACT ON PROFITABILITY

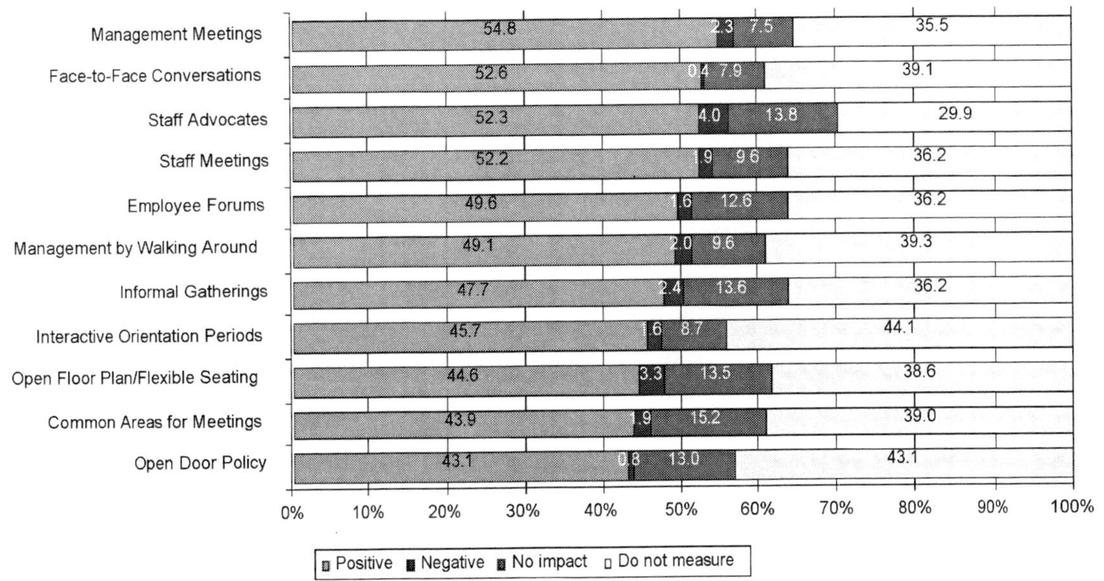

- When looking only at those respondents who measured the impact of their in-person communication practices on profitability, face-to-face conversations are most likely to have a positive impact (86 percent). Respondents are also highly likely to say that management meetings have a positive impact (85 percent). More than 70 percent of those who measured the impact of each practice said that the impact was positive.

TABLE 14 – IN-PERSON IMPACT ON PROFITABILITY AMONG ORGANIZATIONS THAT MEASURE THE IMPACT OF IN-PERSON COMMUNICATION PRACTICES

Practice	Number	Mean	95% Confidence Interval	
			Lower	Upper
Face-to-Face Conversations	322	0.86	0.83	0.90
Management Meetings	311	0.85	0.81	0.89
Staff Meetings	298	0.82	0.77	0.86
Interactive Orientation Periods	213	0.82	0.76	0.87
Management by Walking Around	246	0.81	0.76	0.86
Employee Forums	162	0.78	0.71	0.84
Open Door Policy	280	0.76	0.71	0.81
Informal Gatherings	183	0.75	0.69	0.81
Staff Advocates	122	0.75	0.67	0.82
Open Floor Plan/Flexible Seating	186	0.73	0.66	0.79
Common Areas for Meetings	189	0.72	0.65	0.78

Please indicate whether the following practices had a positive or negative impact on employee behavior:

- The majority of respondents who use each method of in-person communication said that it has had a positive impact on employee behavior. Face-to-face conversations are most likely to have had a positive impact (85.1 percent), followed by informal gatherings (80.5 percent) and an open door policy (79.7 percent). The methods most likely to have a negative impact are staff advocates (5.7 percent), management by walking around (4.7 percent) and management meetings (4.6 percent).

FIGURE 10 – IN-PERSON IMPACT ON EMPLOYEE BEHAVIOR

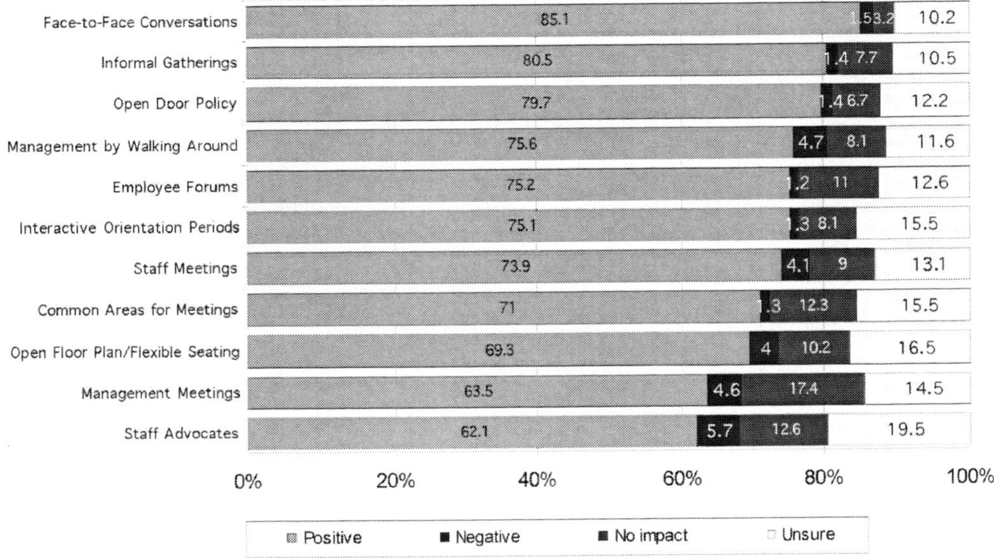

- When looking only at those who measured the impact of their in-person communication practices on employee behavior, face-to-face conversations are the most likely to have a positive impact (95 percent), while 91 percent of those who measured the impact of the open door policy felt that it had a positive impact. A large majority of respondents who measured the impact of their practices said that they have been positive.

TABLE 15 – IN-PERSON IMPACT ON EMPLOYEE BEHAVIOR AMONG ORGANIZATIONS THAT MEASURE THE IMPACT OF IN-PERSON COMMUNICATION PRACTICES

Practice	Number	Mean	95% Confidence Interval	
			Lower	Upper
Face-to-Face Conversations	475	0.95	0.93	0.97
Open Door Policy	432	0.91	0.88	0.93
Informal Gatherings	257	0.90	0.86	0.94
Interactive Orientation Periods	322	0.89	0.85	0.92
Employee Forums	222	0.86	0.81	0.91
Management by Walking Around	358	0.85	0.82	0.89
Staff Meetings	406	0.85	0.81	0.88
Common Areas for Meetings	262	0.84	0.79	0.88
Open Floor Plan/Flexible Seating	253	0.83	0.78	0.88
Staff Advocates	140	0.77	0.70	0.84
Management Meetings	412	0.74	0.70	0.79

- Respondents who are employed by proprietorships found more methods of in-person communication had a positive impact on employee behavior than those employed by partnerships and corporations.

TABLE 16 – IN-PERSON IMPACT ON EMPLOYEE BEHAVIOR BY TYPE OF COMPANY

Impact on Employee Behavior		Type of Company				
		Proprietorship	Partnership	Corporation	Other	Total
Interactive Orientation Periods	Number	43	55	209	15	322
	% Positive	81.4%	87.3%	90.9%	86.7%	88.8%
Face-to-Face Conversations	Number	70	79	295	31	375
	% Positive	94.3%	97.5%	94.6%	90.3%	94.7%
Management Meetings	Number	57	65	266	24	412
	% Positive	84.2%	66.2%	73.3%	83.3%	74.3%
Staff Meetings	Number	63	68	253	22	406
	% Positive	84.1%	83.8%	85.0%	90.9%	85.0%
Employee Forums	Number	30	35	142	15	222
	% Positive	83.3%	82.9%	88.0%	80.0%	86.0%
Informal Gatherings	Number	48	48	146	15	257
	% Positive	93.8%	89.6%	88.4%	93.3%	89.9%
Management by Walking Around	Number	50	55	234	19	358
	% Positive	90.0%	83.6%	87.2%	57.9%	85.5%
Open Door Policy	Number	57	71	281	23	432
	% Positive	94.7%	87.3%	90.7%	91.3%	90.7%
Staff Advocates	Number	21	23	86	10	140
	% Positive	90.5%	69.6%	74.4%	90.0%	77.1%
Common Areas for Meetings	Number	40	58	151	13	262
	% Positive	90.0%	82.8%	83.4%	76.9%	84.0%
Open Floor Plan	Number	32	57	154	10	253
	% Positive	81.3%	89.5%	80.5%	90.0%	83.0%

Please indicate whether the following practices had a positive or negative impact on communications with your customers, the public and the media.

- The methods of in-person communication most likely to have a positive impact on external communications are face-to-face conversations (65.8 percent), staff meetings (58.5 percent) and management meetings (57.1 percent). No more than 4 percent of respondents said that any particular practice has had a negative impact on external communications.

FIGURE 11 – IN-PERSON IMPACT ON EXTERNAL COMMUNICATIONS

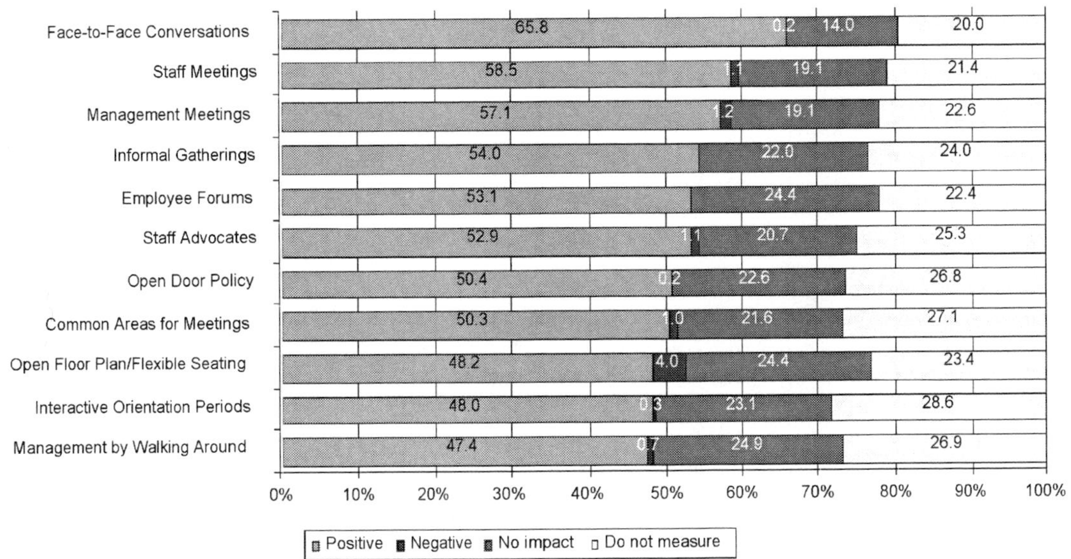

- More than 60 percent of those who measured the impact of their in-person communication practices on external communications said that each impact was positive. Face-to-face conversations were more likely than other practices to have a positive impact (82 percent).

TABLE 17 – IN-PERSON IMPACT ON EXTERNAL COMMUNICATIONS AMONG ORGANIZATIONS THAT MEASURE THE IMPACT OF IN-PERSON COMMUNICATION PRACTICES

Practice	Number	Mean	95% Confidence Interval	
			Lower	Upper
Face-to-Face Conversations	423	0.82	0.79	0.86
Staff Meetings	367	0.74	0.70	0.79
Management Meetings	373	0.74	0.69	0.78
Informal Gatherings	218	0.71	0.65	0.77
Staff Advocates	130	0.71	0.63	0.79
Common Areas for Meetings	226	0.69	0.63	0.75
Open Door Policy	360	0.69	0.64	0.74
Employee Forums	197	0.69	0.62	0.75
Interactive Orientation Periods	272	0.67	0.62	0.73
Management by Walking Around	296	0.65	0.59	0.70
Open Floor Plan/Flexible Seating	232	0.63	0.57	0.69

- When considering all respondents who currently use each practice, face-to-face communication was one of the top three in-person communication practices in each category. Management meetings also rank high in the areas of cost-effectiveness, positive impact on profitability and positive impact on external communications. Shaded cells show the top practices in each category.

TABLE 18 – IN-PERSON SUMMARY TABLE

Practice	% Who Used	% At Least Somewhat Cost-effective	% Positive Impact on:			
			Productivity	Profitability	Employee Behavior	External Comm.
Face-to-Face Conversations	86.9	92.2	75.6	52.6	85.1	65.8
Staff Meetings	76.7	90.1	66.6	52.2	73.9	58.5
Informal Gatherings	47.1	89.5	69.3	47.7	80.5	54
Employee Forums	41.7	85.4	70.1	49.6	75.2	53.1
Management Meetings	79.1	89.9	67.6	54.8	63.5	57.1
Open Door Policy	80.8	89.6	66.7	43.1	79.7	50.4
Management by Walking Around	66.5	89.9	67.2	49.1	75.6	47.4
Interactive Orientation Periods	62.6	84.3	65.6	45.7	75.1	48
Common Areas for Meetings	50.9	86.1	62.6	43.9	71	50.3
Staff Advocates	28.6	81	65.5	52.3	62.1	52.9
Open Floor Plan	49.8	88.5	61.1	44.6	69.3	48.2

PRINT COMMUNICATION PRACTICES / These communication methods relay information through print and hard copy media.

Please indicate the level of current or intended use for the following print communication practices.

- The number of respondents who currently use printed manuals, such as employee handbooks, as a method of print communication is 61.4 percent. Those who use open book management total 41.1 percent, and 35.8 percent use printed publications, such as newspapers or magazines. The least used print methods of communication are anonymous suggestion systems (22 percent) and letters mailed to employees' homes (22.5 percent).

FIGURE 12 – PRINT USAGE

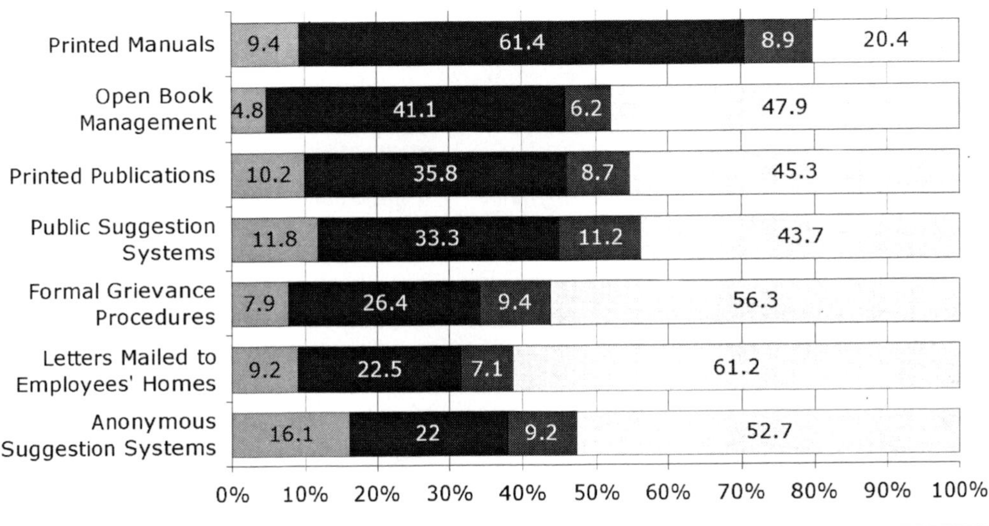

- Companies with more than 200 employees are more likely to use all print communication practices than those with fewer employees, except for anonymous and public suggestion systems, which are most likely to be used by companies with 51 to 200 employees.

TABLE 19 – PRINT USAGE BY NUMBER OF EMPLOYEES

Usage		Number of Employees			
		Up to 50	51 to 200	More than 200	Total
Formal Grievance Procedures	Number	296	163	147	606
	% Currently Use	14.2%	35.0%	42.2%	26.6%
Anonymous Suggestion Systems	Number	296	163	147	606
	% Currently Use	10.8%	34.4%	31.3%	22.1%
Public Suggestion Systems	Number	296	163	147	606
	% Currently Use	27.4%	42.9%	35.4%	33.5%
Printed Publications	Number	296	163	147	606
	% Currently Use	20.9%	46.0%	55.1%	36.0%
Letters Mailed to Employees' Homes	Number	296	163	147	606
	% Currently Use	11.1%	29.4%	38.1%	22.6%
Open Book Management	Number	296	163	147	606
	% Currently Use	31.8%	47.9%	53.1%	41.3%
Printed Manuals	Number	296	163	147	606
	% Currently Use	47.0%	74.2%	77.6%	61.7%

- Organizations based in the U.S. are more likely than those elsewhere to currently use anonymous suggestion systems and letters mailed to employees' homes. Companies based in Canada are most likely to use open book management. Organizations based outside of North America and Europe are most likely to use all other methods of print communication.

TABLE 20 – PRINT USAGE BY LOCATION OF MAIN OFFICE

Usage		Location of Main Office				
		U.S.	Canada	Europe	Other	Total
Formal Grievance Procedures	Number	466	89	26	28	609
	% Currently Use	28.1%	15.7%	19.2%	39.3%	26.4%
Anonymous Suggestion Systems	Number	466	89	26	28	609
	% Currently Use	23.8%	20.2%	7.7%	10.7%	22.0%
Public Suggestion Systems	Number	466	89	26	28	609
	% Currently Use	34.8%	24.7%	23.1%	46.4%	33.3%
Printed Publications	Number	466	89	26	28	609
	% Currently Use	35.8%	39.3%	15.4%	42.9%	35.8%
Letters Mailed to Employees' Homes	Number	466	89	26	28	609
	% Currently Use	27.0%	5.6%	7.7%	14.3%	22.5%
Open Book Management	Number	466	89	26	28	609
	% Currently Use	40.6%	43.8%	42.3%	39.3%	41.1%
Printed Manuals	Number	466	89	26	28	609
	% Currently Use	62.2%	55.1%	57.7%	71.4%	61.4%

- Companies in the manufacturing sector are more likely than those in other sectors to use public suggestion systems, printed publications, letters mailed to employee's homes and printed manuals. Companies in the health care sector are most likely to use formal grievance procedures, while those in the finance sector are most likely to use open book management. Companies in the construction and health care sector were both most likely (at 43.5 percent) to use anonymous suggestion systems.

TABLE 21 – PRINT USAGE BY SECTOR

Usage		Sector								
		Profession-al/Scienti-fic/Technical	Manufac-turing	Finance	Infor-mation Services	Retail	Construc-tion	Health Care	Other	Total
Formal Grievance Procedures	Number	232	67	53	52	39	23	23	120	609
	% Currently Use	16.8%	43.3%	30.2%	25.0%	25.6%	21.7%	56.5%	30.0%	26.4%
Anonymous Suggestion Systems	Number	232	67	53	52	39	23	23	120	609
	% Currently Use	15.5%	31.3%	22.6%	15.4%	33.3%	43.5%	43.5%	20.0%	22.0%
Public Suggestion Systems	Number	232	67	53	52	39	23	23	120	609
	% Currently Use	31.5%	53.7%	32.1%	23.1%	35.9%	34.8%	43.5%	27.5%	33.3%
Printed Publications	Number	232	67	53	52	39	23	23	120	609
	% Currently Use	28.4%	49.3%	43.4%	32.7%	30.8%	43.5%	43.5%	39.2%	35.8%
Letters Mailed to Employees' Homes	Number	232	67	53	52	39	23	23	120	609
	% Currently Use	17.7%	38.8%	15.1%	17.3%	28.2%	30.4%	34.8%	22.5%	22.5%
Open Book Manage-ment	Number	232	67	53	52	39	23	23	120	609
	% Currently Use	37.9%	46.3%	58.5%	44.2%	43.6%	47.8%	39.1%	33.3%	41.1%
Printed Manuals	Number	232	67	53	52	39	23	23	120	609
	% Currently Use	55.6%	82.1%	71.7%	51.9%	71.8%	52.2%	73.9%	56.7%	61.4%

- Corporations are significantly more likely than other types of companies to use all forms of print communication.

TABLE 22 – PRINT USAGE BY TYPE OF COMPANY

Usage		Type of Company				
		Proprietorship	Partnership	Corporation	Other	Total
Formal Grievance Procedures	Number	107	97	365	40	609
	% Currently Use	16.8%	22.7%	31.0%	20.0%	26.4%
Anonymous Suggestion Systems	Number	107	97	365	40	609
	% Currently Use	17.8%	16.5%	25.8%	12.5%	22.0%
Public Suggestion Systems	Number	107	97	365	40	609
	% Currently Use	23.4%	33.0%	37.3%	25.0%	33.3%
Printed Publications	Number	107	97	365	40	609
	% Currently Use	23.4%	36.1%	40.0%	30.0%	35.8%
Letters Mailed to Employees' Homes	Number	107	97	365	40	609
	% Currently Use	16.8%	21.6%	26.0%	7.5%	22.5%
Open Book Management	Number	107	97	365	40	609
	% Currently Use	29.9%	40.2%	44.1%	45.0%	41.1%
Printed Manuals	Number	107	97	365	40	609
	% Currently Use	38.3%	60.8%	69.9%	47.5%	61.4%

Are you using any other print communication strategies in your organization? If so, briefly describe the practice below:

- Seventy-two respondents (11.8 percent) indicated other print communication strategies that they use in their organizations. Of those, the most common types of communication mentioned were bulletin boards, newsletters, memos, brochures and pay inserts.

Please rate the following practices on a scale of 1 to 3 where "1" is *not at all cost-effective*, "2" is *somewhat cost-effective* and "3" is *very cost-effective*. Cost-effectiveness refers to those practices that were worth the cost of implementing:

- The majority of respondents who currently use each print communication practice said that it is cost-effective, giving ratings of 2 or 3 out of 3. The practices most likely to be cost-effective are public suggestion systems (82.7 percent), open book management (79.6 percent) and printed manuals (77.5 percent). Formal grievance procedures are least likely to be cost-effective, with only 62.7 percent of those who use them giving a rating of 2 or 3 out of 3.

FIGURE 13 – PRINT COST-EFFECTIVENESS

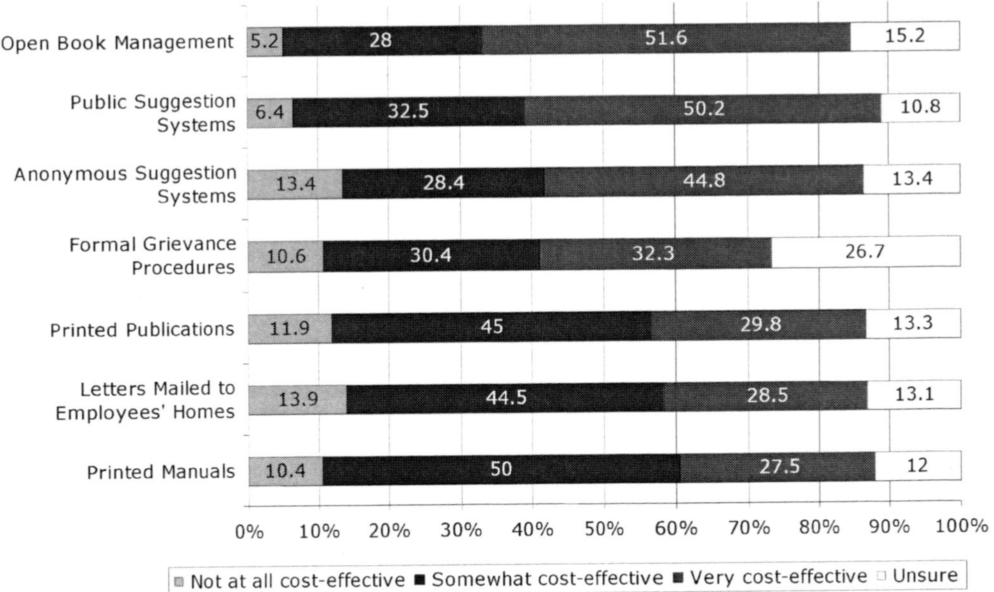

- Considering those respondents who gave cost-effectiveness ratings for their print communication practices, open book management is most likely to be seen as somewhat or very cost-effective (94 percent), followed by public suggestion systems (93 percent). The practices least likely to be seen as cost-effective are anonymous suggestion systems and letters mailed to employees' homes (84 percent each).

TABLE 23 – PRINT COST-EFFECTIVENESS

Practice	Number	Mean	95% Confidence Interval	
			Lower	Upper
Open Book Management	212	0.94	0.91	0.97
Public Suggestion Systems	181	0.93	0.89	0.97
Printed Manuals	329	0.88	0.85	0.92
Printed Publications	189	0.86	0.81	0.91
Formal Grievance Procedures	118	0.86	0.79	0.92
Anonymous Suggestion Systems	116	0.84	0.78	0.91
Letters Mailed to Employees' Homes	119	0.84	0.77	0.91

Please indicate whether the following practices had a positive or negative impact on the productivity of your organization.

- Of those whose organizations use public suggestion systems, 60.1 percent said that they have had a positive impact on productivity. Of those who use open book management, 59.6 percent said that it has had a positive impact. The practices least likely to have a positive effect on an organization's productivity are formal grievance procedures (43.5 percent) and letters mailed to employees' homes (48.2 percent).

FIGURE 14 – PRINT IMPACT ON PRODUCTIVITY

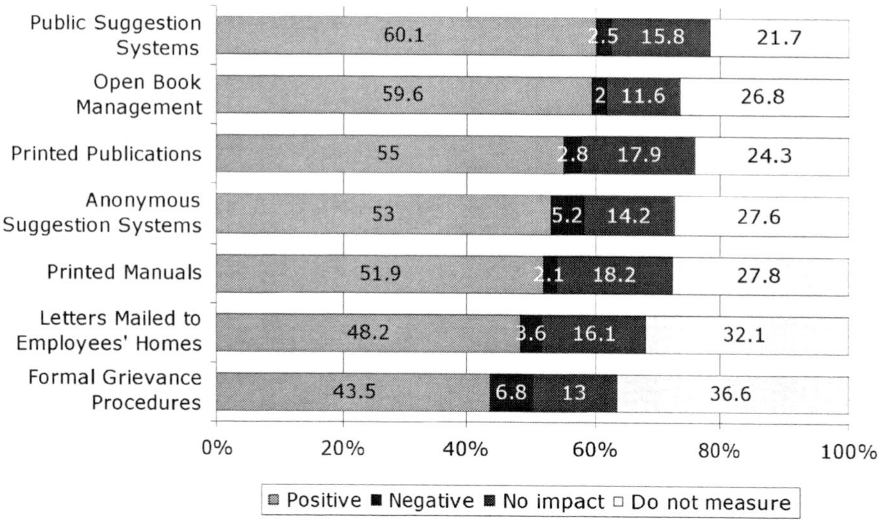

- When looking only at those who measured the impact of each print communication practice on productivity, open book management is most likely to have a positive impact (81 percent), followed by public suggestion systems (77 percent). At 69 percent, formal grievance procedures are least likely to have a positive impact on productivity.

TABLE 24 – PRINT IMPACT ON PRODUCTIVITY AMONG ORGANIZATIONS THAT MEASURE THE IMPACT OF PRINT COMMUNICATION PRACTICES

Practice	Number	Mean	95% Confidence Interval	
			Lower	Upper
Open Book Management	183	0.81	0.76	0.87
Public Suggestion Systems	159	0.77	0.70	0.83
Anonymous Suggestion Systems	97	0.73	0.64	0.82
Printed Publications	165	0.73	0.66	0.80
Printed Manuals	270	0.72	0.66	0.77
Letters Mailed to Employees' Homes	93	0.71	0.62	0.80
Formal Grievance Procedures	102	0.69	0.59	0.78

Please indicate whether the following practices had a positive or negative impact on the profitability of your organization.

- Less than half of the respondents who use each print communication practice said that using it has had a positive impact on the profitability of their organization. The practices most likely to have a positive impact are public suggestion systems (48.8 percent) and open book management (47.2 percent). The practices most likely to have a negative impact on profitability are letters mailed to employees' homes (7.3 percent), printed publications (5.5 percent) and anonymous suggestion systems (5.2 percent).

FIGURE 15 – PRINT IMPACT ON PROFITABILITY

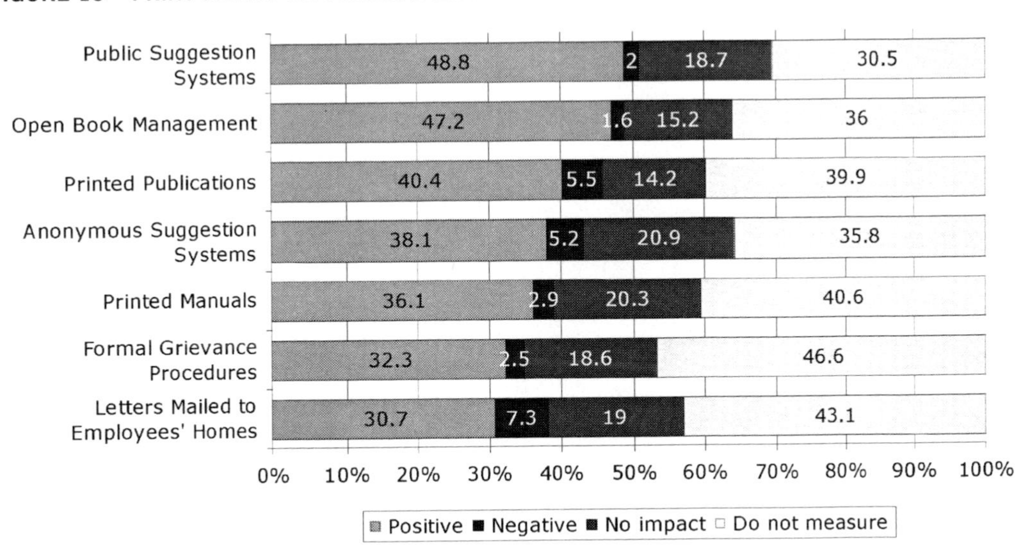

- When considering only those who measured the impact of their print communication practices on profitability, open book management is the most likely to have a positive impact (74 percent), followed by public suggestion systems (70 percent). Only 54 percent of those who measured the impact of sending letters to employees' homes said that the impact was positive.

TABLE 25 – PRINT IMPACT ON PROFITABILITY AMONG ORGANIZATIONS THAT MEASURE THE IMPACT OF PRINT COMMUNICATION PRACTICES

Practice	Number	Mean	95% Confidence Interval	
			Lower	Upper
Open Book Management	160	0.74	0.67	0.81
Public Suggestion Systems	141	0.70	0.63	0.78
Printed Publications	131	0.67	0.59	0.75
Printed Manuals	222	0.61	0.54	0.67
Formal Grievance Procedures	86	0.60	0.50	0.71
Anonymous Suggestion Systems	86	0.59	0.49	0.70
Letters Mailed to Employees' Homes	78	0.54	0.43	0.65

Please indicate whether the following practices had a positive or negative impact on employee behavior:

- The majority of respondents who currently use each method of print communication said that it has had a positive impact on employee behavior. The practices most likely to have a positive impact on employee behavior are public suggestion systems (71.9 percent) and open book management (69.6 percent).

FIGURE 16 – PRINT IMPACT ON EMPLOYEE BEHAVIOR

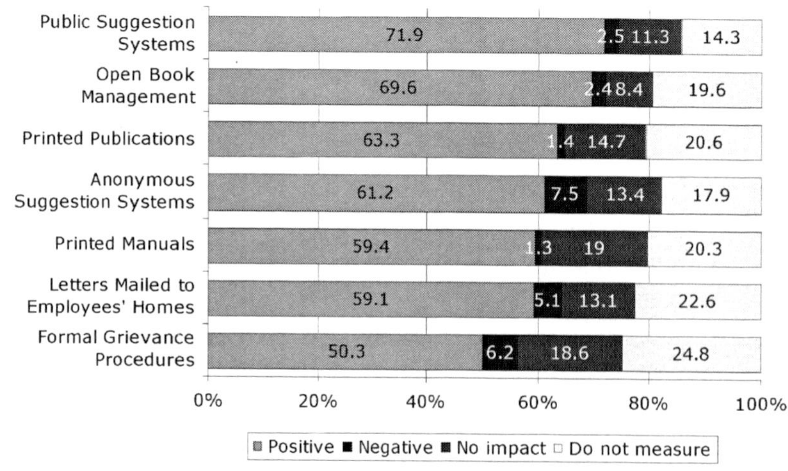

- When looking at those who measured the impact of their print communication practices on employee behavior, open book management is the most likely to have a positive impact (87 percent), followed by public suggestion systems (84 percent). Formal grievance procedures are least likely to have a positive impact on employee behavior (67 percent).

TABLE 26 – PRINT IMPACT ON EMPLOYEE BEHAVIOR AMONG ORGANIZATIONS THAT MEASURE THE IMPACT OF PRINT COMMUNICATION PRACTICES

Practice	Number	Mean	95% Confidence Interval	
			Lower	Upper
Open Book Management	201	0.87	0.82	0.91
Public Suggestion Systems	174	0.84	0.78	0.89
Printed Publications	173	0.80	0.74	0.86
Letters Mailed to Employees' Homes	106	0.76	0.68	0.85
Anonymous Suggestion Systems	110	0.75	0.66	0.83
Printed Manuals	298	0.74	0.70	0.79
Formal Grievance Procedures	121	0.67	0.58	0.75

Please indicate whether the following practices had a positive or negative impact on communications with your customers, the public and the media.

- No more than 55 percent of respondents whose organizations use particular print communication practice said that they have had a positive impact on external communications. Printed publications are most likely to have a positive impact (55 percent), while formal grievance procedures are least likely (26.7 percent). Mailing letters to employees' homes was most likely to have a negative impact (5.1 percent).

FIGURE 17 – PRINT IMPACT ON EXTERNAL COMMUNICATIONS

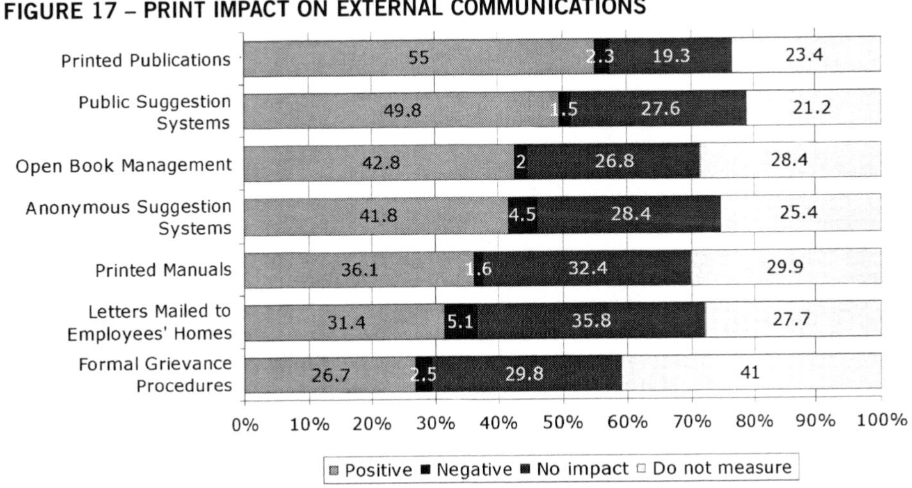

- When looking only at those who measured the impact of their print communication practices on external communications, printed publications are most likely to have a positive impact (72 percent), followed by public suggestion systems (63 percent) and open book management (60 percent). Less than half of those who measured the impact of formal grievance procedures and letters mailed to employees' homes felt that the impact was positive.

TABLE 27 – PRINT IMPACT ON EXTERNAL COMMUNICATIONS AMONG ORGANIZATIONS THAT MEASURE THE IMPACT OF PRINT COMMUNICATION PRACTICES

Practice	Number	Mean	95% Confidence Interval	
			Lower	Upper
Printed Publications	167	0.72	0.65	0.79
Public Suggestion Systems	160	0.63	0.56	0.71
Open Book Management	179	0.60	0.53	0.67
Anonymous Suggestion Systems	100	0.56	0.46	0.66
Printed Manuals	262	0.52	0.45	0.58
Formal Grievance Procedures	95	0.45	0.35	0.55
Letters Mailed to Employees' Homes	99	0.43	0.33	0.53

- The impact of print practices on external communications by sector was quite mixed. Respondents from the construction sector found that more print communication practices had a positive impact on external communications than those from other sectors. Respondents from the health care sector were least likely to find that most of the print communication practices had a positive impact on external communications.

TABLE 28 – PRINT IMPACT ON EXTERNAL COMMUNICATIONS BY SECTOR

Impact on External Communications		Sector								
		Professional/ Scientific/ Technical	Manufacturing	Finance	Information Services	Retail	Construction	Health Care	Other	Total
Formal Grievance Procedures	Number	22	12	8	10	10	3	8	22	95
	% Positive	36.4%	41.7%	75.0%	30.0%	50.0%	66.7%	50.0%	45.5%	45.3 %
Anonymous Suggestion Systems	Number	26	17	9	8	10	9	6	15	100
	% Positive	53.9%	58.8%	44.4%	50.0%	70.0%	77.8%	16.7%	60.0%	56.0 %
Public Suggestion Systems	Number	58	25	13	10	12	8	8	26	160
	% Positive	70.7%	56.0%	46.2%	80.0%	75.0%	75.0%	37.5%	53.9%	63.1 %
Printed Publications	Number	47	27	17	11	12	9	7	37	167
	% Positive	76.6%	59.3%	94.1%	63.6%	83.3%	77.8%	42.9%	67.6%	71.9 %
Letters Mailed to Employees' Homes	Number	30	15	5	9	10	5	5	20	99
	% Positive	40.0%	53.3%	80.0%	33.3%	50.0%	80.0%	20.0%	30.0%	43.4 %
Open Book Management	Number	64	21	18	20	14	8	6	28	179
	% Positive	54.7%	76.2%	72.2%	45.0%	78.6%	87.5%	33.3%	50.0%	59.8 %
Printed Manuals	Number	84	41	27	18	22	11	13	46	262
	% Positive	53.6%	56.1%	40.7%	33.3%	68.2%	72.7%	38.5%	47.8%	51.5 %

- Considering respondents whose organizations use each practice, open book management is within the top three practices in each category. Printed publications and public suggestion systems are ranked within the top three in the majority of categories.

TABLE 29 – PRINT SUMMARY TABLE

Practice	% Who Used	% At Least Somewhat Cost - effective	% Positive Impact on:			
			Productivity	Profitability	Employee Behavior	External Comm.
Public Suggestion Systems	33.3	82.7	60.1	48.8	71.9	49.8
Open Book Management	41.1	79.6	59.6	47.2	69.6	42.8
Printed Publications	35.8	74.8	55	40.4	63.3	55
Anonymous Suggestion Systems	22	73.2	53	38.1	61.2	41.8
Printed Manuals	61.4	77.5	51.9	36.1	59.4	36.1
Letters Mailed to Employees' Homes	22.5	73	48.2	30.7	59.1	31.4
Formal Grievance Procedures	26.4	62.7	43.5	32.3	50.3	26.7

ELECTRONIC COMMUNICATION PRACTICES / These communication methods involve the use of electronic devices and media to relay and exchange information.

Please indicate the level of current or intended use for the following electronic communication strategies.

- E-mail is currently the most commonly used electronic communication strategy (78.5 percent); followed by portable devices, such as cell phones or laptops (75.5 percent); and a company web site (74.5 percent). The least used electronic communication strategies are employee blogs (9.4 percent) and telephone hotlines (11.8 percent).
- Eighteen respondents named other electronic communication strategies that their company uses. Please see page 216 for a complete list.

FIGURE 18 – ELECTRONIC COMMUNICATION USAGE

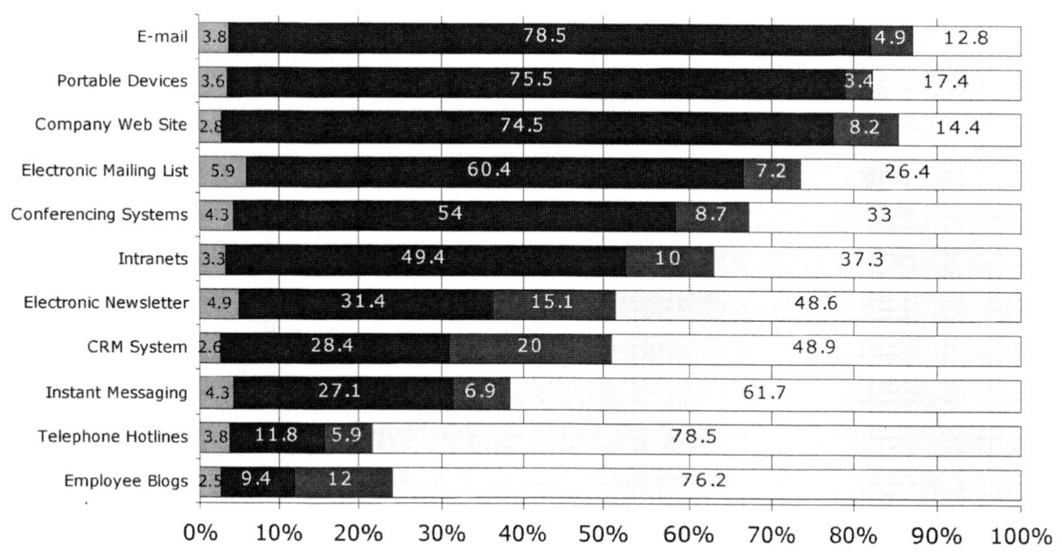

- Companies with more than 200 employees were most likely to use all of the electronic communication practices, except for employee blogs, instant messaging and CRM systems, which companies with 51 to 200 employees were most likely to use.

TABLE 30 – ELECTRONIC COMMUNICATION USAGE BY NUMBER OF EMPLOYEES

Usage		Number of Employees			
		Up to 50	51 to 200	More than 200	Total
Electronic Mailing List	Number	296	163	147	606
	% Currently Use	48.0%	66.3%	80.3%	60.7%
Electronic Newsletter	Number	296	163	147	606
	% Currently Use	17.6%	41.1%	49.0%	31.5%
Telephone Hotlines	Number	296	163	147	606
	% Currently Use	7.4%	9.2%	23.8%	11.9%
E-mail	Number	296	163	147	606
	% Currently Use	72.0%	81.6%	89.8%	78.9%
Employee Blogs	Number	296	163	147	606
	% Currently Use	7.1%	13.5%	9.5%	9.4%
Instant Messaging	Number	296	163	147	606
	% Currently Use	25.0%	33.7%	24.5%	27.2%
Intranets	Number	296	163	147	606
	% Currently Use	29.7%	58.9%	79.6%	49.7%
Company Web Site	Number	296	163	147	606
	% Currently Use	65.2%	80.4%	88.4%	74.9%
CRM System	Number	296	163	147	606
	% Currently Use	19.9%	36.8%	36.7%	28.5%
Conferencing Systems	Number	296	163	147	606
	% Currently Use	41.2%	63.8%	70.1%	54.3%
Portable Devices	Number	296	163	147	606
	% Currently Use	67.2%	81.6%	87.1%	75.9%

- Corporations are most likely to currently use company web sites, CRM systems, conferencing systems, portable devices, electronic newsletters and intranets. Partnerships are most likely to use electronic mailing lists, telephone hotlines, e-mail, employee blogs and instant messaging.

TABLE 31 – ELECTRONIC COMMUNICATION USAGE BY TYPE OF COMPANY

Usage		Type of Company				
		Proprietorship	Partnership	Corporation	Other	Total
Electronic Mailing List	Number	107	97	365	40	609
	% Currently Use	39.3%	71.1%	64.4%	55.0%	60.4%
Electronic Newsletter	Number	107	97	365	40	609
	% Currently Use	24.3%	30.9%	34.2%	25.0%	31.4%
Telephone Hotlines	Number	107	97	365	40	609
	% Currently Use	7.5%	13.4%	12.6%	12.5%	11.8%
E-mail	Number	107	97	365	40	609
	% Currently Use	63.6%	84.5%	82.2%	70.0%	78.5%
Employee Blogs	Number	107	97	365	40	609
	% Currently Use	8.4%	16.5%	7.9%	7.5%	9.4%
Instant Messaging	Number	107	97	365	40	609
	% Currently Use	26.2%	30.9%	26.8%	22.5%	27.1%
Intranets	Number	107	97	365	40	609
	% Currently Use	34.6%	45.4%	55.3%	45.0%	49.4%
Company Web Site	Number	107	97	365	40	609
	% Currently Use	53.3%	74.2%	81.6%	67.5%	74.5%
CRM System	Number	107	97	365	40	609
	% Currently Use	19.6%	25.8%	32.1%	25.0%	28.4%
Conferencing Systems	Number	107	97	365	40	609
	% Currently Use	33.6%	50.5%	61.1%	52.5%	54.0%
Portable Devices	Number	107	97	365	40	609
	% Currently Use	55.1%	80.4%	80.8%	70.0%	75.5%

Please rate the following practices on a scale of 1 to 3 where "1" is *not at all cost-effective*, "2" is *somewhat cost-effective* and "3" is *very cost-effective*. Cost-effectiveness refers to those practices that were worth the cost of implementing:

- The electronic communication practice most likely to be considered very cost-effective is e-mail, with 81.6 percent of respondents giving it a rating of 3 out of 3. Electronic mailing lists are next at 70.9 percent. The practice least likely to be considered very cost-effective is telephone hotlines (34.7 percent).

FIGURE 19 – ELECTRONIC COMMUNICATION COST-EFFECTIVENESS

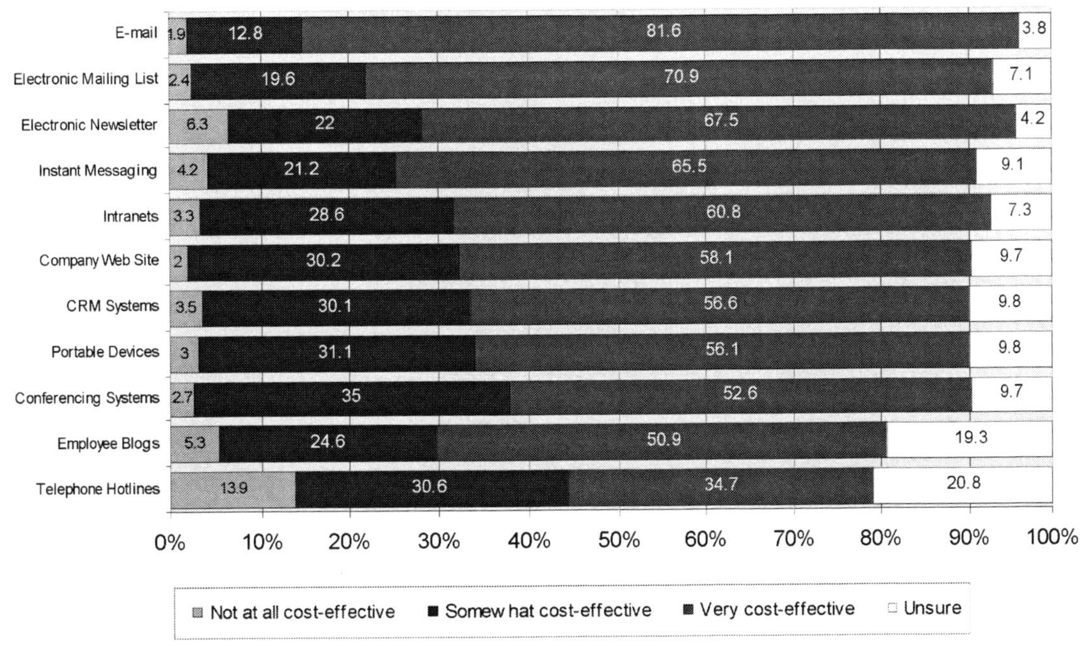

- Considering only those respondents who gave their electronic communication practices cost-effectiveness ratings, e-mail and company web sites are most likely to be seen as cost-effective, with 98 percent of respondents giving ratings of 2 or 3 out of 3. Again, telephone hotlines are least likely to be seen as cost-effective (82 percent).

TABLE 32 – ELECTRONIC COMMUNICATION COST-EFFECTIVENESS

Practice	Number	Mean	95% Confidence Interval	
			Lower	Upper
E-mail	460	0.98	0.97	0.99
Company Web Site	410	0.98	0.96	0.99
Electronic Mailing List	342	0.97	0.96	0.99
Conferencing Systems	297	0.97	0.95	0.99
Portable Devices	415	0.97	0.95	0.98
Intranets	279	0.96	0.94	0.99
CRM System	156	0.96	0.93	0.99
Instant Messaging	150	0.95	0.92	0.99
Employee Blogs	46	0.93	0.86	1.01
Electronic Newsletter	183	0.93	0.90	0.97
Telephone Hotlines	57	0.82	0.72	0.93

- Cost-effectiveness ratings for electronic communication practices by the number of employees in an organization were quite mixed, with companies with more than 200 employees and organizations with up to 50 employees splitting most of the highest cost-effectiveness ratings.

TABLE 33 – ELECTRONIC COMMUNICATION COST-EFFECTIVENESS BY NUMBER OF EMPLOYEES

Cost-effectiveness		Number of Employees			
		Up to 50	51 to 200	More than 200	Total
Electronic Mailing List	Number	137	98	107	342
	% Somewhat or Very	99.3%	94.9%	97.2%	97.4%
Electronic Newsletter	Number	50	65	68	183
	% Somewhat or Very	92.0%	90.8%	97.1%	93.4%
Telephone Hotlines	Number	19	14	24	57
	% Somewhat or Very	84.2%	85.7%	79.2%	82.5%
E-mail	Number	208	129	123	460
	% Somewhat or Very	98.6%	96.9%	98.4%	98.0%
Employee Blogs	Number	19	16	11	46
	% Somewhat or Very	94.7%	87.5%	100.0%	93.5%
Instant Messaging	Number	71	53	26	150
	% Somewhat or Very	95.8%	92.5%	100.0%	95.3%
Intranets	Number	79	93	107	279
	% Somewhat or Very	96.2%	92.5%	100.0%	96.4%
Company Web Site	Number	176	120	114	410
	% Somewhat or Very	98.9%	95.8%	98.2%	97.8%
CRM System	Number	54	57	45	156
	% Somewhat or Very	98.1%	91.2%	100.0%	96.2%
Conferencing Systems	Number	114	95	88	297
	% Somewhat or Very	96.5%	94.7%	100.0%	97.0%
Portable Devices	Number	183	123	109	415
	% Somewhat or Very	97.8%	94.3%	97.2%	96.6%

- Cost-effectiveness ratings by type of company were also quite mixed.

TABLE 34 – ELECTRONIC COMMUNICATION COST-EFFECTIVENESS BY TYPE OF COMPANY

Cost-effective		Type of Company				
		Proprietorship	Partnership	Corporation	Other	Total
Electronic Mailing List	Number	39	66	215	22	342
	% Somewhat or Very	100.0%	97.0%	97.2%	95.5%	97.4%
Electronic Newsletter	Number	24	30	119	10	183
	% Somewhat or Very	91.7%	93.3%	93.3%	100.0%	93.4%
Telephone Hotlines	Number	8	13	33	3	57
	% Somewhat or Very	87.5%	76.9%	84.8%	66.7%	82.5%
E-mail	Number	65	78	290	27	460
	% Somewhat or Very	98.5%	97.4%	97.9%	100.0%	98.0%
Employee Blogs	Number	8	12	24	2	46
	% Somewhat or Very	100.0%	91.7%	100.0%	0.0%	93.5%
Instant Messaging	Number	28	28	86	8	150
	% Somewhat or Very	96.4%	96.4%	94.2%	100.0%	95.3%
Intranets	Number	32	43	188	16	279
	% Somewhat or Very	96.9%	95.3%	96.3%	100.0%	96.4%
Company Web Site	Number	52	66	267	25	410
	% Somewhat or Very	100.0%	98.5%	97.4%	96.0%	97.8%
CRM System	Number	18	24	106	8	156
	% Somewhat or Very	100.0%	100.0%	94.3%	100.0%	96.2%
Conferencing Systems	Number	34	44	202	17	297
	% Somewhat or Very	97.1%	95.5%	97.0%	100.0%	97.0%
Portable Devices	Number	52	75	264	24	415
	% Somewhat or Very	98.1%	100.0%	95.1%	100.0%	96.6%

Please indicate whether the following practices had a positive or negative impact on the productivity in your organization.

- Approximately three-quarters of respondents whose organizations use portable devices or e-mail said that these practices have had a positive impact on productivity. Telephone hotlines are least likely to have a positive impact on productivity (51.4 percent), followed by employee blogs (54.4 percent).

FIGURE 20 – ELECTRONIC COMMUNICATION IMPACT ON PRODUCTIVITY

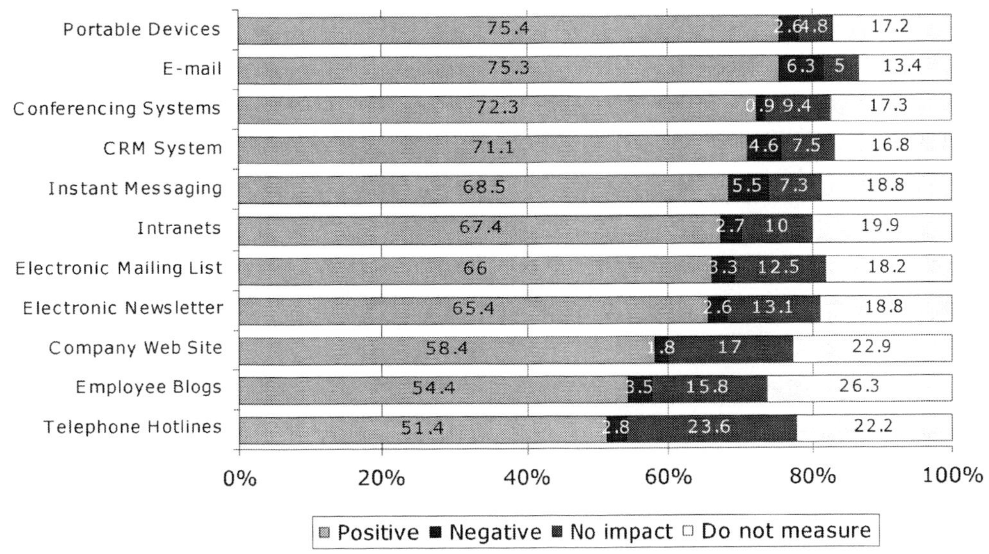

- When considering only those respondents who measured the impact of their organization's electronic communication practices on productivity, portable devices were the most likely to have a positive impact (91 percent), followed by conferencing systems (88 percent) and e-mail (87 percent). Telephone hotlines are least likely to have a positive impact on productivity (66 percent).

TABLE 35 – ELECTRONIC COMMUNICATION IMPACT ON PRODUCTIVITY AMONG ORGANIZATIONS THAT MEASURE THE IMPACT OF ELECTRONIC COMMUNICATION PRACTICES

Practice	Number	Mean	95% Confidence Interval	
			Lower	Upper
Portable Devices	381	0.91	0.88	0.94
Conferencing Systems	272	0.88	0.84	0.91
E-mail	414	0.87	0.84	0.90
CRM System	144	0.85	0.80	0.91
Instant Messaging	134	0.84	0.78	0.91
Intranets	241	0.84	0.80	0.89
Electronic Mailing List	301	0.81	0.76	0.85
Electronic Newsletter	155	0.81	0.74	0.87
Company Web Site	350	0.76	0.71	0.80
Employee Blogs	42	0.74	0.60	0.88
Telephone Hotlines	56	0.66	0.53	0.79

Please indicate whether the following practices had a positive or negative impact on the profitability in your organization.

- Of the respondents whose organizations use a CRM system, 64.2 percent said that it has had a positive impact on profitability. Telephone hotlines are least likely to have a positive impact (45.8 percent), followed by electronic newsletters (49.2 percent).

FIGURE 21 – ELECTRONIC COMMUNICATION IMPACT ON PROFITABILITY

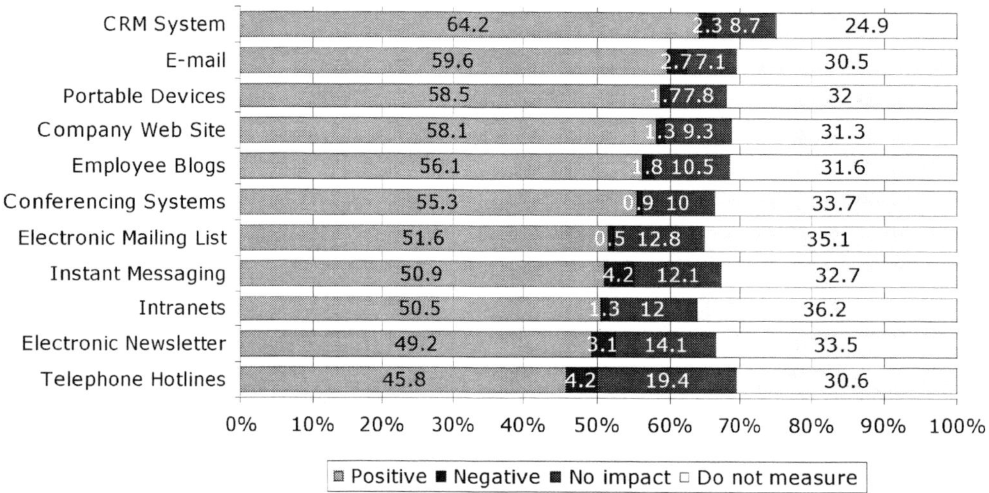

- Looking only at those companies that measured the impact of their organization's electronic communication practices on profitability, portable devices and e-mail are the most likely to have a positive impact (86 percent each). Also, 85 percent of respondents who use CRM systems or company web sites said that they have a positive impact on profitability. Telephone hotlines are least likely to be seen as having a positive impact on profitability (66 percent).

TABLE 36 – ELECTRONIC COMMUNICATION IMPACT ON PROFITABILITY AMONG ORGANIZATIONS THAT MEASURE THE IMPACT OF ELECTRONIC COMMUNICATION PRACTICES

Practice	Number	Mean	95% Confidence Interval	
			Lower	Upper
Portable Devices	313	0.86	0.82	0.90
E-mail	332	0.86	0.82	0.90
CRM System	130	0.85	0.79	0.92
Company Web Site	312	0.85	0.81	0.89
Conferencing Systems	218	0.83	0.79	0.88
Employee Blogs	39	0.82	0.69	0.95
Electronic Mailing List	239	0.79	0.74	0.85
Intranets	192	0.79	0.73	0.85
Instant Messaging	111	0.76	0.68	0.84
Electronic Newsletter	127	0.74	0.66	0.82
Telephone Hotlines	50	0.66	0.52	0.80

Please indicate whether the following practices had a positive or negative impact on employee behavior:

- Approximately three-quarters of respondents whose organization uses electronic newsletters said that this practice has a positive impact on employee behavior. E-mail and instant messaging are also highly likely to have a positive impact on employee behavior (70.5 percent and 70.3 percent respectively). Company web sites are least likely to have a positive impact on employee behavior (52 percent), followed by telephone hotlines (55.6 percent).

FIGURE 22 – ELECTRONIC COMMUNICATION IMPACT ON EMPLOYEE BEHAVIOR

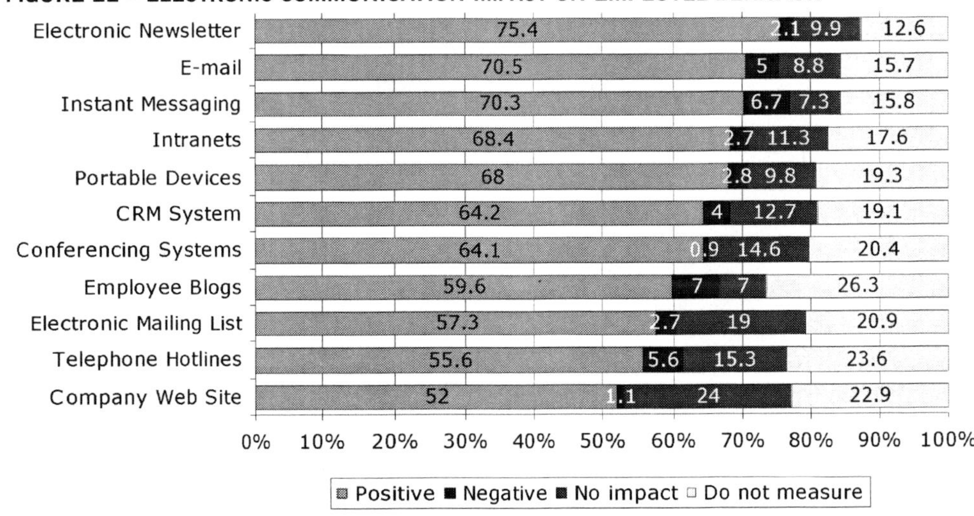

- When considering only those who measured the impact of their organization's electronic communication practices on employee behavior, electronic newsletters are most likely to have a positive impact (86 percent), followed by portable devices and e-mail (84 percent each). The practice least likely to have a positive impact is company web sites (67 percent).

TABLE 37 – ELECTRONIC COMMUNICATION IMPACT ON EMPLOYEE BEHAVIOR AMONG ORGANIZATIONS THAT MEASURE THE IMPACT OF ELECTRONIC COMMUNICATION PRACTICES

Practice	Number	Mean	95% Confidence Interval	
			Lower	Upper
Electronic Newsletter	167	0.86	0.81	0.92
Portable Devices	371	0.84	0.81	0.88
E-mail	403	0.84	0.80	0.87
Instant Messaging	139	0.83	0.77	0.90
Intranets	248	0.83	0.78	0.88
Employee Blogs	42	0.81	0.69	0.93
Conferencing Systems	262	0.81	0.76	0.85
CRM System	140	0.79	0.72	0.86
Telephone Hotlines	55	0.73	0.61	0.85
Electronic Mailing List	291	0.73	0.67	0.78
Company Web Site	350	0.67	0.62	0.72

Please indicate whether the following practices had a positive or negative impact on communications with your customers, the public and the media.

- Respondents whose organizations have a company web site are most likely to say that it has a positive impact on external communications (81.5 percent), followed by e-mail (72.2 percent). Intranets are least likely to have a positive impact (38.5 percent), followed by telephone hotlines and instant messaging (44.4 percent and 45.5 percent respectively).

FIGURE 23 – ELECTRONIC COMMUNICATION IMPACT ON EXTERNAL COMMUNICATIONS

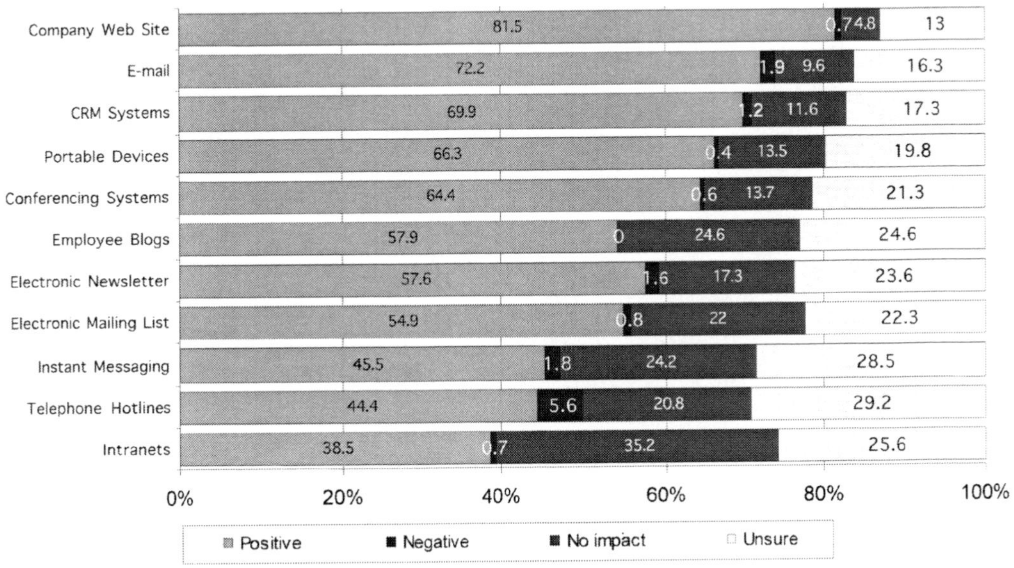

- Considering only those who measured the impact of electronic communication practices on external communications, company web sites are significantly more likely than all other practices to have a positive impact (94 percent). Eighty-six percent of those who measured the impact of e-mail on external relations said the impact was positive, followed by 85 percent of those who measured the impact of CRM systems. Intranets are the least likely to have a positive impact on external communications (52 percent).

TABLE 38 – ELECTRONIC COMMUNICATION IMPACT ON EXTERNAL COMMUNICATIONS AMONG ORGANIZATIONS THAT MEASURE THE IMPACT OF ELECTRONIC COMMUNICATION PRACTICES

Practice	Number	Mean	95% Confidence Interval	
			Lower	Upper
Company Web Site	395	0.94	0.91	0.96
E-mail	400	0.86	0.83	0.90
CRM System	143	0.85	0.79	0.91
Portable Devices	369	0.83	0.79	0.87
Conferencing Systems	259	0.82	0.77	0.87
Employee Blogs	43	0.77	0.64	0.90
Electronic Newsletters	146	0.75	0.68	0.82
Electronic Mailing List	286	0.71	0.65	0.76
Instant Messaging	118	0.64	0.55	0.72
Telephone Hotlines	51	0.63	0.49	0.76
Intranets	224	0.52	0.45	0.58

- Respondents from companies with more than 200 employees were most likely to find that employee blogs and instant messaging had a positive impact on external communications. Respondents from companies with 51 to 200 employees were most likely to find that telephone hotlines and company web sites had a positive impact on external communications. Respondents from companies with up to 50 employees were most likely to find that the remainder of electronic communication practices had a positive impact on external communications.

TABLE 39 – ELECTRONIC COMMUNICATION IMPACT ON EXTERNAL COMMUNICATIONS BY NUMBER OF EMPLOYEES

Impact on External Communications		Number of Employees			
		Up to 50	51 to 200	More than 200	Total
Electronic Mailing List	Number	121	93	72	286
	% Positive	76.0%	68.8%	63.9%	70.6%
Electronic Newsletter	Number	39	61	46	146
	% Positive	84.6%	73.8%	69.6%	75.3%
Telephone Hotlines	Number	17	13	21	51
	% Positive	76.5%	76.9%	42.9%	62.7%
E-mail	Number	192	117	91	400
	% Positive	91.1%	84.6%	78.0%	86.3%
Employee Blogs	Number	15	16	12	43
	% Positive	80.0%	68.8%	83.3%	76.7%
Instant Messaging	Number	52	46	20	118
	% Positive	65.4%	58.7%	70.0%	63.6%
Intranets	Number	71	75	78	224
	% Positive	57.7%	49.3%	48.7%	51.8%
Company Web Site	Number	172	118	105	395
	% Positive	94.2%	94.9%	91.4%	93.7%
CRM System	Number	46	53	44	143
	% Positive	87.0%	81.1%	86.4%	84.6%
Conferencing Systems	Number	103	88	68	259
	% Positive	93.2%	76.1%	72.1%	81.9%
Portable Devices	Number	169	113	87	369
	% Positive	85.8%	79.6%	80.5%	82.7%

- Considering all respondents whose organizations use each practice, e-mail is one of the top three practices in every category. Telephone hotlines are one of the bottom two methods in every category. Shaded cells show the top practices in each category.

TABLE 40 – ELECTRONIC COMMUNICATION SUMMARY TABLE

Practice	% Who Used	% At Least Somewhat Cost - effective	% Positive Impact on:			
			Productivity	Profitability	Employee Behavior	External Comm.
E-mail	78.5	94.4	75.3	59.6	70.5	72.2
CRM System	28.4	88.7	71.1	64.2	64.2	69.9
Portable Devices	75.5	87.2	75.4	58.5	68	66.3
Conferencing Systems	54	87.6	72.3	55.3	64.1	64.4
Company Web Site	74.5	88.3	58.4	58.1	52	81.5
Electronic Newsletter	31.4	89.5	65.4	49.2	75.4	57.6
Instant Messaging	27.1	86.7	68.5	50.9	70.3	45.5
Electronic Mailing List	60.4	90.5	66	51.6	57.3	54.9
Intranets	49.4	89.4	67.4	50.5	68.4	38.5
Employee Blogs	9.4	75.5	54.4	56.1	59.6	57.9
Telephone Hotline	11.8	65.3	51.4	45.8	55.6	44.4

COMMUNICATION RESEARCH PRACTICES / These communication methods involve internal studies and analyses of the ways employees exchange information amongst themselves and of their perceptions regarding their work and the company.

Please indicate the level of current or intended use for the following communication research practices.

- Currently, 36.5 percent of respondents use customer satisfaction surveys as a method of communication research. The percentage using employee opinion surveys is 25.3 percent, and 15.4 percent use communication audits.
- Thirty-two respondents named other communication research practices used by their company. Please see page 217 for a complete list.

FIGURE 24 – RESEARCH USAGE

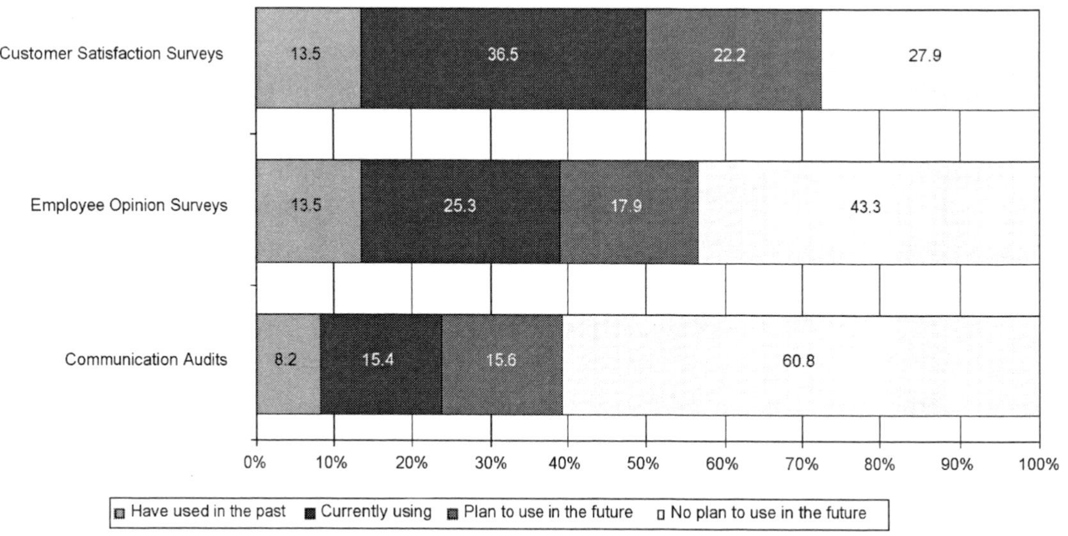

- Organizations with male CEOs are significantly more likely than those with female CEOs to currently use all communication research practices.

TABLE 41 – RESEARCH USAGE BY CEO GENDER

Usage		Gender of CEO		
		Male	Female	Total
Communication Audits	Number	460	138	598
	% Currently Use	16.1%	13.8%	15.6%
Employee Opinion Surveys	Number	460	138	598
	% Currently Use	28.0%	17.4%	25.6%
Customer Satisfaction Surveys	Number	460	138	598
	% Currently Use	39.6%	27.5%	36.8%

- Companies with more than 200 employees are more likely than those with fewer employees to use all communication research practices.

TABLE 42 – RESEARCH USAGE BY NUMBER OF EMPLOYEES

Usage		Number of Employees			
		Up to 50	51 to 200	More than 200	Total
Communication Audits	Number	296	163	147	606
	% Currently Use	10.1%	17.8%	23.8%	15.5%
Employee Opinion Surveys	Number	296	163	147	606
	% Currently Use	14.5%	30.1%	42.2%	25.4%
Customer Satisfaction Surveys	Number	296	163	147	606
	% Currently Use	27.7%	39.9%	51.0%	36.6%

- Corporations are more likely than other types of companies to use all communication research practices.

TABLE 43 – RESEARCH USAGE BY TYPE OF COMPANY

Usage		Type of Company				
		Proprietorship	Partnership	Corporation	Other	Total
Communication Audits	Number	107	97	365	40	609
	% Currently Use	11.2%	14.4%	17.0%	15.0%	15.4%
Employee Opinion Surveys	Number	107	97	365	40	609
	% Currently Use	15.0%	22.7%	28.8%	27.5%	25.3%
Customer Satisfaction Surveys	Number	107	97	365	40	609
	% Currently Use	24.3%	38.1%	40.5%	27.5%	36.5%

Please rate the following practices on a scale of 1 to 3 where "1" is *not at all cost-effective*, "2" is *somewhat cost-effective* and "3" is *very cost-effective.* Cost-effectiveness refers to those practices that were worth the cost of implementing:

- All three methods of communication research are likely to be considered very cost-effective, with more than half of the respondents who use them giving ratings of 3 out of 3. Employee opinion surveys are most likely to be considered not at all cost-effective (8.4 percent).

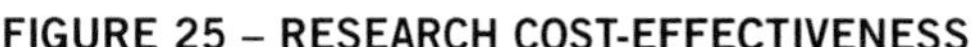
FIGURE 25 – RESEARCH COST-EFFECTIVENESS

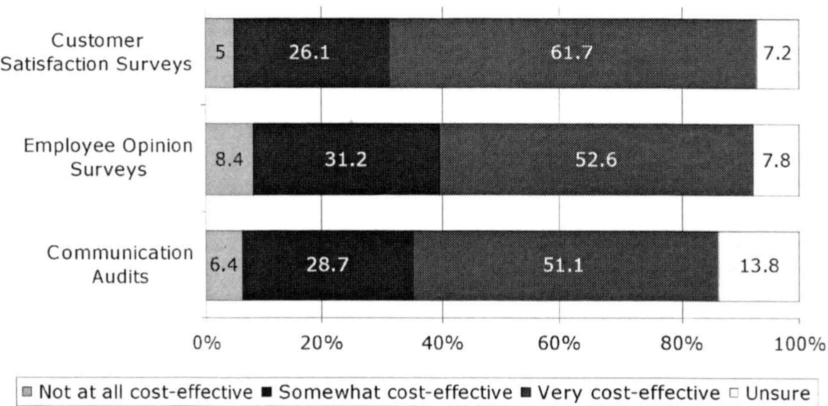

- Considering only those respondents who gave cost-effectiveness ratings for their communication research practices, all three practices are extremely likely to be seen as cost-effective, with over 90 percent of those who use them giving ratings of 2 or 3 out of 3.

TABLE 44 – RESEARCH COST-EFFECTIVENESS

Practice	Number	Mean	95% Confidence Interval	
			Lower	Upper
Customer Satisfaction Surveys	206	0.95	0.92	0.98
Communication Audits	81	0.93	0.87	0.98
Employee Opinion Surveys	142	0.91	0.86	0.96

- Respondents who work for a corporation are more likely those who work for partnerships and proprietorships to say that employee opinion surveys and communication audits are cost-effective. Respondents who work for proprietorships are most likely to find customer satisfaction surveys cost-effective.

TABLE 45 – RESEARCH COST-EFFECTIVENESS BY TYPE OF COMPANY

Cost-effectiveness		Type of Company				
		Proprietorship	Partnership	Corporation	Other	Total
Communication Audit	Number	12	13	50	6	81
	% Somewhat or Very	91.7%	92.3%	94.0%	83.3%	92.6%
Employee Opinion Surveys	Number	16	22	95	9	142
	% Somewhat or Very	81.3%	81.8%	93.7%	100.0%	90.8%
Customer Satisfaction Surveys	Number	25	36	136	9	206
	% Somewhat or Very	96.0%	91.7%	94.9%	100.0%	94.7%

Please indicate whether the following practices had a positive or negative impact on the productivity of your organization.

- More than three-quarters of those who use customer satisfaction surveys as a method of communication research said that this practice has had a positive impact on productivity. Employee opinion surveys are most likely to have a negative impact on productivity (6.5 percent).

FIGURE 26 – RESEARCH IMPACT ON PRODUCTIVITY

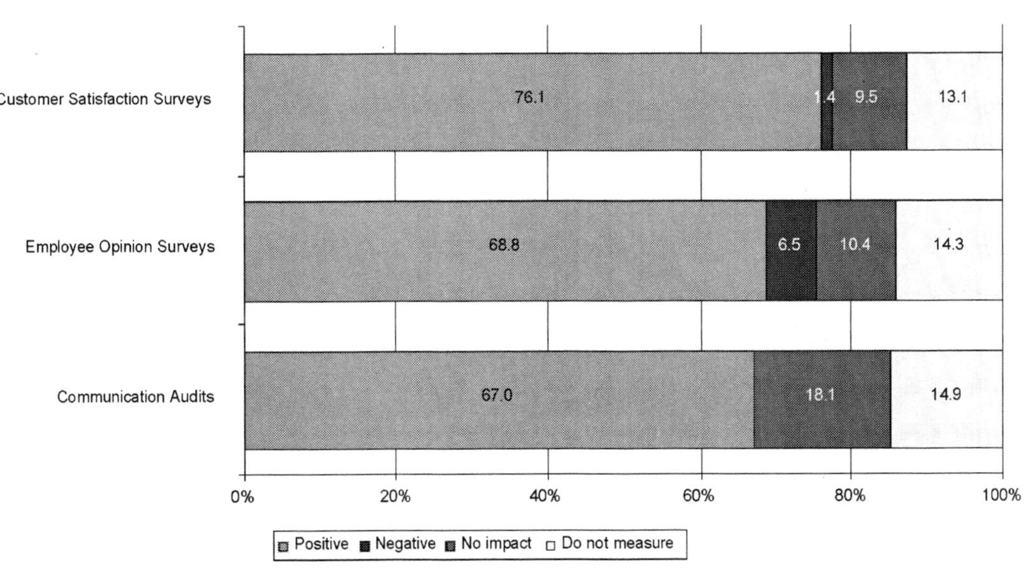

- Considering only those who measured the impact of communication research practices on productivity, customer satisfaction surveys are the most likely to have a positive impact (88 percent), while communication audits are least likely (79 percent).

TABLE 46 – RESEARCH IMPACT ON PRODUCTIVITY AMONG ORGANIZATIONS THAT MEASURE THE IMPACT OF RESEARCH

Practice	Number	Mean	95% Confidence Interval	
			Lower	Upper
Customer Satisfaction Surveys	193	0.88	0.83	0.92
Employee Opinion Surveys	132	0.80	0.73	0.87
Communication Audit	80	0.79	0.70	0.88

Please indicate whether the following practices had a positive or negative impact on the profitability in your organization.

- Customer satisfaction surveys are most likely to have a positive impact on profitability (70.7 percent), while employee opinion surveys are least likely (52.6 percent).

FIGURE 27 – RESEARCH IMPACT ON PROFITABILITY

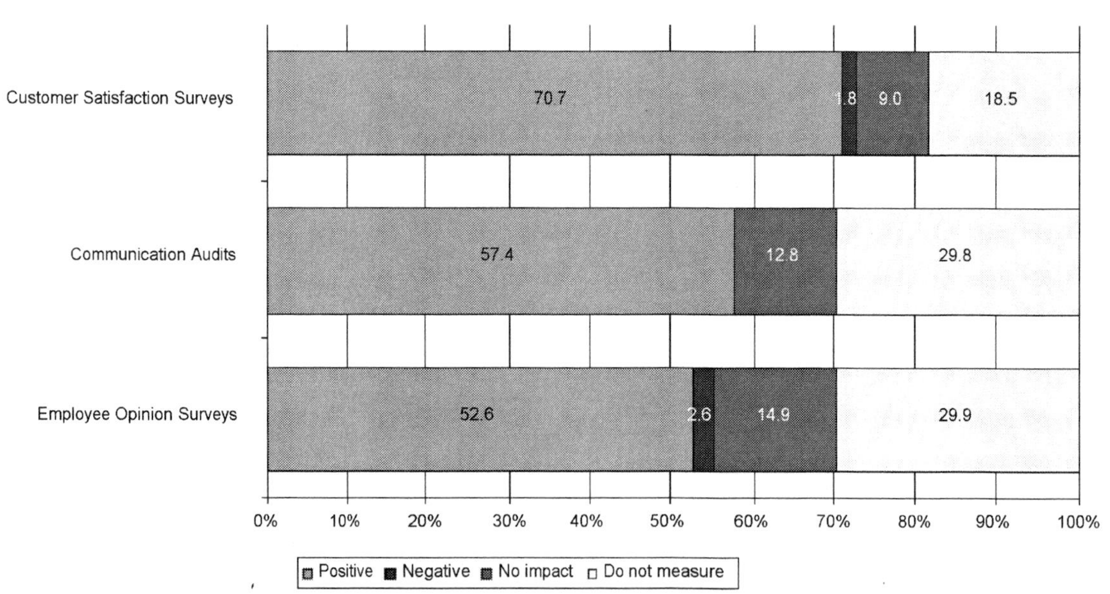

- Considering only those who measured the impact of communication research practices on profitability, customer satisfaction surveys are most likely to have a positive impact (87 percent), while employee opinion surveys are least likely (75 percent).

TABLE 47 – RESEARCH IMPACT ON PROFITABILITY AMONG ORGANIZATIONS THAT MEASURE THE IMPACT OF RESEARCH

Practice	Number	Mean	95% Confidence Interval	
			Lower	Upper
Customer Satisfaction Surveys	181	0.87	0.82	0.92
Communication Audits	66	0.82	0.72	0.91
Employee Opinion Surveys	108	0.75	0.67	0.83

Please indicate whether the following practices had a positive or negative impact on employee behavior:

- Over 70 percent of respondents who use each practice said that it has a positive impact on employee behavior. Employee opinion surveys are most likely to have a negative impact on employee behavior (5.2 percent).

FIGURE 28 – RESEARCH IMPACT ON EMPLOYEE BEHAVIOR

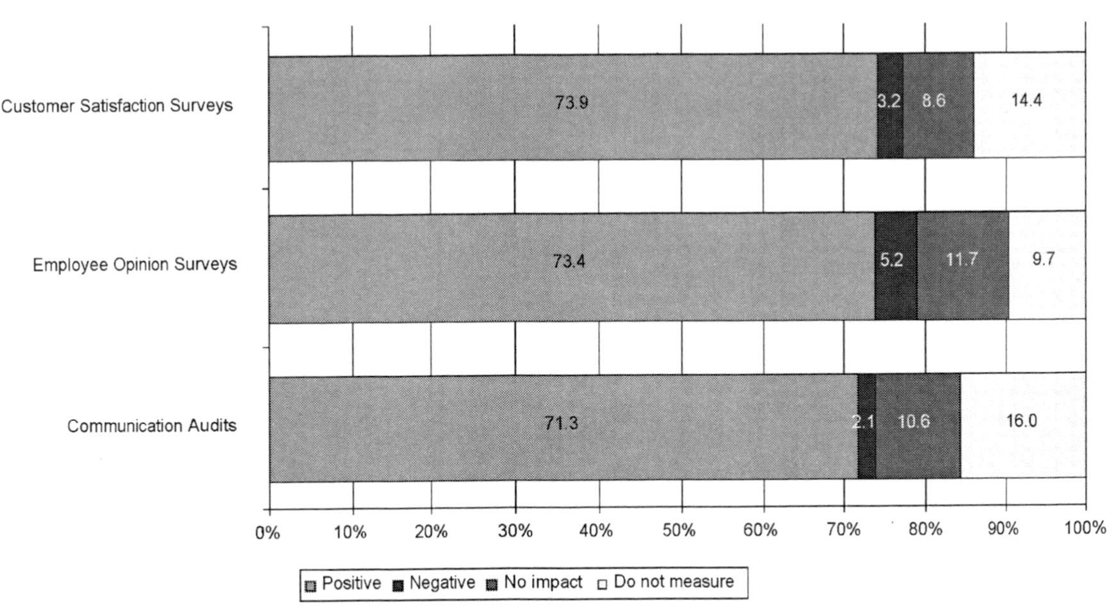

- Considering only those respondents who measured the impact of their communication research practices on employee behavior, customer satisfaction surveys are most likely to have a positive impact (86 percent), while employee opinion surveys are least likely (81 percent).

TABLE 48 – RESEARCH IMPACT ON EMPLOYEE BEHAVIOR AMONG ORGANIZATIONS THAT MEASURE THE IMPACT OF RESEARCH

Practice	Number	Mean	95% Confidence Interval	
			Lower	Upper
Customer Satisfaction Surveys	190	0.86	0.81	0.91
Communication Audits	79	0.85	0.77	0.93
Employee Opinion Surveys	139	0.81	0.75	0.88

Please indicate whether the following practices had a positive or negative impact on communication with your customers, the public and the media.

- Customer satisfaction surveys are most likely to have a positive impact on external communications (82.9 percent), while employee opinion surveys are least likely to have a positive impact (47.4 percent).

FIGURE 29 – RESEARCH IMPACT ON EXTERNAL COMMUNICATIONS

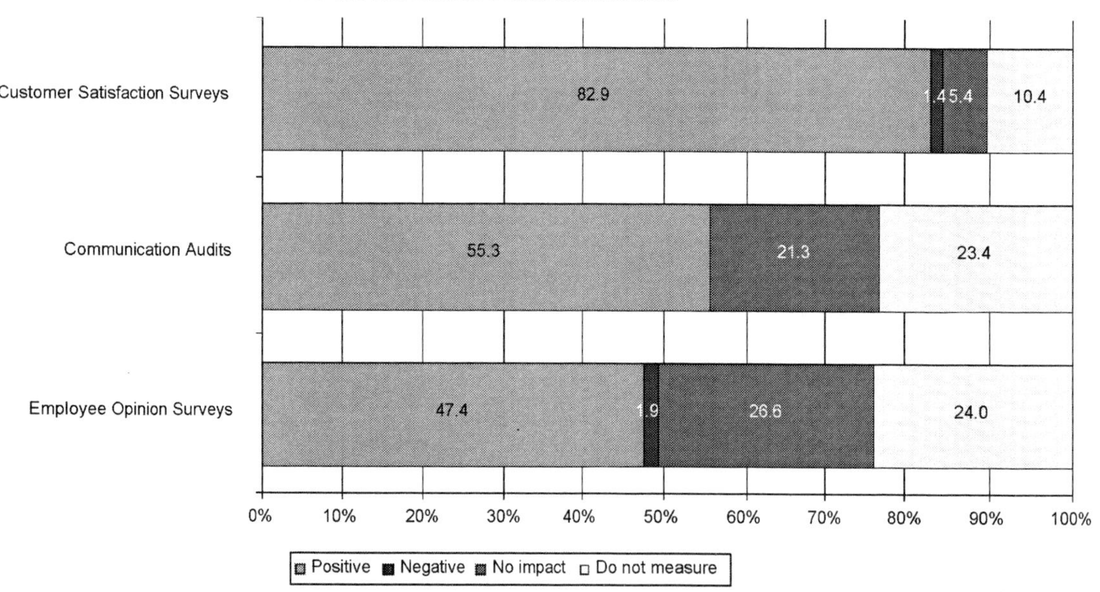

- Considering only those who measured the impact of their communication research practices on external communications, customer satisfaction surveys were significantly more likely than the other practices to have a positive impact (92 percent).

TABLE 49 – RESEARCH IMPACT ON EXTERNAL COMMUNICATIONS AMONG ORGANIZATIONS THAT MEASURE THE IMPACT OF RESEARCH

Practice	Number	Mean	95% Confidence Interval	
			Lower	Upper
Customer Satisfaction Surveys	199	0.92	0.89	0.96
Communication Audit	72	0.72	0.62	0.83
Employee Opinion Surveys	117	0.62	0.53	0.71

- Customer satisfaction surveys are the most used method of communication research and the most likely to be considered cost-effective. Customer satisfaction surveys are also most likely to be seen as having a positive impact on productivity, profitability, employee behavior and external communications. Communication audits are least likely to be considered cost-effective. Employee opinion surveys are least likely to be seen as having a positive impact on profitability and external communication.

TABLE 50 – RESEARCH SUMMARY TABLE

Practice	% Who Used	% At Least Somewhat Cost-effective	% Positive Impact on:			
			Productivity	Profitability	Employee Behavior	External Comm.
Customer Satisfaction Surveys	36.5	87.8	76.1	70.7	73.9	82.9
Communication Audits	15.4	79.8	67	57.4	71.3	55.3
Employee Opinion Surveys	25.3	83.8	68.8	52.6	73.4	47.4

BUSINESS SUCCESS / The following is a list of functions in a typical business. Please indicate how important the functions are to your business success by allocating 100 points among each of the following eight functions. Please allocate more points to those functions you view as being more important. Business success is defined in terms of personal satisfaction with your enterprise.

- The function that respondents said is most important to their business success is sales and marketing, with 24 percent giving it more than 25 points. Research and development is viewed as being the least important business function with 33.5 percent of respondents giving it no points, and only 14.1 percent giving it 11 to 25 points.

FIGURE 30 – IMPORTANCE OF BUSINESS FUNCTIONS

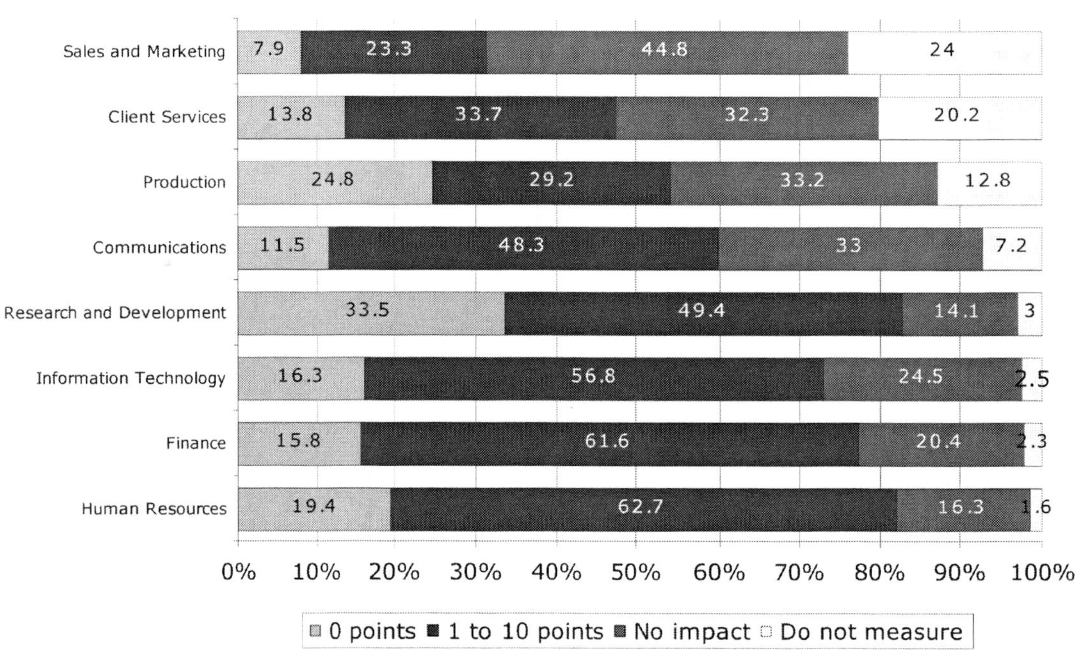

- On average, sales and marketing received significantly more points than any other business function, at 21.1. Client services is perceived as the second most important function, with an average of 18.1 points.

TABLE 51 – IMPORTANCE OF BUSINESS FUNCTIONS

Business Function	Mean	95% Confidence Interval	
		Lower	Upper
Sales and Marketing	21.1	19.8	22.4
Client Services	18.1	16.7	19.5
Production	14.1	12.9	15.3
Communications	12.7	11.8	13.6
Information Technology	9.7	9.0	10.3
Finance	9.2	8.5	9.9
Human Resources	8.1	7.4	8.8
Research and Development	7.0	6.4	7.7

Overall, what employee communication strategy has really made a difference in your firm? Please describe this strategy and the impact it has had on your business.

- Of those who responded, approximately one-quarter said that open communication has really made a difference in their firm. Seventeen percent said personal and face-to-face communication has made a difference, and 16.3 percent said meetings have made a difference. Those who said that e-mail, video or telecommunications has really made a difference in their firm totaled 12.9 percent.

FIGURE 31 – COMMUNICATION STRATEGY THAT HAS MADE THE BIGGEST DIFFERENCE

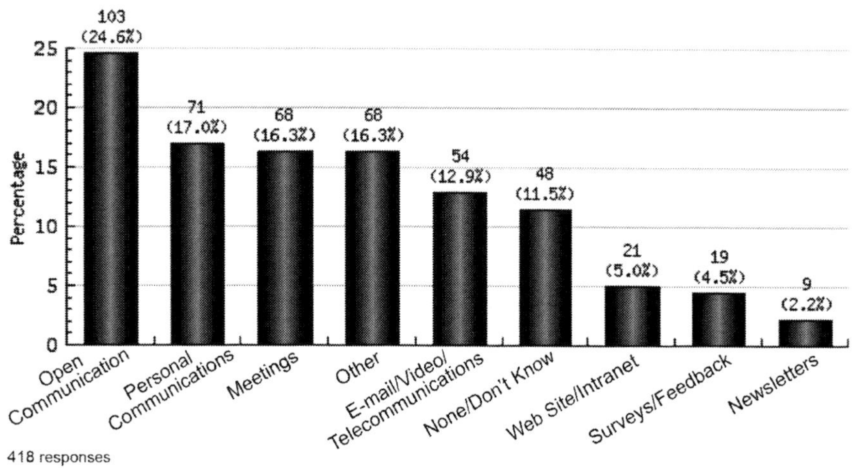

TABLE 52 – COMMUNICATION STRATEGY THAT HAS MADE THE BIGGEST DIFFERENCE

Description	Total #	% of Responses
Open communication, open door policy	103	24.6
Personal and face-to-face communication	71	17.0
Meetings with staff, team, managers, company, and/or CEO; focus groups	68	16.3
Retreats, training, stakeholders	68	16.3
E-mail, video, telecommunications	54	12.9
None, Not Applicable, Don't Know	48	11.5
Company web site for employees and/or customers	21	5.0
Employee and/or customer surveys, reviews, evaluations, audits	19	4.5
Electronic or print newsletters	9	2.2
Total	**418**	**100**

- The following is a list of selected responses from categories that had more than 50 responses. Please see Appendix A for a complete list of responses.

Open Communication

"Our open door policy has had the biggest impact for us. We encourage its use, and our employees are very responsive. Productivity and morale are high."

"Open discussion of internal and client issues in a team environment. Impact: makes everyone feel they are 'in this together.' Everyone takes ownership and understands the challenges of a small consulting organization."

Personal and Face-to-Face Communication

"Informal gatherings amongst employees. It tends to surface issues, leads to discussion of potential solutions to issues, allows for an exchange of ideas and just boosts morale. There is no formal strategy for implementing gatherings—employees seek out the opportunities themselves."

"Teamwork and face-to-face communications have made a difference in our firm since we are just a few people. We are consultants, so the more we share the work we are doing, the better service we provide to our clients."

Meetings

"Management meetings: weekly meetings of team managers to discuss issues, exchange ideas for the company, etc. Top-down and bottom-up communications allow decisions to be made faster and collectively. Positive impact on managers' motivation."

"Monthly meetings where employees can voice their concerns and comments have had such a positive impact on business; the employees are the front line, and they know where to make changes for the better."

Other

"Monthly new employee orientation—our company is growing so rapidly that it is vital that new employees are introduced to the company, its culture and corporate goals at the start of their employment."

"Sending memoranda with relevant information to all departments. It has kept all employees advised of all general and some specific data about the activities and programs of the organization."

E-mail, Video, Telecommunications

"Moving from print to electronic. We are a bank with 19 branches in three states, and this allows us to provide more timely and targeted communications."

"Weekly e-mail and quarterly company updates keep people connected to the company and each other while assessing our progress to date and what to expect moving forward."

Does your firm currently have a budget for communication in place?

- The percentage of respondents who indicated that their firm currently has a budget for communication in place was 38.1 percent, while 49.1 percent indicated that their firm does not have a communication budget. The remaining 12.8 percent are unsure.

FIGURE 32 – BUDGET FOR COMMUNICATION IN PLACE

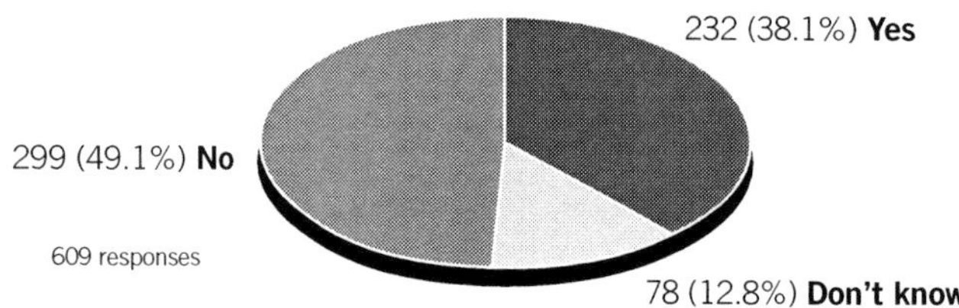

What percentage is the budget for communication?

- Of those who have a budget for communication, 37.5 percent indicated that less than 5 percent of their firm's budget is for communication, 15.9 percent said 5 to 9 percent, and 28.9 percent said 10 to 19 percent. Those who said 20 percent or more totaled 17.7 percent. The mean percentage is 10.4 percent, and the median is 6.5 percent.

TABLE 53 – PERCENTAGE OF BUDGET FOR COMMUNICATION

% of Budget for Communication	Frequency	Percent	Cumulative Percent
Less than 5%	87	37.5	37.5
5% to 9%	37	15.9	53.4
10% to 19%	67	28.9	82.3
20% or more	41	17.7	100.0
Total	232	100.0	

Does your firm currently have a strategic communication plan in place?

- Fifty-six percent of respondents said that their firm does not currently have a strategic communication plan in place, while 32.7 percent said that their firm has a plan in place. The remaining 11.3 percent are unsure.

FIGURE 33 – STRATEGIC COMMUNICATION PLAN IN PLACE

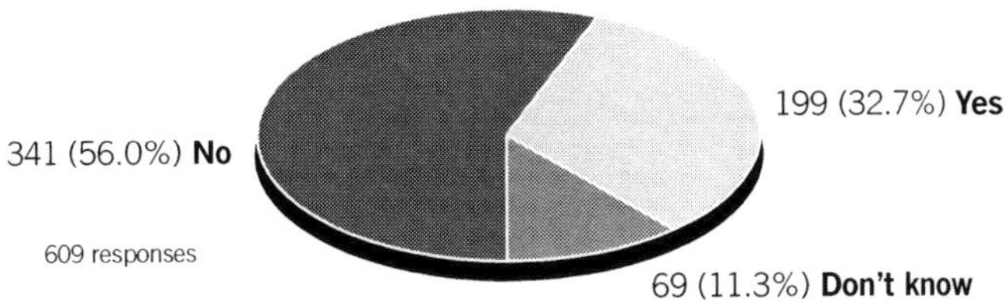

Please rate the formal and organizational level of your strategic communication plan on a scale of 1 to 10, with "1" being *somewhat formal and organized* and "10" being *extremely formal and organized.*

- Of those who have a strategic communication plan in place, 19.5 percent gave it a rating of 1 to 3. Those who gave their plan a rating of 4 to 7 totaled 55.4 percent, and 25.1 percent gave their plan a rating of 8 to 10. The majority of respondents said that their strategic communication plan is more than somewhat formal and organized, but that it could be improved.

FIGURE 34 – FORMAL AND ORGANIZATIONAL LEVEL OF STRATEGIC COMMUNICATION PLAN

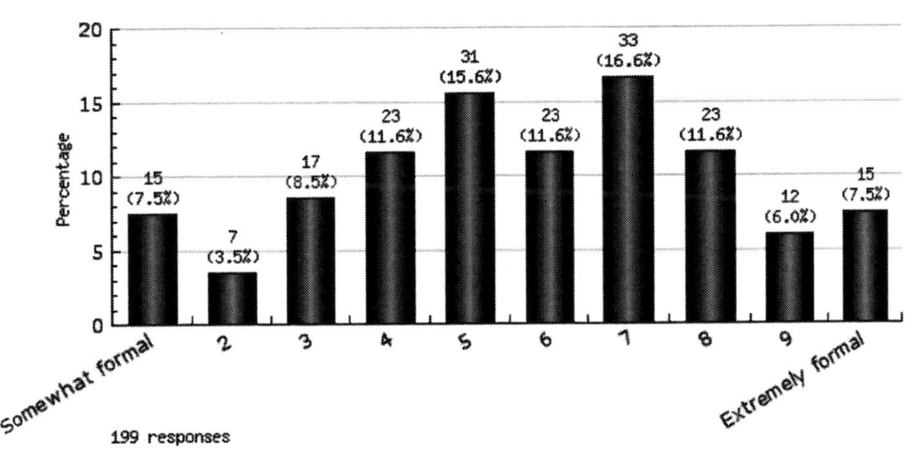

What was your firm's pre-tax profit margin in the most recent fiscal year as a percentage of total revenue?

- The percentage of respondents who could not provide their firm's pre-tax profit margin was 40.6 percent. Of those who could provide this information, 14.3 percent (87 of 362 respondents) indicated that it was more than 20 percent. Another 21 percent (128 of 362 respondents) said that it was between 11 and 20 percent, while 19.6 percent (119 of 362 respondents) were between 1 and 10 percent. Those whose organization had a profit margin of 0 or incurred a loss totaled 4.6 percent (28 of 362 respondents).

FIGURE 35 – PRE-TAX PROFIT MARGIN

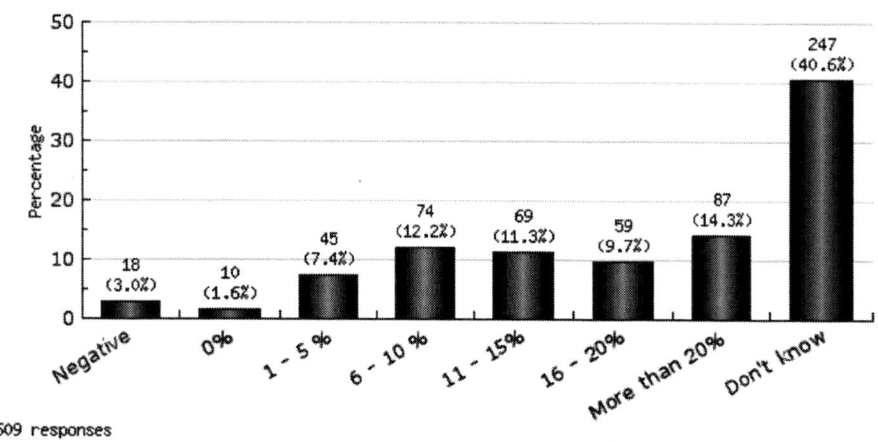

Overall, how has your pre-tax profit margin changed over the past five years?

- Of those who were able to say how their pre-tax profit margin has changed, 42.4 percent (258 of 401 respondents) said that it has increased, 14.1 percent (86 of 401 respondents) said that it has stayed the same, and 9.4 percent (57 of 401 respondents) said that it has decreased.

FIGURE 36 – HOW HAS YOUR FIRM'S PRE-TAX PROFIT MARGIN CHANGED?

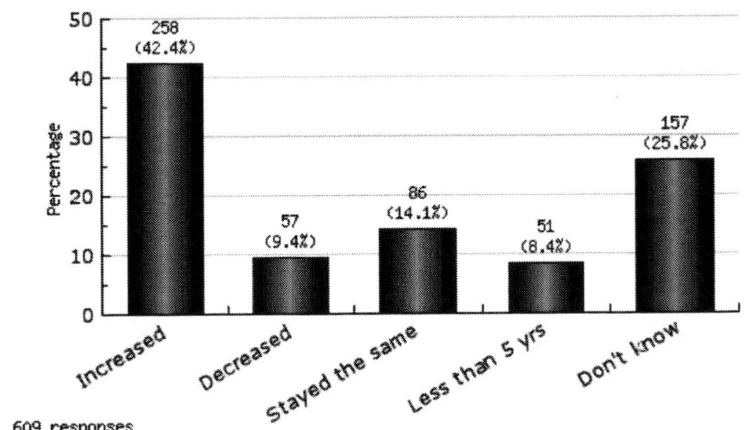

What percentage describes your firm's revenue growth in the most recent fiscal year?

- Of those who know what percentage describes their firm's revenue growth in the most recent fiscal year, 17.2 percent (105 of 432 respondents) said growth was 6 to 10 percent, and 13.5 percent (82 of 432 respondents) said growth was 1 to 5 percent.

FIGURE 37 – PERCENTAGE OF REVENUE GROWTH

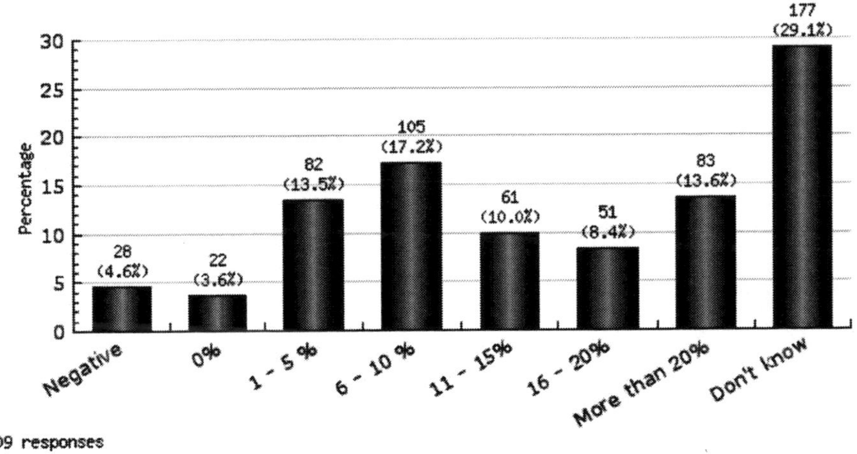

Overall, how has your revenue growth changed over the past five years?

- The majority of respondents said that their revenue growth has increased over the past five years (58 percent). Those who said it had stayed the same totaled 11.5 percent, while 6.9 percent said it had decreased. Those who are unsure totaled 15.4 percent, and 8.2 percent are part of a company that has been around for less than five years.

FIGURE 38 – HOW HAS YOUR FIRM'S REVENUE GROWTH CHANGED?

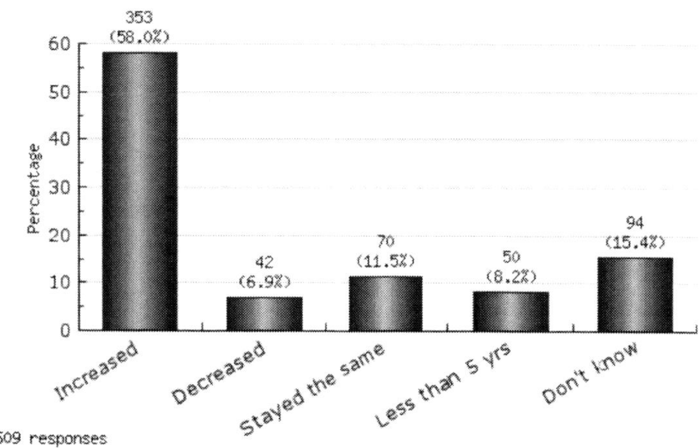

Is all or a portion of your workforce unionized?

- The percentage of respondents who indicated that no portion of their workforce is unionized was 88.8 percent, while 8.4 percent said that all or a portion of their workforce is unionized.

FIGURE 39 – WORKFORCE UNIONIZED

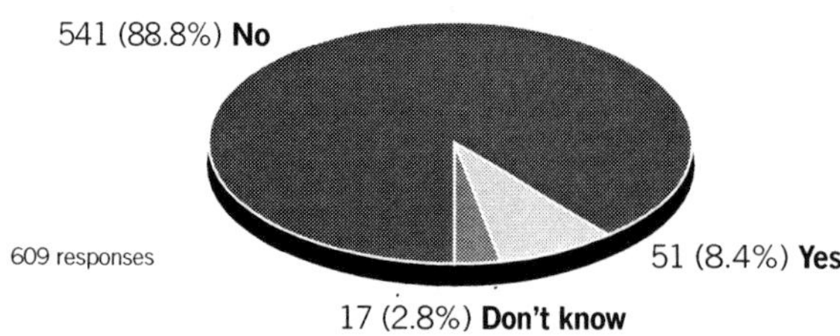

APPENDIX B / Open-Ended Survey Responses

ARE YOU USING ANY OTHER IN-PERSON COMMUNICATION STRATEGIES IN YOUR ORGANIZATION? IF SO, BRIEFLY DESCRIBE THE PRACTICE BELOW.

No: 49 responses

Meetings: 37 responses (Meetings with staff, team, management and/or CEO, focus groups)

(3) One-on-one meetings.

(1) All-employee "boot camps" where executive management relays upcoming initiatives, how we're doing, corporate goals and objectives. Employee committees and councils give updates on their projects and initiatives. Includes mingle time and lots of fun.

(1) Annual (relaxation) reward trip for "star" salespeople accompanied by at least three partners. Annual companywide off-site meeting to update, train, communicate and bond.

(1) Annual companywide meeting. All associates (and a guest, if they wish) are flown to a nice location (i.e., Orlando, Florida; The Bahamas; or Cancun, Mexico) for three days of meetings, networking, social events, team building events and free time.

(1) Annual employee retreat, quarterly business planning meetings, annual employee evaluations.

(1) Annual strategy meeting for senior executives.

(1) CEO, president and two VPs meet quarterly in officer meetings. President and two VPs provide direct input for online CEO newsletter. Meet as account teams and monthly department meetings.

(1) Conferences for communicators, car show events.

(1) Daily shift start meetings with management and employees.

(1) Daily staff meetings in each office, linked to other offices by phone.

(1) Employee meetings to roll out new policies and/or benefit plans.

(1) Encouragement, focus groups.

(1) Face-to-face staff meetings.

(1) Having sit-down meetings one-on-one, making goals and benchmarks clear at that time.

(1) Human resources does an active follow-up of new hires at intervals. We have informal celebrations of awards, goals, achievements and community contributions. Employee information meetings. Survey to improve methods and types of communication. Newsletters.

(1) Internal events, communication meets by senior management, birthday celebrations, internal recognition meetings, etc.

(1) Monthly board meeting in an open forum with senior management and external members.

(1) No, seeing that we are a relatively small company there has been no need to formalize the employee communication. There are no secrets about that. The management certainly has meetings among themselves concerning the strategies the company will adopt in the future. We are still growing so the main concern is how to find competent staff.

(1) One-on-one meetings between supervisor and employee.

(1) Pre-shift meetings.

(1) Monthly Q&A with the owners.

(1) Quarterly employee meetings to discuss the business.

(1) Random in-depth meetings with employee, name picked at random and asked if he or she has input.

(1) Roundtable discussions with members of the senior team and randomly selected people from throughout the organization.

(1) Small group meetings with six to eight employees, president/CEO, HR director (and another manager where appropriate).

(1) Town hall sessions where management reports on quarterly results/events, and staff has the opportunity to ask questions.

(1) Town halls monthly, strategy road show presentation annually.

(1) Town halls, CEO roundtables, skip level meetings.

(1) We also do an off-site meeting twice a year.

(1) We have staff meetings every day; the owner of the company comes once a day, and we can talk to him freely.

(1) We place a great deal of emphasis on involving employees in strategy formulation and business planning. Therefore, we have a quarterly all-company meeting where we do fun exercises that solicit opinions and input from employees. This plays an important role in helping to make the link between someone's day-to-day role and the direction of the business.

(1) We set up lunches for new employees that are hosted by our top executives. We also facilitate brown bag lunches that are focused on sharing knowledge between departments and/or between management and staff.

(1) Weekly staff meetings.

(1) Weekly team meetings with managers and staff.

(1) WIP—weekly work-in-progress meeting.

Other: 25 responses (Road Shows, Retreats, Incentives, Other)

(1) Three people communicate with each aspect of the company production/packing/shipping/selling office.

(1) All-employee "boot camps" where executive management relays upcoming initiatives, how we're doing, corporate goals and objectives. Employee committees and councils give updates on their projects and initiatives. Includes mingle time and lots of fun.

(1) Annual (relaxation) reward trip for "star" salespeople accompanied by at least three partners. Annual companywide off-site meeting to update, train, communicate and bond.

(1) Annual employee retreat, quarterly business planning meetings, annual employee evaluations.

(1) Any member of the staff can make an appointment to meet with the owner to voice a grievance of a delicate nature or that requires top management discussion.

(1) Conferences for communicators, car show events.

(1) Different committees and quarterly training sessions.

(1) Employees are free to talk to management at any time.

(1) Encouragement, focus groups.

(1) Face-to-face conversations.

(1) I use them all on a daily basis, talking with the people who work under me.

(1) If we have any issue, we are encouraged to talk to our manager to get things fixed.

(1) Literally, we don't have doors within the office.

(1) Make it a practice to always have open and in-person communication.

(1) My door is always open to all who work for me.

(1) Once a year "kickoff" where management communicates strategy to employees, usually in January.

(1) Road shows: a brief session (usually one hour) on an upcoming project or initiative with employee impacts, usually delivered by a senior leader, with opportunities for dialogue between employees. The "show" travels to all teams in the organization prior to formal training. There are substantial employee learning opportunities.

(1) Supervisor visitation of off-site employees. Paychecks are delivered to employees face-to-face.

(1) The face-to-face communication framework I work within uses a combination of these tactics and others to solicit employee input and facilitate two-way communication.

(1) The owner and GM both will go around to various people and ask how they're doing, if they need anything, etc.

(1) This is a business that goes off-site. We try to be available when out of the office.

(1) Monthly town halls, strategy road show presentation annually.

(1) We also use cross-functional teams for various corporate or change initiatives.

(1) We are a small company. There is a lot of in-person communication on an informal basis.

(1) We have face-to-face conversations.

Personal/Social: 21 responses (Informal/Social gatherings)

(1) Annual companywide meeting. All associates (and a guest, if they wish) are flown to a nice location (i.e., Orlando, Florida; The Bahamas; or Cancun, Mexico) for three days of meetings, networking, social events, team building events and free time.

(1) Annual staff appreciation event where performance awards and attendance awards are presented, along with a speech from the CEO outlining our successes over the past year and our goals for the upcoming year.

(1) Monthly breakfast,with the CEO.

(1) Frequent one-on-one casual discussions, such as taking an employee to lunch. As a small company, we have the ability to air concerns on a personal basis.

(1) Happy hours at the local bar and VFW.

(1) Holiday parties; CEO travels to development offices to boost morale.

(1) Human resources does an active follow-up of new hires at intervals. We have informal celebrations of awards, goals, achievements and community contributions. Employee information meetings. Survey to improve methods and types of communication. Newsletters.

(1) Informal and formal gatherings to celebrate associates' birthdays, anniversaries and other significant events.

(1) Informal gatherings, get-togethers, having non-work–related activities together.

(1) Internal events, communication meets by senior management, birthday celebrations, internal recognition meets, etc.

(1) Management is encouraged to spend time regularly with individual employees over coffee or lunch to find out how things are working for them and to hear their ideas on what could be improved.

(1) One-on-one luncheons to review performance and set goals.

(1) One-on-one staff lunches (informal); office social events (with and without spouses and significant others).

(1) Personal lunch meetings.

(1) Staff e-mails, lunch room, employee lounge, off- and on-site celebrations of success.

(1) Supervisor visitation of off-site employees. Paychecks are delivered to employees face-to-face.

(1) Team buildings for a weekend.

(1) Team building sessions in which praise is openly given. Group training sessions or workshops. We also have "lunch 'n learn" in which trainers present a topic in a workshop setting. Face-to-face communication ensues.

(1) We have a cheesecake contest, charity golf tournament, pizza and beer lunches, martini lounges, a chili cook-off for charity, summer BBQ and two holiday parties (one for kids, one more formal for adults).

(1) We set up lunches for new employees that are hosted by our top executives. We also facilitate brown bag lunches, that are focused on sharing knowledge between departments and/or between management and staff.

(1) Yes, we have yearly lunches with our boss, when the boss takes an employee out to lunch to discuss their job and anything else they want to talk about.

Training/Reviews: 14 responses (Training, coaching, evaluations)

(1) Annual employee retreat, quarterly business planning meetings, annual employee evaluations.

(1) Coaching sessions to take the place of annual performance reviews.

(1) Communication training.

(1) Computer training, administrative procedures.

(1) Different committees and quarterly training sessions.

(1) Human resources does an active follow-up of new hires at intervals. We have informal celebrations of awards, goals, achievements and community contributions. Employee information meetings. Survey to improve methods and types of communication. Newsletters.

(1) Mentoring program for junior staff to get support from experienced team members. It's called the "Jelly Buddy" program, and each month it involves Jelly Buddies presenting their personal achievements to the rest of the company.

(1) Mentoring/coaching/shadowing.

(1) Monthly employee evaluations. This lets them know and understand the standards, tells them their strengths, and encourages help to address any weaknesses.

(1) Face-to-face performance evaluations.

(1) Performance reviews, one-on-one reviews.

(1) Performance reviews. Personal coaching and support.

(1) Quarterly individual company and individual performance feedback sessions where employees can raise issues or areas of concern relating to productivity and profitability.

(1) We are a two-person shop with a handful of outside suppliers and collaborators. It's pretty informal. I do a lot of coaching, which is pretty well covered by face-to-face conversations, though it is a conversation about goals and development, not necessarily day-to-day business.

ARE YOU USING ANY OTHER PRINT COMMUNICATION STRATEGIES IN YOUR ORGANIZATION? IF SO, BRIEFLY DESCRIBE THE PRACTICE BELOW.

No/Nonprint: 58 responses (No, not applicable, use nonprint strategies)

Other: 27 responses (Benefits information, reports)

(1) 360 feedback.

(1) Annual report.

(1) Background check authorization, NDA, CSOW, SOW, miscellaneous HR information and paperwork generated from outsourced HR firm.

(1) Clearly written goals help keep employees on task.

(1) Contracts and role descriptions. Performance reviews. Marketing campaigns (internalization).

(1) Cost savings forms—turn in and you receive a percentage of what you save the company.

(1) Employees can nominate other employees for going beyond the call of duty. They get a printed certificate of appreciation and are entered into a monthly drawing for movie passes.

(1) Financial reports and status only given to senior management. These are overviews. Managers for a particular area are given more in-depth reports for their area of responsibility.

(1) Form we would fill out.

(1) Have distributed a midyear report to employees, which was a scaled-down version of our annual report to shareholders.

(1) Health care and prescription drug information.

(1) Health publications.

(1) Mouse pads and other collateral to reinforce communications, such as posters, flyers, etc.

(1) Placing notices in on-site employee mailboxes.

(1) Printed brochure outlining corporate vision, corporate "placemats" that communicate annual objectives and measurements.

(1) Process maps.

(1) Rebate and incentive information is organized into a booklet by a clerical staff member for use, and updated as needed.

(1) Sales tools for product launches.

(1) Special Filofax pages are printed for each team member. These are company-specific and are often personalized to each individual. They include key contacts, company structure, business plan summary for 2006, training program, 360 feedback data, monthly financial results, photo pages of team events and parties, IT guidelines, and much more.

(1) Tailgate training.

(1) Templates.

(1) Thank-you notes for excellent work, birthday, anniversary; bulletin board with client forum for excellent satisfaction; employee of the quarter; schedules.

(1) Handwritten thank-you notes for excellent work.

(1) Too small to worry about this much. However, we do receive a yearly comp statement listing pay, benefits and fringe.

(1) We have educational tools such as a manipulative cube and a desktop display that celebrates the winning of an award from "Companies that Care" and includes the reasons why we won the award. We also give each new associate a framed copy of our mission, vision and core values.

(1) We use our own printing.

(1) Work-in-progress flow charts.

Bulletin Board: 21 responses (Bulletin Board)

(2) Bulletin boards.

(1) Brochures, memos, circulars and information boards.

(1) Bulletin board notices/postings.

(1) Bulletin board and e-mail postings of various company information.

(1) Bulletin board postings, e-mail.

(1) Bulletin board postings, inserts with paychecks, interoffice mail.

(1) Bulletin board, payroll stuffers.

(1) Bulletin boards—examples of good work, professional development articles, etc., are posted for all to see and read; distributed articles—we route professional development articles to those who may be interested.

(1) Bulletin boards to post our electronic newsletters and customer feedback.

(1) Communication boards.

(1) E-mail and bulletin boards.

(1) Information posted on common wall. Notes on paychecks.

(1) Mass e-mail communications, postings on employee bulletin boards.

(1) Meeting notices posted in employee lunch areas and sign-up sheets for meetings.

(1) Payroll stuffers, bulletin board postings.

(1) Poster board.

(1) Press releases, analyst reports and news coverage are often printed out and posted for employees to read. The lunchroom bulletin board is used to post information that anyone wants to share (business and beyond).

(1) Thank-you notes for excellent work, birthday, anniversary; bulletin board with client forum for excellent satisfaction; employee of the quarter; schedules.

(1) We have a community bulletin board in our kitchen area where we can post all kinds of stuff, like a list of holidays for the year, volunteer committee updates, menus for local restaurants and a help line phone number to report any kind of concerns about employees or the company.

(1) Weekly e-bulletin e-mailed to employees, hard copy posted for remote sites/sites with employees with no e-mail access to pin to bulletin boards.

Newsletter: 13 responses (Newsletter)

(2) Company newsletter.

(2) Monthly employee newsletter.

(1) E-mails with general information. Company newsletter. Company and employee web site.

(1) Internal communication newsletters, greeting cards, etc.

(1) Memos faxed to stores. Monthly newsletter to all employees.

(1) Monthly employee newsletter.

(1) Monthly updates.

(1) Newsletter.

(1) No employees; print advertising in group newsletters is used to reach potential clients where applicable.

(1) Periodical newsletters.

(1) Weekly news updates—daily e-mails if necessary.

Memos/Brochures: 8 responses (Memos, brochures, pamphlets)

(1) Briefing documents for managers relating to HR initiatives.

(1) Brochures, memos, circulars and information boards.

(1) Memo.

(1) Memos faxed to stores. Monthly newsletter to all employees.

(1) Mouse pads and other collateral to reinforce communications, such as posters, flyers, etc.

(1) Pamphlets of issues such as EEO issues. Bonus programs.

(1) Printed brochure outlining corporate vision, corporate "placemats" that communicate annual objectives and measurements.

(1) Project plan that is shared with the team on a weekly basis.

Pay inserts: 6 responses (Inserts/stuffers with paycheck)

(1) Bulletin board postings, inserts with paychecks, interoffice mail.

(1) Bulletin board, payroll stuffers.

(1) Information posted on common wall. Notes on paychecks.

(1) Letter to all staff of current happenings in monthly paycheck.

(1) Paycheck stuffers (a method of communicating with employees when their paycheck stubs are issued).

(1) Payroll stuffers, bulletin board postings.

ARE YOU USING ANY OTHER ELECTRONIC COMMUNICATION STRATEGIES IN YOUR ORGANIZATION? IF SO, BRIEFLY DESCRIBE THE PRACTICE BELOW.

(1) CEO blog, streaming video.

(1) Collaborative unified communication applications.

(1) Communication stations in factory locations.

(1) Computer software programs designed for law firms.

(1) Digital camera, scanner. Sometimes it's easier to take a snapshot of something and send it as a jpg or PDF than to describe it in an e-mail.

(1) Electronic support help desk.

(1) Electronic surveys.

(1) Films and video recordings of events shared with employees.

(1) FTP sites.

(1) Kiosk in common area.

(1) Once every four months, the employees are given an employee satisfaction survey. They call an 800 number, do not give their names, and answer about 25 questions. The questions address different issues the employee may be facing, and the employee then has the opportunity to address his or her concern, with no fear of reprisal.

(1) Online meeting system (VIA3) used to hold senior management meetings, employee forums.

(1) Podcasting.

(1) QuickTime movies, internal home web site, internal calendars, FTP site, client sites on company web site.

(1) SDF.

(1) Skype.

(1) Skype (VOIP) when one is traveling outside North America. Toll-free telephone line in North America. Mobile calls to each other are free when we're within Canada. Various collaborative project management tools from www.37seconds.com (Backpack, Campfire, etc.), Outlook meeting scheduler.

(1) Webcasting, surveying.

ARE YOU USING ANY OTHER COMMUNICATION RESEARCH STRATEGIES IN YOUR ORGANIZATION? IF SO, BRIEFLY DESCRIBE THE PRACTICE BELOW.

(3) Focus groups.

(2) Web site tracking.

(1) Business relationships, constant communication.

(1) Customer focus groups.

(1) Customer service hotline records.

(1) Direct calling to customer.

(1) Discussion with colleagues. Searching the Internet.

(1) Feedback is required.

(1) Focus group meetings.

(1) Focus groups. Formal consumer research.

(1) Informal follow-up with clients.

(1) Informal research—conversations at the water cooler.

(1) Informal telephone contacts.

(1) Just verbal communication.

(1) Mainly informal and anecdotal, but we have used employee advisory teams in the past.

(1) Ongoing contacts with clients and asking for satisfaction levels, case studies and referrals at the end of projects.

(1) Referrals.

(1) Regular survey and customer visits.

(1) Roundtable discussions with employees and clients on industry topics.

(1) Talk with my employees and customers.

(1) We follow our internal surveys with feedback groups to address major issues.

(1) We have a customer suggestion in place (where our larger customers can ask us to look into obtaining given products that are not currently listed on our catalogs).

(1) We keep logs of all communications between employees through e-mail.

(1) We monitor our external web site usage and trends and also have an online customer community where we exchange info with our customers. For external perspective, we also monitor public discussion about our product.

(1) We talk to each other every day.

(1) We use meetings to determine employee needs and concerns.

(1) Web forums and opinion surveys.

(1) Working with communication/workflow consultants to increase productivity.

OVERALL, WHAT EMPLOYEE COMMUNICATION STRATEGY HAS REALLY MADE A DIFFERENCE IN YOUR FIRM? PLEASE DESCRIBE THIS STRATEGY AND THE IMPACT IT HAS HAD ON YOUR BUSINESS.

Open Communication: 103 responses (Open communication, open door policy)

(3) Open door policy.

(2) Open door.

(1) All-hands communication meetings with open Q&A sessions.

(1) An open communication strategy with the right mix of print, electronic and personal communications and internal events, all measured for effectiveness. Communication has actually helped the organization to face change head-on and make a smooth transition from being an old traditional organization to a vibrant and active organization.

(1) At one time, everyone had a closed-off space. When we moved into a larger office, we went with a more open floor plan. People didn't like it at first but productivity went way up.

(1) Business-as-usual culture of openness, honesty and freedom of expression.

(1) By sharing company strategy and directional information on a regular basis, employees can align their own behaviors toward the goal.

(1) Celebrating every win, recognizing contributions of staff and open communication with all staff on nearly everything.

(1) CEO has open door policy and regular monthly all-staff meetings. His passion for the business is felt by all.

(1) Communication between management and staff.

(1) Communication. Talking when needed and solving problems, accepting suggestions, etc.

(1) Complete accessibility; no question is a dumb question; completely free and open communication.

(1) Constant communication with employees helps sales.

(1) Direct speaking from employee to manager. You get their full opinions, whereas surveys just touch on the main issue.

(1) E-mail, staff meetings, informal gatherings and an open door policy have been key to communication.

(1) Employee suggestions for improvement plus recognition of coworkers for going "above and beyond." It was getting mundane until we had a near disastrous fire. It became evident that the "line staff" knew what the deal was, and their input has since been sought in a more serious manner.

(1) Encouraging employees to share their ideas with management has made them feel more useful, and since they have input to help the company grow, this is a great tool for management.

(1) Encouraging employees to come forward to management with any problems they are experiencing has been the most effective.

(1) Everyone working together as a team and openness. If there is a problem, I want to know, and we'll work it out together. I'm not one to get upset easily. I'd rather teach the young employees it's better to talk when a problem arises and that it is possible to work it out together.

(1) Focused, deliberate internal communications to all staff, pertaining to all aspects of our business. The more they know, the better they function.

(1) Giving each employee the opportunity to speak to the administration about any problems they may have.

(1) Having a very clear vision of what we are trying to achieve and the role we each play. This is discussed daily, and each of us is responsible for ensuring the success of the others—no secrets, no egos and no hidden agendas are the strategy.

(1) Having an honest, open culture. Very flat organizational structure. Open books, research and results-oriented.

(1) I would say it's mostly verbal communications among employees—open approach system in which anybody can approach anybody any time with concerns, questions, suggestions, etc.

(1) Increasing information sharing about the company's objectives and how we are achieving them, as well as the work of other departments.

(1) Informal meetings and open policy to discuss every concern of employees because they feel free to express every issue that can add value to their work.

(1) Involvement and open book management: This makes people feel that they have a stake in the outcome and builds ownership. Aligning communication around team bonuses and rewards, together with plenty of public recognition for individual achievements.

(1) Keeping employee communications open has had a huge positive effect on our business in that we are able to embrace any issues at any time.

(1) Keeping employees informed on the direction and progress of the company. Listening to ideas, concerns, etc., of employees.

(1) Management accessibility to the staff. In a high turnover industry like ours, extra attention to the staff is critical.

(1) Manager-employee communications.

(1) Monthly meetings and an open door policy.

(1) Networking, surveys and open two-way communication.

(1) An open door policy allows employees to voice their opinions and doesn't make them feel uneasy.

(1) Open and clear communication; alignment.

(1) Open and honest communication when a new policy is being implemented or any concerns we have about productivity.

(1) An open and honest communication environment, keeping employees in the loop to avoid surprises. Timely feedback; using electronic, paper-based and in-person avenues to communicate with employees.

(1) Open book and open door policy that the owner embraces. Employees are aware of the challenges and successes of the business. They participate in the strategies and implementation of plans and programs.

(1) Open book management. We are an employee-owned company with a fairly flat management structure (not very many layers of management bureaucracy). We share business goals, financial information and strategy with all employees, encourage them to ask questions so that they understand the business, and have them design personal development plans that line up their daily tasks and goals with the overall business goals for the year.

(1) Open communication about company successes, obstacles and plans for the future.

(1) Open communication and utilization of the chain of command to solve problems and disseminate information.

(1) Open communication between management and employees.

(1) Open communication with the ability to discuss issues, concerns and new ideas in person or electronically.

(1) Open communication. Plenty of one-on-one, combined with group staff meetings and e-mail communication.

(1) Open communication: open door, open book, open access.

(1) Open communication across the organization, vertical and horizontal. New ideas surface and are rapidly reviewed, and those that survive are implemented.

(1) Open communication: sharing of the firm's results and plans on a monthly basis at an all-associate staff meeting.

(1) Open conversations and regular meetings/discussions on certain projects and issues—the employees are better informed, feel important and are more responsible.

(1) Open discussion of internal and client issues in a team environment. Impact: makes everyone feel they are "in this together." Everyone takes ownership and understands the challenges of a small consulting organization.

(1) Open door and open discussions have worked great, but there are only two of us in the company.

(1) Open door policies upheld by all in management.

(1) Open door policy and face-to-face communication that enable brainstorming and troubleshooting. It creates a good company culture around the office.

(1) Open door policy—everyone has a say and is listened to.

(1) Open door policy with CEO and senior managers.

(1) Open door policy has worked well for us.

(1) Open door policy. Employees are free to voice opinions at any time. Doing this makes for happy employees, and they stay longer. This will cost far less than constantly having to hire and train.

(1) Open door policy. It keeps all avenues open and allows people to speak up.

(1) Open door policy. The employees seem to feel more a part of the company. It also allows us to show each individual how important they are to the company as a whole.

(1) Open door policy and routine social meetings.

(1) Open door works best.

(1) Open floor communication—the salespeople can interact easily with the customers and management in an open environment that creates a safe and comfortable experience for the customer.

(1) Open forum in which employees regularly meet with the CEO for open discussion. Improved employees' perceptions of the stability of the business, removing the stress of job security and allowing them to focus on productivity.

(1) Open line of communication between staff and management.

(1) Open line of communication with all employees. Anyone is free to visit with the boss about any subject. Nobody has gone postal in 25 years.

(1) Open management. Financial and management decisions are made with all employees knowing what is going on, and they are able to provide input anytime.

(1) Open office—it allows us to share information and ideas—both easily and accessibly.

(1) Open walls/office configuration.

(1) Open, frequent, interpersonal communication afforded by size.

(1) Open, honest communication regarding business results and competitive conditions.

(1) Open, honest relationships.

(1) Openness is the best vehicle and is visible in much of our communication plan. Physically, we have low "walls" and no actual walls around personal work spaces. The environment is very open, which really fosters a positive feeling. Approachable management and employees who feel empowered that what they do on a daily basis really matters to the company.

(1) Openness. Sharing information freely and honestly. An example is our One Company—One Voice meetings, which are all-company meetings that openly share the strategic issues facing our companies, concluding with an open forum where people ask questions regarding our company's strategies, future and key issues.

(1) Opportunities for staff to interact with management and share ideas. Informal setting of an event (breakfast with president, all-employee events, etc).

(1) Our open door policy has had the biggest impact for us. We encourage its use, and our employees are very responsive. Productivity and morale are high.

(1) Our philosophy is one of transparent communication. Our senior team is strong in providing clear and consistent messaging to our employees. We use all-staff e-mails to communicate important messages, and those are followed up with brown bag events or smaller breakout sessions, if necessary, where employees can ask questions. This approach works very well for our company at its headquarters location. Our challenge now is how we take that messaging to our global offices and still be consistent.

(1) Policy of open, honest and multidirectional communication has promoted a working climate of confidence, responsibility, teamwork and productivity.

(1) Several. First, sharing of financial status with management. Second, management by walking around. Third, staff meetings.

(1) Simply being open and proactive. Why make it complicated?

(1) Strategy: fostering open communication; tactic: publication of firm newsletter, written by and for employees; impact: Both morale and the number of employees participating in the writing of the newsletter have increased.

(1) Surveys and open communication. Data gathering is important.

(1) Taking care of my employees, listening to their concerns and treating them like people. It has increased my sales by 30 percent over the years.

(1) Tell it like it is at all times. Never hide the truth.

(1) The ability to reach upper management by just knocking on their door.

(1) The belief that employees at all levels need to be informed about the business to perform their jobs well.

(1) The best is complete communication between employees and management. This allows changes to be made if necessary for a smoother working environment.

(1) The employees feel like they are part of the firm and can provide input and be heard.

(1) The open and honest flow of information—financial, policies, etc.—throughout the company, led by the chairman.

(1) The open door policy where employees can make suggestions to improve other areas of work development. It allows everyone to work as a team and not have so much hostility in the workplace.

(1) The open door policy; any employee can feel free to come to my office and speak to me about anything (suggestions, complaints, etc.).

(1) The open environment where people are encouraged to be candid/real and speak the truth about "reality." Leaders demonstrate by example.

(1) The two communication strategies that have the most impact for employees are the open door policy and the employee communication forum.

(1) There is no formal communication strategy. However, I have never worked for a company that communicates internally as well as this one. Management is open, inclusive, sociable and accessible—it's like joining a family.

(1) To just communicate with each other better. Say what has to be said.

(1) To let employees know that you are always there to listen and willing to make changes if you can. If they trust you, then they will talk to you.

(1) Total connectivity for all key players.

(1) Training, open communication with employees and clients.

(1) We encourage employee input concerning management practices.

(1) We have an open door policy, a flat organization structure and a culture of deep respect. Employees have no hesitation talking to management and sharing their ideas.

(1) We have an open door policy. Our employees are encouraged to voice their opinions.

(1) The president/CEO sits down once a year with every employee to talk about various issues and the direction they see the firm growing.

Personal Communication: 71 responses (Personal and face-to-face communication)

(9) Face-to-face communications.

(2) One-on-one.

(1) An honest relationship on a more personal level.

(1) As a small company, most communication is face-to-face, especially small meetings. The intranet could be more helpful if it were more closely linked to the business mission and business-critical information that is communicated face-to-face. This area has not been assigned to my department.

(1) As a sole proprietor, one-on-one communication has been best in talking with clients.

(1) As we are a very small firm, the best communication strategy is regular team building and face-to-face communication with colleagues and management.

(1) At least daily "check-ins" with each employee.

(1) Combination of a lot of face-to-face communication with e-mail.

(1) Constant informal verbal communication; we often have to change plans rapidly in response to client requests and the environment. There is no time for formal communication. This works best during our busy "action" season.

(1) Daily face-to-face communication. Knowing your employees as more than a badge or an extension of their equipment. Thanking your employees for a job well done.

(1) Direct communication up, down and sideways in the organization.

(1) Direct face-to-face communication has a great impact since the company is so small.

(1) E-mail, staff meetings, informal gatherings and an open door policy have been key to communication.

(1) Enhancing personal trust.

(1) Face-to-face communication builds trust, which enables positive change to occur.

(1) Face-to-face communication; with only two staff members (who are also husband and wife), this is really the best strategy.

(1) Face-to-face conversation. Listening as well as talking.

(1) Face-to-face meetings.

(1) Face-to-face or voice-to-voice at the very minimum. Everyone on the team knows what everyone else is doing and contributes ideas to the team's success on a regular basis.

(1) Face-to-face. Being a company of two, that is the main way we communicate everything.

(1) Face-to-face, immediate communication; get verbal and nonverbal feedback; can clarify and get "commitment."

(1) Face-to-face communication framework that facilitates two-way communication, employee input and the rollout of initiatives, etc.

(1) Face-to-face or forum sessions. The information and knowledge are directly linked to productivity.

(1) Face-to-face time with employees. It is time-consuming and slows production at the moment, but employees hear the same message instead of someone else's interpretation of the message. We are in the process of implementing processed-based leadership, which includes many of these questions about communication.

(1) Face-to-face with examples.

(1) Face-to-face and walking around.

(1) Formal and informal meetings, face-to-face meetings, focus groups.

(1) Happy people, happy customers. Monthly catered luncheon meetings that assure people and let them voice their concerns. Recognizing anniversaries and achievements. Updates about projects. People feel like progress is being made and are encouraged to go out and keep it up.

(1) Highly respectful, personal, one-on-one communication with staff. Listening to staff concerns and making process changes in response to valid concerns. Holding staff meetings to discuss new policies and procedures and to answer staff questions.

(1) I have a small business, and everybody talks to everybody all the time. If we consider this as part of a communication strategy, the impact of this kind of culture is powerful!

(1) I work with associates and subcontractors, not employees, but the three most important communication strategies, in order, have been: 1. e-mail, 2. phone and 3. face-to-face.

(1) Improved face-to-face communication between supervisors and their employees.

(1) In-person management communicating employee news face-to-face, backed by marketing materials that support it.

(1) In-person brainstorming.

(1) Informal communication. Sitting, chatting, listening, then acting on input from employees.

(1) Informal gatherings amongst employees. It tends to surface issues, leads to discussion of potential solutions to issues, allows for an exchange of ideas and just boosts morale. There is no formal strategy for implementing gatherings—employees seek out the opportunities themselves.

(1) Not only is our company small, but we're quite young in our business cycle. We have few formal employee communication methods, yet we should because we have employees scattered across four states. We frequently use conference calls for small groups with a specific task. For nearly anything else, it's one-on-one phone calls or in-person meetings if the participants are in the same location.

(1) One-on-one contact with each individual employee on a daily basis and good working communication with one another.

(1) One-on-one and face-to-face conversation. Keep employees informed of what is going on in the company. This will increase productivity and employee satisfaction.

(1) Open door policy and face-to-face communication that enables brainstorming and troubleshooting. It creates a good company culture around the office.

(1) Periodic, candid face-to-face interaction and recognition. Employees feel they are being empowered with ownership of the work they are doing and are inspired to do more.

(1) Person-to-person.

(1) Person-to-person talk.

(1) Personal communication—one-on-one allows employees to freely share ideas and concerns, and eliminates problems before they become major.

(1) Personal contact.

(1) Personal interaction with employees and customers. Making everything personal creates a positive environment for everyone involved.

(1) Plain, open, face-to-face communication between owners and staff. Easy to do with a tiny organization.

(1) Simple, direct, brief conversations are most effective. We are a small business of two people and are both busy, so we get to the point.

(1) Talking to employees has had a great positive impact because I hear what they are thinking, and we can share ideas.

(1) Teamwork and face-to-face communication have made a difference in our firm since we are just a few people. We are consultants, so the more we share the work we are doing, the better service we provide to our clients.

(1) The most effective has been face-to-face meetings with staff. They have produced the best results and made us all more in line and in focus with our business goals.

(1) The willingness of senior management to spend time on one-on-one communication. It's rare that a company's management will see the value of this and not try to replace it with something they see as more effective at reaching the masses.

(1) This company is owned and staffed by immigrant Chinese. Employee communications tend to be less strategic than cultural—informal, colloquial, verbal.

(1) Treating each employee with the highest respect possible. They were hired to be an asset to us, and we respect that. We feel it's that important.

(1) Treating others as I would want to be treated.

(1) Verbal and written strategies have been equally effective. Face-to-face contact with our employees and a firm policy of discipline/acknowledgement have increased our productivity and client/employee satisfaction.

(1) Walking through the office and the plant, and talking to employees.

(1) We are a recycling facility for latex paint and occupy a small space with very few employees who rely mostly on face-to-face communication with the operations manager. I am the only person doing all administration/sales/marketing/etc.

(1) We do a lot of face-to-face communication and try to make all associates feel included and important to the business. It is a family-owned operation, and the atmosphere is very informal and inclusive.

(1) We're a very small firm, so the majority of our communication is face-to-face; however, with a specialization in commercial real estate, our employees are often out of the office conducting tours and attending meetings. We use e-mail and electronic messaging to convey information in a timely and convenient fashion. As the director of research and communication, I have broadened the range of information that is delivered to the brokers, enabling them to stay more informed about what we're doing internally, as well as what is happening in the industry as a whole. I send bimonthly newsletters reviewing the real estate activity in the market, as well as e-mail links to pertinent stories that spark conversation about improvements in our workplace or productivity.

(1) We're still small enough to talk to each other. We relate well, and we're open and honest about where things are.

(1) With a small firm, we don't have a lot of internal communication mediums available. Of course, you can talk face-to-face with your boss in a small company, but more important is having someone who listens to what you say and acts upon your suggestions for success.

Meetings: 68 responses (Meetings with staff, team, managers, company, and/or CEO; focus groups)

(2) Meetings.

(1) All corporate employees go through a communication seminar that has three sessions. It teaches us how to communicate effectively to our external customers as well as our internal coworkers. In addition, we have monthly meetings to go over the company as a whole—everything from finances to "what's new." At the end, the CEO and management answer any questions (they can either be submitted anonymously or not, or people can raise their hands and ask at the forum).

(1) All-employee meetings on an annual basis have had the most impact. At these meetings, financials for the previous year are discussed, and management discusses goals for the coming year.

(1) All-hands meetings held each quarter followed by lunch keep employees up-to-date, allow for questions, usually acknowledge contribution of star employees, and get everyone together.

(1) As we are a very small firm, the best communication strategy is regular team building and face-to-face communication with colleagues and management.

(1) Because of our size, the implementation of weekly staff and management meetings is invaluable in order to keep everyone on the same page and to keep morale high.

(1) Bimonthly staff meetings keep everyone informed of what's happening with the business. This allows everyone to serve the customers better.

(1) The CEO has an open door policy and regular monthly all-staff meetings. His passion for the business is felt by all.

(1) Creating employee forums that include roundtable discussions with employees every month and quarterly all-employee meetings to discuss the business and financial results.

(1) E-mail, staff meetings, informal gatherings and an open door policy have been key to communication.

(1) Each week, all 16 of our employees crowd around the conference table and discuss, client-for-client, each project that's in the works. It keeps everyone up-to-speed and gives us a chance to socialize.

(1) Employee meetings on a regular basis and managers communicating more often with the owner.

(1) Employee meetings and informational e-mails. The strategy is to involve employees in the company and to make them feel like a part of the business. This has improved morale. Constant communication also helps morale.

(1) Face-to-face and regular work-in-progress meetings.

(1) Face-to-face employee meetings. We have shift meetings with members of management or benefit providers, which give employees insight into what the company's goals/future/prospects are and what we are trying to accomplish.

(1) Face-to-face meetings.

(1) Face-to-face shift meetings providing financial status and the outlook for our plant and the company as a whole. The meetings have a strong impact on a plant status; they have less impact when they concern company status.

(1) Face-to-face, well-designed and orchestrated meetings.

(1) Focus group meetings aimed strictly at improving workplace safety.

(1) Formal and informal meetings, face-to-face meetings, focus groups.

(1) Getting together as a team and talking face-to-face.

(1) Having a weekly team meeting with all staff and agents that is informative and motivating keeps people focused and working together.

(1) Highly respectful, personal, one-on-one communication with staff. Listening to staff concerns and making process changes in response to valid concerns. Holding staff meetings to discuss new policies and procedures and to answer staff questions.

(1) Impromptu team meetings to share the latest information.

(1) Informal company meetings every Friday morning.

(1) Informal gatherings. They foster good relationships between employer and employees and amongst colleagues. The team sees each other as more than just colleagues. They see each other as people and get to understand each other's strengths and weaknesses better. As an employer, I understand what motivates and drives them. These insights enable me to get the team together and channel their capabilities into the right areas.

(1) Informal meetings and open policy to discuss every concern of employees because they feel free to express every issue that can add value to their work.

(1) Informal, out-of-office planning and work sessions. They have injected new life into an old and solid company.

(1) Live and in-person meetings.

(1) Management meetings: weekly meetings of team managers to discuss issues, exchange ideas for the company, etc. Top-down and bottom-up communication allows decisions to be made faster and collectively. Positive impact on managers' motivation.

(1) Manager meetings once a month. There is a companywide meeting once or twice a year—personal contact goes a long way!

(1) Meetings with the CEO.

(1) Meetings: Management meetings have been very instrumental to good organizational strategies and implementation. Management and staff meetings have also been very productive in the execution of the organizational strategies and tactics. Moreover, the meetings bring the interpersonal interactions, cordiality and the human touch necessary in communication.

(1) Monthly full-staff pizza luncheons with company news and information. Keeps everyone on the same general page; employees feel like they have a good sense of where the company is going and what is going on.

(1) Monthly meetings and an open door policy.

(1) Monthly meetings where employees can voice their concerns and comments. It has had such a positive impact on business. The employees are the front line, and they know where to make changes for the better.

(1) Monthly meetings with all members present. We go over the suggestion box, ask them how they think we can better our service and try out some of their ideas. This makes them feel their opinions are valued, and that we are working together as one team.

(1) Monthly staff meeting, employee stock ownership committee, management listening/walking around.

(1) Not only is our company small, but we're quite young in our business cycle. We have few formal employee communication methods, yet we should because we have employees scattered across four states. We frequently use conference calls for small groups with a specific task. For nearly anything else, it's one-on-one phone calls or in-person meetings if the participants are in the same location.

(1) Nothing has really made a big difference, except that we have a morning meeting of department heads to discuss problems and potential shortages.

(1) Open communication: plenty of one-on-one combined with group staff meetings and e-mail communication.

(1) Open communications: sharing of firm's results, plans on a monthly basis at all-associate staff meeting.

(1) Open conversations and regular meetings/discussions on certain projects and issues. The employees are better informed, feel important and are more responsible.

(1) Our annual companywide meeting is the one time each year when the entire company comes together. Being that our employees are spread across the country at various client sites, it is an opportunity for them to see themselves as a part of the bigger picture. It is a great opportunity for information-sharing, networking and culture-building. Employees leave with a better understanding of corporate initiatives and strategies, a feeling that this is a company that cares about them, and a true sense of contributing to something bigger than themselves. This time together builds employee morale and connection, which contributes to low turnover.

(1) Our strategy is to meet with employees and explain what we expect from them.

(1) Quarterly business meetings at which financial information and strategic business information is shared with associates. Our associates feel more a part of the business and understand how their performance counts toward achieving corporate goals.

(1) Quarterly face-to-face business reviews with management, weekly e-newsletter, weekly briefs on industry news and challenges.

(1) Quarterly planning sessions with all employees. Every quarter, we meet for a whole morning and report on the past quarter and plan for the next one. Each employee is responsible for implementing and managing a task. It gets everyone involved, and they become a part of the company's success.

(1) Regular and impromptu team meetings keep projects running smoothly and keep the finish line/vision in front of everyone at the same time. With a staff this small, it is important to maximize teamwork. Free-flowing updates and information make achieving the vision more of an ongoing motivation than some distant "like to have."

(1) Regular all-staff meetings combined with walk-around by management for one-on-ones. The combination of those two is essential.

(1) Regular staff meetings assure open communication, accountability and execution.

(1) Sales and staff meetings. Communication is the key to success.

(1) Sales meeting, production meeting, employee benefit meetings, 401k meetings, daily production meetings. Constant clear communication throughout the business!

(1) Several. First, sharing of financial status with management. Second, management by walking around. Third, staff meetings.

(1) Sharing of information through quarterly employee meetings conducted by upper management. Job-related communication delivered by frontline supervisors.

(1) Small focus groups discussing a shared problem and developing alternate resolutions.

(1) Staff and manager's meetings.

(1) Staff meeting.

(1) Staff meetings and remote e-mail accessibility keep all employees informed and allow all of us to serve clients whether we work directly on these accounts or not.

(1) Team meetings and reviews.

(1) Team meetings have strengthened each department and strengthened the "whole."

(1) The meetings are good as long as they aren't repetitive. The newsletter has received positive feedback so we will rely on that more.

(1) Face-to-face meetings with staff have been most effective and have produced the best results, making us all more in line and focused on our business goals.

(1) We are a small organization, and our once-weekly reviews, sharing of information and group involvement in direction and change make the greatest impact on employee communication and the overall business.

(1) We operate in a very entrepreneurial atmosphere with little formal structure. Institution of a monthly meeting for the business development function has resulted in the ability to track sales calls, account status, etc.

(1) Weekly meetings with the managing partner.

(1) Weekly one-on-one meetings.

Other: 68 responses (Retreats, training, stakeholders)

(1) A system for employees to see in an instant all the data relevant to the achievement of specified goals.

(1) Achieving goal alignment across the business.

(1) Aligning messages to enhance our credibility and communicate understanding among employees. Our branding strategy has given our employees something to connect to and identify with.

(1) All corporate employees go through a communication seminar that has three sessions. It teaches us how to communicate effectively to our external customers as well as to our internal coworkers. In addition, we have monthly meetings to go over the company as a whole—everything from finances to "what's new." At the end, the CEO and management answer any questions (they can either be submitted anonymously or not, or people can raise their hands and ask at the forum).

(1) Annual picnics, softball team.

(1) Back-office automation for sharing and archiving information.

(1) Being human.

(1) Blog—seems to get the employees thinking and talking.

(1) Brochures given to the customers and updated as necessary.

(1) Case studies published in respected trade journals have increased my company's exposure in target markets and generated viable leads.

(1) Celebrating every win, recognizing contributions of staff and open communication with all staff on nearly everything.

(1) Communicating core competencies to prospective customers.

(1) Company retreat.

(1) Constant contact with client base.

(1) CRM implementation.

(1) Daily employee communications on systems, practice or process changes. Short and sweet. Always relevant and topical. Necessary information in palatable bite-size pieces, stored in a searchable database.

(1) Developing a strategic plan with ongoing employee input, including their leadership on various teams.

(1) Easy communication.

(1) Efficient communication is essential. We pride ourselves in the fact that we don't spend all day in meetings. We communicate essential business with no political agendas, and we get on with the work.

(1) Ensuring that all communication is bilingual, consistent and timely.

(1) External communications: campaigning the industry clientele and audience on how our firm differs from our competitors, but that has more to do with external communication than internal.

(1) Focus on involvement. Communicating the level of staff utilization has allowed folks to look at profitability, over which they have ownership within a profit sharing program.

(1) Formalizing the need for regular employee communication has resulted in better overall coordination, less rework and more on-time delivery.

(1) Good communication skills with the boss.

(1) I have to be very specific about what I want done.

(1) I think having a more laid-back management process has helped our business immensely. We like to stop problems before they start to keep problems to a minimum.

(1) Implementation of a change management program to communicate better with staff around all major projects and processes. The outcome of the program embedded the importance of internal communication throughout the organization.

(1) Interactive communication with employees about defining strategic communication goals and defining a communication vision.

(1) Involvement and open book management—this makes people feel that they have a stake in the outcome and builds ownership. Aligning communication around team bonuses and rewards, together with plenty of public recognition for individual achievements.

(1) Involvement of middle management and team leaders in the strategic planning process.

(1) Involving employees in the day-to-day realities of the business, as well as the longer-term strategic vision, is essential for securing employee engagement.

(1) It gives an idea about where the employees are, provides a very good matrix about the management vision, and employees' goals can be measured and the gaps can be identified.

(1) It's hard to say. Printed manuals have probably had the greatest impact. We work in a highly regulated environment, and proper procedures are very important. Creation of procedure manuals for standard processes helped communicate with employees and customers. It also substantially helps with training new employees.

(1) Since we are a small firm, leadership by consensus has led to good business decisions and employee support of the çorporate objectives.

(1) Listening to what the client wants.

(1) Listening. Responding with a plan and being seen to implement that plan. Regularly reporting against objectives.

(1) Manager departmental goals and objectives/plans for their improvement within their departments to help the company as a whole!

(1) Manager training audio conferences for our recent merger/acquisition prepared managers and spokespeople to support employees and customers through the change.

(1) Mentoring new employees.

(1) Monthly new employee orientation—our company is growing so rapidly, it is vital that new employees are introduced to the company, its culture and corporate goals at the start of their employment.

(1) Monthly staff meetings, employee stock ownership committee, management listening/walking around.

(1) Networking; surveys; open, two-way communication.

(1) Not only is our company small, but we're also quite young in our business cycle. We have few formal employee communication methods, yet we should because we have employees scattered across four states. We frequently use conference calls for small groups with a specific task. For nearly anything else, it's one-on-one phone calls or in-person meetings if the participants are in the same location.

(1) Ongoing communication with clients and prospects.

(1) Open communication and utilization of the chain of command to solve problems and disseminate information.

(1) Our current strategy is to work on our internal communication. We, by the nature of our business, work hard on external communication. Therefore, if we can make the conscious effort to communicate better internally, we will improve all the way around.

(1) Our strategy is defined by our senior management and in line with the business priorities. Their emphasis on our customers has set the tone for the entire organization and created alignment in our actions. The messaging is consistent as an outcome of the culturally-driven actions that are demonstrated on a daily basis. Our singular focus on our business vision allows us to consistently tell our story across different geographic regions and throughout each department and role level.

(1) Overall friendly, positive and open environment.

(1) Positive reinforcement.

(1) Providing a spectrum of communication mediums.

(1) Quality of care.

(1) Respect, confidence and communication are our values.

(1) Sending memoranda with relevant information to all departments. It has kept employees informed of all general and some specific data about the activities and programs of the organization.

(1) Several. First, sharing of financial status with management. Second, management by walking around. Third, staff meetings.

(1) Straightforward, timely communications. This has stopped the rumor mill, reduced stress, made employees more comfortable, and therefore increased their productivity and improved human relations.

(1) Targeting management-level employees with key messages and briefings, etc., has been very effective, although we mainly communicate broadly to employees by e-mail.

(1) Teamwork and face-to-face communications have made a difference in our firm since we are just a few people. We are consultants so the more we share the work we are doing the better service we provide to our clients.

(1) Teleconferencing/working from home.

(1) The notes on the walls. All employees can read about good work being done. It lets employees know how we are doing with our customers.

(1) The two communication strategies that have the most impact for employees are the open door policy and the employee communication forum.

(1) There are weekly reports that every department does; they let us know where we are and where we are going.

(1) Training, open communication with employees and clients.

(1) Union/management working groups—representatives of both (not executives) work together to sort out a number of issues including communication improvement.

(1) Walk by talk and individual briefings.

(1) Walking the talk, discussing client issues, getting feedback on what is the best way of doing things.

(1) We are a creative group, so giving employees wide latitude in nonclient matters, such as dress, time flexibility and an open, interactive environment is essential. Freedom of expression and style equals creative spark and greater profits for all.

(1) We continuously re-energize the team with activities that encourage them to look at what they are doing with fresh eyes. It is important that we focus on innovation in our creativity, quality consulting and business skills. Our strategy is to always move forward, try new ideas but to allow for failure and learn the lesson.

(1) We created a think tank that's a comfortable, physical space where we discuss new and ongoing ideas.

E-mail/Video/Telecommunications: 54 responses (E-mail, video, telecommunications)

(3) Cell phones.

(3) E-mail.

(1) By e-mailing employees, we are certain that information is reaching all.

(1) Cell phones, e-mail and electronic means of communication.

(1) Cell phones. Our foremen and crew can stay in constant contact.

(1) Combination of a lot of face-to-face communications with e-mail.

(1) Consistent updates on business opportunities and real-time dialogue with IM.

(1) Constant contact and involvement in the projects on the table. We are a virtual agency and could not survive without constant electronic discussion and updates.

(1) Direct e-mail-improved productivity.

(1) E-mail and instant messaging are the most convenient and easiest to use.

(1) E-mail gives us quick and accurate answers to problems occurring during production.

(1) E-mail, staff meetings, informal gatherings and an open door policy have been key to communication.

(1) Electronic communications.

(1) E-mail announcements and posting of procedures, forms, sales and marketing information, and tools to the intranet.

(1) E-mail communications.

(1) E-mail followed by a phone call.

(1) E-mail has made the biggest difference in our employee communications. We are a small company that is spread out, and this is generally how we get our information. We tried doing a staff newsletter but after two issues it was apparent that nobody was reading it, and it was shelved.

(1) E-mail system. Provides for more efficient communication within the company.

(1) E-mail using the intranet. Less costly than mailing and less time consuming.

(1) E-mail, Internet and a client approval site on our web page have eased the approval process and the stress of deadlines.

(1) E-mail—increased productivity due to less time being spent on the phone and the ability to print out information.

(1) E-mail: cost-effective, can respond at your convenience, can send information/memos/files electronically.

(1) E-mails from the CEO, including consistent repeating of the company's strategy objectives across all communications in an easy to understand manner.

(1) Employee forums. Video streaming (featuring CEO).

(1) I think e-mail has been the best. It eliminates walking from office to office and saves time and energy.

(1) I think e-mail has made the biggest difference because it lets everyone communicate quickly.

(1) I work with associates and subcontractors, not employees, but the three most important communication strategies, in order, have been: 1. e-mail, 2. phone, and 3. face-to-face.

(1) Implementing a Q&A with the president so employees can hear his real voice and his real opinions, instead of just reading dry corporate communication.

(1) Keeping a firm our size that's spread out across many time zones up-to-date on the latest information regarding the company is difficult. E-mail efforts seem to be the best method.

(1) Manager briefings on major initiatives and projects available via teleconference if managers can't attend.

(1) Monthly teleconference with all staff, led by the CEO and COO. Present financials, topics of board and executive committee meetings, human resources news (e.g., recruiting progress, training opportunities), reports on marketing and project wins from the practice area leaders. Staff members feel informed and feel that management is open and honest.

(1) Mostly e-mail has been the most effective of all. With e-mail, communication is very fast, and the ability to document all the correspondence has been very convenient.

(1) Moving everything humanly possible from offline to online.

(1) Moving from print to electronic. We are a bank with 19 branches in three states, and this allows us to provide more timely and targeted communications.

(1) Online communications via the intranet, e-mail and electronic newsletters have been most helpful. It was a cost-effective way to communicate and keep everyone informed about what is going on companywide so that everyone is speaking the same language, especially to customers.

(1) Portable communication, e-mail, cell phones, PDAs, anything that can keep business flowing while on job sites or out of the office.

(1) Redefining e-mail communications and limiting access to global messaging.

(1) Since we have one office in Florida and one in California, Internet and telecommunications are essential for us. Our business couldn't function without them.

(1) Staff meetings and remote e-mail accessibility keep all employees informed and allow all of us to serve clients whether we work directly on these accounts or not.

(1) Targeting management-level employees with key messages and briefings, etc., has been very effective, although we mainly communicate broadly to employees by e-mail.

(1) Teleconferencing/working from home.

(1) The ability to communicate with our customers and vendors throughout the world on a timely basis via electronic means.

(1) The fact that our clients can contact our employees via e-mail through our web site has eased our communication problem completely.

(1) The most effective is e-mail and instant messaging.

(1) Use of cell phones.

(1) We all have Blackberries.

(1) We have done very little in the field of employee communication; however, e-mail has emerged as the favored form of communication, and we will work on ensuring it is used more effectively by everyone in the organization.

(1) We're a very small firm so the majority of our communication is face-to-face; however, with a specialization in commercial real estate, our employees are often out of the office conducting tours and attending meetings. We use e-mail and electronic messaging to convey information in a timely and convenient fashion. As the director of research and communication, I have broadened the range of information delivered to the brokers, enabling them to stay more informed about what

we're doing internally, as well as what is happening in the industry as a whole. I send bimonthly newsletters reviewing the real estate activity in the market, as well as e-mail links to pertinent stories that spark conversation about improvements in our workplace or productivity.

(1) Weekly e-mail and quarterly company updates keep people connected to the company and each other while assessing our progress to date and what to expect moving forward.

(1) Weekly e-mail updates from the president and CEO about various successes for the company.

None/Don't Know: 48 responses (None, Don't Know)

Web site/Intranet: 21 responses (Company web site for employees and/or customers)

(1) Building an intranet that has become the first point of reference for staff.

(1) Creation of an intranet, as all employees are Net-enabled. It makes it easy to have interactive communication: top-down, down-up and peer-to-peer. We have recently even included business process automation. We plan to use this medium to capture employee feedback, control the grapevine and improve employee efficiencies.

(1) Intranet.

(1) Intranet—getting people the information they need to do their job in the most efficient manner possible.

(1) Intranet CRM system.

(1) Intranet web site that is updated daily. Eye-catching and informative with one-stop shopping for most corporate information in a fun format.

(1) Launching the company's intranet to employees.

(1) My web site has had the most important impact on my business. Since I work from my home, it is essentially my storefront. Not only does it attract clients, but it has also been the source of several inquiries from other writers about working with me on projects in the future. This list of inquirers will be the basis of my network of subcontractors as the business expands.

(1) Once we set up a system that could be accessed off-site, productivity improved dramatically. The e-mail system alone has improved the efficiency of the client/staff relationship, and all paperwork can be accessed and sent in via the Internet.

(1) Online communications via the intranet, e-mail and electronic newsletters have been most helpful. It was a cost-effective way to communicate and keep everyone informed about what is going on companywide so everyone is speaking the same language, especially to customers.

(1) Our company web site, which allows our membership interactive capabilities (requesting claim forms, etc.).

(1) Our intranet is becoming a more robust communication vehicle, thanks to the efforts of the internal communication team. We are working to have this as our central repository for all information needed on the job. As this occurs, the business will gain efficiencies and productivity as a result of the most current information being easily and centrally accessible and available.

(1) Our web site. It's much more dynamic than most sites and tells our story in an engaging manner. We plan on adding a team blog to the site within the next three months.

(1) Relaunch of our intranet home page about one year ago so that it contains daily news updates from within and outside the organization. Notable reduction in e-mails, better understanding of corporate objectives and major projects, more focus on employee recognition, easy way for anyone in the organization to convey information.

(1) The fact that our clients can contact our employees via e-mail through our web site has eased our communication problem completely.

(1) The web site is now very user-friendly.

(1) We are struggling with our strategy because of a difference of opinion in our company's leadership. Before the current administration, the employee web site was most useful in providing information and requesting feedback from employees.

(1) We have an information strategy on our web site, rather than an online brochure or e-commerce. Employees and customers can go to the web site for useful technical and practical information on our industrial equipment.

(1) We use an intranet to communicate internally and keep our company ISO-certified.

(1) Web site and pushing clients to it.

(1) Web site.

Surveys/Feedback: 19 responses (Employee and/or customer surveys, reviews, evaluations, audits)

(1) A communication audit identified what employees were thinking, where we could improve and how we could move forward.

(1) Actively listening to feedback from employee surveys and implementing changes where appropriate have convinced employees that their voices will be heard; thus improving attitudes and a sense of ownership and accountability.

(1) By putting a survey on the final bill.

(1) Conducting an annual audit.

(1) Conducting pulse surveys and doing something about the results.

(1) Consulting with and getting feedback from the sales staff and the support staff in terms of what they need to help the business grow.

(1) Customer feedback and internal debate about service/product quality improvement.

(1) Employee surveys.

(1) Getting employee feedback through surveys and making real changes based on that feedback. Satisfaction levels with communication have gone up as our communications have become timelier, and we've given the rationale behind management decisions.

(1) Internal employee satisfaction surveys.

(1) Networking; surveys; open, two-way communication.

(1) Quarterly employee evaluations administered by each supervisor have forced supervisors to evaluate and communicate that performance evaluation to each employee. These evaluations let employees know what areas need work and give them some input and time lines for improvement.

(1) Surveys and open communication. Data gathering is important.

(1) Team meetings and reviews.

(1) The reflective practice survey that was given to several employees. They responded in a positive manner, and as a result, the company has put some practices in place to combat the inefficiencies that we were experiencing.

(1) Walking the talk, discussing client issues, getting feedback on what is the best way of doing things.

(1) We have yearly evaluations in which employees can voice their opinions concerning their positions and operations inside and outside the company.

(1) Weekly review of job list/client requests with sales and production area managers and the allocation of appropriate resources.

(1) Written reviews have increased employee conscientiousness.

Newsletters: 9 responses (Electronic or print newsletters)

(1) A biweekly newsletter e-mailed to employees. It helps keep everybody tuned in to what others are doing. We coordinate better.

(1) Beginning a company newsletter. Employees look forward to each issue, and it has become a place to introduce new people and ideas.

(1) In 2005, the company developed an internal employee newsletter that focused on educating employees on the different aspects of the business. Overall, it provided employees with the knowledge to speak intelligently to our clients about the company's different business units. In the past, the employees wouldn't feel comfortable talking about the other services because they didn't know much about them. It also created dialog between employees who work in different business units.

(1) Online communications via the intranet, e-mail and electronic newsletters have been most helpful. It was a cost-effective way to communicate and keep everyone informed about what is going on companywide so everyone is speaking the same language, especially to customers.

(1) Quarterly face-to-face business reviews with management, weekly e-newsletter, weekly briefs on industry news and challenges.

(1) Regular monthly employee newsletter, which recently moved from e-mail-based to web-based delivery format. Extremely popular.

(1) Strategy: fostering open communication; tactic: publication of firm newsletter, written by and for employees; impact: both morale and the number of employees participating in the writing of the newsletter have increased.

(1) The electronic employee newsletter and intranet.

(1) The meetings are good as long as they aren't repetitive. The newsletter has received positive feedback so we will rely on that more.

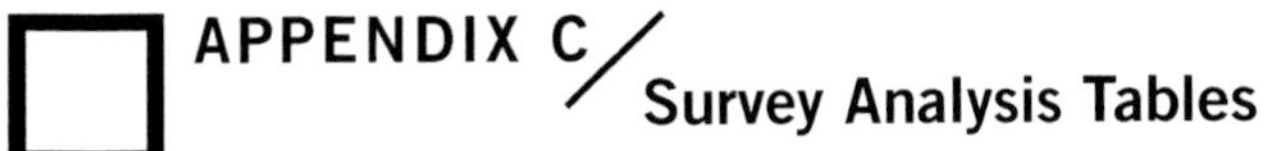

APPENDIX C / Survey Analysis Tables

IN-PERSON COMMUNICATION PRACTICES

IN-PERSON USAGE BY SECTOR

Usage		Sector								
		Profession-al/Scientific/Technical	Manufac-turing	Finance	Infor-mation services	Retail	Construc-tion	Health Care	Other	Total
Interactive Orientation Periods	Number	232	67	53	52	39	23	23	120	609
	% Currently Use	63.4%	68.7%	79.2%	61.5%	53.8%	65.2%	60.9%	53.3%	62.6%
Face-to-Face Conver-sations	Number	232	67	53	52	39	23	23	120	609
	% Currently Use	87.9%	88.1%	90.6%	84.6%	87.2%	87.0%	82.6%	84.2%	86.9%
Manage-ment Meetings	Number	232	67	53	52	39	23	23	120	609
	% Currently Use	79.3%	80.6%	92.5%	78.8%	84.6%	69.6%	73.9%	73.3%	79.1%
Staff Meetings	Number	232	67	53	52	39	23	23	120	609
	% Currently Use	80.6%	77.6%	84.9%	75.0%	74.4%	60.9%	73.9%	70.0%	76.7%
Employee Forums	Number	232	67	53	52	39	23	23	120	609
	% Currently Use	37.9%	49.3%	45.3%	53.8%	46.2%	47.8%	43.5%	35.0%	41.7%
Informal Gatherings	Number	232	67	53	52	39	23	23	120	609
	% Currently Use	54.3%	37.3%	37.7%	53.8%	33.3%	56.5%	43.5%	43.3%	47.1%
Manage-ment by Walking Around	Number	232	67	53	52	39	23	23	120	609
	% Currently Use	64.7%	85.1%	64.2%	59.6%	76.9%	65.2%	69.6%	60.0%	66.5%
Open Door Policy	Number	232	67	53	52	39	23	23	120	609
	% Currently Use	80.6%	91.0%	90.6%	76.9%	84.6%	65.2%	82.6%	74.2%	80.8%
Staff Advocates	Number	232	67	53	52	39	23	23	120	609
	% Currently Use	21.6%	37.3%	32.1%	28.8%	46.2%	26.1%	26.1%	30.8%	28.6%
Common Areas for Meetings	Number	232	67	53	52	39	23	23	120	609
	% Currently Use	54.3%	46.3%	39.6%	53.8%	64.1%	52.2%	65.2%	43.3%	50.9%
Open Floor Plan	Number	232	67	53	52	39	23	23	120	609
	% Currently Use	53.4%	56.7%	35.8%	46.2%	56.4%	43.5%	43.5%	46.7%	49.8%

COST-EFFECTIVENESS BY TYPE OF COMPANY

Cost-effectiveness		Type of Company				
		Proprietorship	Partnership	Corporation	Other	Total
Interactive Orientation Periods	Number	46	58	214	17	335
	% Somewhat or Very	97.8%	94.8%	96.3%	88.2%	95.8%
Face-to-Face Conversations	Number	79	85	308	32	504
	% Somewhat or Very	97.5%	96.5%	96.4%	100.0%	96.8%
Management Meetings	Number	64	75	289	25	453
	% Somewhat or Very	98.4%	98.7%	94.1%	96.0%	95.6%
Staff Meetings	Number	69	80	276	24	449
	% Somewhat or Very	87.0%	91.3%	96.0%	95.8%	93.8%
Employee Forums	Number	37	37	149	13	236
	% Somewhat or Very	97.3%	86.5%	91.3%	100.0%	91.9%
Informal Gatherings	Number	54	49	153	15	271
	% Somewhat or Very	98.1%	93.9%	93.5%	100.0%	94.8%
Management by Walking Around	Number	56	62	243	20	381
	% Somewhat or Very	96.4%	98.4%	94.7%	95.0%	95.5%
Open Door Policy	Number	63	75	294	28	460
	% Somewhat or Very	93.7%	96.0%	95.9%	100.0%	95.9%
Staff Advocates	Number	26	23	97	12	158
	% Somewhat or Very	88.5%	91.3%	87.6%	100.0%	89.2%
Common Areas for Meetings	Number	49	61	162	11	283
	% Somewhat or Very	95.9%	95.1%	93.2%	100.0%	94.3%
Open Floor Plan	Number	43	62	164	11	280
	% Somewhat or Very	95.3%	96.8%	95.1%	100.0%	95.7%

COST-EFFECTIVENESS BY SECTOR

Cost-effectiveness		Profession-al/Scientific/Technical	Manufac-turing	Finance	Information Services	Retail	Construction	Health Care	Other	Total
		Sector								
Interactive Orientation Periods	Number	127	42	39	28	19	12	12	56	335
	% Somewhat or Very	93.7%	97.6%	94.9%	100.0%	100.0 %	100.0%	100.0%	94.6%	95.8%
Face-to-Face Conversations	Number	197	58	46	41	32	20	16	94	504
	% Somewhat or Very	99.5%	96.6%	93.5%	97.6%	96.9%	95.0%	93.8%	93.6%	96.8%
Management Meetings	Number	171	52	47	38	33	14	15	83	453
	% Somewhat or Very	97.1%	98.1%	87.2%	100.0%	97.0%	92.9%	86.7%	95.2%	95.6%
Staff Meetings	Number	180	51	43	38	29	14	14	80	449
	% Somewhat or Very	93.9%	96.1%	90.7%	92.1%	100.0 %	100.0%	100.0%	90.0%	93.8%
Employee Forums	Number	80	31	22	28	17	9	10	39	236
	% Somewhat or Very	96.3%	93.5%	86.4%	92.9%	88.2%	88.9%	100.0%	84.6%	91.9%
Informal Gatherings	Number	122	25	18	28	12	11	8	47	271
	% Somewhat or Very	95.1%	92.0%	94.4%	100.0%	100.0 %	100.0%	100.0%	89.4%	94.8%
Management by Walking Around	Number	143	54	31	29	30	15	13	66	381
	% Somewhat or Very	95.8%	98.1%	87.1%	100.0%	93.3%	100.0%	100.0%	93.9%	95.5%
Open Door Policy	Number	174	56	47	37	33	14	16	83	460
	% Somewhat or Very	97.1%	96.4%	97.9%	94.6%	93.9%	100.0%	93.8%	92.8%	95.9%
Staff Advocates	Number	45	23	15	13	17	5	5	35	158
	% Somewhat or Very	91.1%	87.0%	86.7%	84.6%	94.1%	80.0%	80.0%	91.4%	89.2%
Common Areas for Meetings	Number	118	28	19	25	24	11	12	46	283
	% Somewhat or Very	96.6%	96.4%	94.7%	92.0%	83.3%	90.9%	100.0%	93.5%	94.3%
Open Floor Plan	Number	117	36	18	23	21	8	8	49	280
	% Somewhat or Very	96.6%	91.7%	94.4%	91.3%	95.2%	100.0%	100.0%	98.0%	95.7%

IMPACT ON PRODUCTIVITY BY TYPE OF COMPANY

Impact on Productivity		Type of Company				
		Proprietorship	Partnership	Corporation	Other	Total
Interactive Orientation Periods	Number	42	50	185	14	291
	% Positive	73.8%	78.0%	89.7%	100.0%	85.9%
Face-to-Face Conversations	Number	65	74	266	26	431
	% Positive	90.8%	91.9%	93.6%	92.3%	92.8%
Management Meetings	Number	55	66	246	19	386
	% Positive	87.3%	78.8%	86.2%	73.7%	84.5%
Staff Meetings	Number	59	66	228	20	373
	% Positive	79.7%	75.8%	86.8%	80.0%	83.4%
Employee Forums	Number	31	34	135	12	212
	% Positive	77.4%	79.4%	86.7%	83.3%	84.0%
Informal Gatherings	Number	43	45	121	14	223
	% Positive	90.7%	84.4%	90.9%	85.7%	89.2%
Management by Walking Around	Number	44	53	197	16	310
	% Positive	79.6%	88.7%	90.4%	75.0%	87.7%
Open Door Policy	Number	52	67	236	20	375
	% Positive	84.6%	85.1%	89.4%	80.0%	87.5%
Staff Advocates	Number	25	24	88	11	148
	% Positive	72.0%	62.5%	80.7%	90.9%	77.0%
Common Areas for Meetings	Number	38	56	134	11	239
	% Positive	79.0%	80.4%	82.1%	81.8%	81.2%
Open Floor Plan	Number	31	56	145	8	240
	% Positive	71.0%	82.1%	75.9%	87.5%	77.1%

IMPACT ON PRODUCTIVITY BY NUMBER OF EMPLOYEES

Impact on Productivity		Number of Employees			
		Up to 50	51 to 200	More than 200	Total
Interactive Orientation Periods	Number	101	55	57	213
	% Positive	80.2%	80.0%	86.0%	81.7%
Face-to-Face Conversations	Number	224	112	95	431
	% Positive	94.2%	90.2%	92.6%	92.8%
Management Meetings	Number	175	108	103	386
	% Positive	85.1%	79.6%	88.3%	84.5%
Staff Meetings	Number	186	100	87	373
	% Positive	82.8%	84.0%	83.9%	83.4%
Employee Forums	Number	92	62	58	212
	% Positive	80.4%	85.5%	87.9%	84.0%
Informal Gatherings	Number	126	53	44	223
	% Positive	92.1%	84.9%	86.4%	89.2%
Management by Walking Around	Number	149	87	74	310
	% Positive	88.6%	86.2%	87.8%	87.7%
Open Door Policy	Number	187	102	86	375
	% Positive	86.1%	91.2%	86.0%	87.5%
Staff Advocates	Number	67	42	39	148
	% Positive	73.1%	88.1%	71.8%	77.0%
Common Areas for Meetings	Number	127	62	50	239
	% Positive	81.1%	79.0%	84.0%	81.2%
Open Floor Plan	Number	126	66	48	240
	% Positive	77.0%	72.7%	83.3%	77.1%

IMPACT ON PRODUCTIVITY BY SECTOR

Impact on Productivity		Sector								
		Profession-al/Scientific/Technical	Manufac-turing	Finance	Informa-tion Services	Retail	Construc-tion	Health Care	Other	Total
Interactive Orientation Periods	Number	111	34	28	27	18	11	11	51	291
	% Positive	88.3%	82.4%	78.6%	81.5%	88.9%	81.8%	90.9%	88.2%	85.9%
Face-to-Face Conversations	Number	172	50	32	34	29	17	12	85	431
	% Positive	95.9%	92.0%	87.5%	97.1%	86.2%	94.1%	91.7%	89.4%	92.8%
Management Meetings	Number	146	45	35	32	28	12	12	76	386
	% Positive	85.6%	86.7%	91.4%	81.3%	85.7%	75.0%	83.3%	80.3%	84.5%
Staff Meetings	Number	149	43	30	31	28	10	11	71	373
	% Positive	88.6%	79.1%	83.3%	77.4%	89.3%	80.0%	90.9%	74.6%	83.4%
Employee Forums	Number	72	30	17	25	17	9	7	35	212
	% Positive	87.5%	90.0%	82.4%	80.0%	88.2%	77.8%	85.7%	74.3%	84.0%
Informal Gatherings	Number	104	17	13	18	13	8	6	44	223
	% Positive	94.2%	88.2%	92.3%	77.8%	84.6%	100.0%	100.0%	79.5%	89.2%
Management by Walking Around	Number	115	48	23	23	21	10	12	58	310
	% Positive	90.4%	91.7%	78.3%	87.0%	76.2%	100.0%	91.7%	84.5%	87.7%
Open Door Policy	Number	147	47	30	28	27	10	14	72	375
	% Positive	87.8%	91.5%	83.3%	85.7%	92.6%	100.0%	85.7%	83.3%	87.5%
Staff Advocates	Number	46	21	12	13	18	4	4	30	148
	% Positive	80.4%	90.5%	58.3%	76.9%	77.8%	75.0%	75.0%	70.0%	77.0%
Common Areas for Meetings	Number	103	20	13	20	22	10	10	41	239
	% Positive	84.5%	85.0%	84.6%	80.0%	81.8%	80.0%	80.0%	70.7%	81.2%
Open Floor Plan	Number	99	30	12	19	19	8	6	47	240
	% Positive	77.8%	76.7%	66.7%	63.2%	94.7%	75.0%	66.7%	78.7%	77.1%

IMPACT ON PROFITABILITY BY TYPE OF COMPANY

Impact on Profitability		Type of Company				
		Proprietorship	Partnership	Corporation	Other	Total
Interactive Orientation Periods	Number	34	36	134	9	213
	% Positive	82.4%	72.2%	83.6%	88.9%	81.7%
Face-to-Face Conversations	Number	51	60	192	19	322
	% Positive	86.3%	85.0%	85.9%	94.7%	86.3%
Management Meetings	Number	47	55	195	14	311
	% Positive	83.0%	89.1%	84.6%	78.6%	84.9%
Staff Meetings	Number	49	57	180	12	298
	% Positive	83.7%	73.7%	69.5%	92.3%	74.9%
Employee Forums	Number	24	29	100	9	162
	% Positive	70.8%	72.4%	80.0%	88.9%	77.8%
Informal Gatherings	Number	37	38	95	13	183
	% Positive	83.8%	73.7%	69.5%	92.3%	74.9%
Management by Walking Around	Number	36	46	150	14	246
	% Positive	86.1%	80.4%	80.0%	78.6%	80.9%
Open Door Policy	Number	38	55	174	13	280
	% Positive	84.2%	74.6%	74.1%	76.9%	75.7%
Staff Advocates	Number	19	21	74	8	122
	% Positive	68.4%	76.2%	74.3%	87.5%	74.6%
Common Areas for Meetings	Number	30	46	105	8	189
	% Positive	80.0%	69.6%	71.4%	62.5%	72.0%
Open Floor Plan	Number	28	46	105	7	186
	% Positive	81.4%	87.3%	90.9%	86.7%	88.8%

IMPACT ON PROFITABILITY BY NUMBER OF EMPLOYEES

Impact on Profitability		Number of Employees			
		Up to 50	51 to 200	More than 200	Total
Interactive Orientation Periods	Number	130	84	77	291
	% Positive	86.9%	82.1%	88.3%	85.9%
Face-to-Face Conversations	Number	169	86	67	322
	% Positive	88.2%	83.7%	85.1%	86.3%
Management Meetings	Number	142	91	78	311
	% Positive	85.2%	80.2%	89.7%	84.9%
Staff Meetings	Number	146	85	67	298
	% Positive	81.5%	83.5%	80.6%	81.9%
Employee Forums	Number	73	49	40	162
	% Positive	67.1%	85.7%	87.5%	77.8%
Informal Gatherings	Number	97	52	34	183
	% Positive	79.4%	67.3%	73.5%	74.9%
Management by Walking Around	Number	121	73	52	246
	% Positive	77.7%	84.9%	82.7%	80.9%
Open Door Policy	Number	140	81	59	280
	% Positive	76.4%	70.4%	81.4%	75.7%
Staff Advocates	Number	56	37	29	122
	% Positive	69.6%	81.1%	75.9%	74.6%
Common Areas for Meetings	Number	97	53	39	189
	% Positive	74.2%	67.9%	71.8%	72.0%
Open Floor Plan	Number	98	49	39	186
	% Positive	72.4%	65.3%	82.1%	72.6%

IMPACT ON PROFITABILITY BY LOCATION OF MAIN OFFICE

Impact on Profitability		Location of Main Office				
		U.S.	Canada	Europe	Other	Total
Interactive Orientation Periods	Number	173	22	5	13	213
	% Positive	82.1%	86.4%	60.0%	76.9%	81.7%
Face-to-Face Conversations	Number	256	40	10	16	322
	% Positive	86.3%	85.0%	100.0%	81.3%	86.3%
Management Meetings	Number	246	39	10	16	311
	% Positive	84.6%	89.7%	80.0%	81.3%	84.9%
Staff Meetings	Number	237	37	8	16	298
	% Positive	81.9%	83.8%	87.5%	75.0%	81.9%
Employee Forums	Number	135	18	2	7	162
	% Positive	79.3%	72.2%	50.0%	71.4%	77.8%
Informal Gatherings	Number	143	23	6	11	183
	% Positive	72.7%	91.3%	83.3%	63.6%	74.9%
Management by Walking Around	Number	204	25	7	10	246
	% Positive	81.4%	84.0%	85.7%	60.0%	80.9%
Open Door Policy	Number	228	30	8	14	280
	% Positive	76.3%	73.3%	87.5%	64.3%	75.7%
Staff Advocates	Number	103	13	0	6	122
	% Positive	77.7%	69.2%	N/A	33.3%	74.6%
Common Areas for Meetings	Number	153	21	7	8	189
	% Positive	71.9%	71.4%	85.7%	62.5%	72.0%
Open Floor Plan	Number	152	17	8	9	186
	% Positive	71.7%	76.5%	75.0%	77.8%	72.6%

IMPACT ON PROFITABILITY BY SECTOR

Impact on Profitability		Sector								
		Profession-al/Scientific/Technical	Manufac-turing	Finance	Infor-mation Services	Retail	Construc-tion	Health Care	Other	Total
Interactive Orientation Periods	Number	76	28	17	21	15	9	8	39	213
	% Positive	78.9%	96.4%	70.6%	85.7%	86.7%	88.9%	87.5%	74.4%	81.7%
Face-to-Face Conversations	Number	121	39	19	27	28	11	10	67	322
	% Positive	88.4%	94.9%	84.2%	96.3%	75.0%	81.8%	90.0%	79.1%	86.3%
Management Meetings	Number	112	39	23	28	27	11	11	60	311
	% Positive	85.7%	87.2%	91.3%	78.6%	81.5%	90.9%	90.9%	81.7%	84.9%
Staff Meetings	Number	116	38	18	27	26	9	9	55	298
	% Positive	82.8%	92.1%	72.2%	81.5%	80.8%	88.9%	88.9%	74.5%	81.9%
Employee Forums	Number	53	24	11	18	17	7	6	26	162
	% Positive	73.6%	87.5%	90.9%	72.2%	64.7%	100.0%	83.3%	76.9%	77.8%
Informal Gatherings	Number	78	15	10	15	13	7	5	40	183
	% Positive	79.5%	73.3%	80.0%	73.3%	61.5%	85.7%	100.0%	65.0%	74.9%
Management by Walking Around	Number	90	38	14	20	24	6	10	44	246
	% Positive	82.2%	92.1%	71.4%	70.0%	70.8%	100.0%	90.0%	77.3%	80.9%
Open Door Policy	Number	106	37	18	23	24	7	11	54	280
	% Positive	75.5%	83.8%	72.2%	73.9%	79.2%	71.4%	90.9%	68.5%	75.7%
Staff Advocates	Number	37	18	8	10	15	4	3	27	122
	% Positive	73.0%	77.8%	75.0%	80.0%	80.0%	75.0%	66.7%	70.4%	74.6%
Common Areas for Meetings	Number	76	21	8	14	21	9	9	31	189
	% Positive	73.7%	57.1%	37.5%	85.7%	71.4%	88.9%	88.9%	71.0%	72.0%
Open Floor Plan	Number	74	24	9	12	19	6	7	35	186
	% Positive	71.6%	66.7%	88.9%	75.0%	78.9%	83.3%	71.4%	68.6%	72.6%

IMPACT ON EMPLOYEE BEHAVIOR BY NUMBER OF EMPLOYEES

Impact on Employee Behavior		Number of Employees			
		Up to 50	51 to 200	More than 200	Total
Interactive Orientation Periods	Number	136	94	92	322
	% Positive	88.2%	90.4%	88.0%	88.8%
Face-to-Face Conversations	Number	229	132	114	475
	% Positive	95.6%	93.9%	93.9%	94.7%
Management Meetings	Number	180	120	112	412
	% Positive	78.3%	66.7%	75.9%	74.3%
Staff Meetings	Number	186	115	105	406
	% Positive	86.6%	84.3%	82.9%	85.0%
Employee Forums	Number	90	66	66	222
	% Positive	81.1%	90.9%	87.9%	86.0%
Informal Gatherings	Number	138	65	54	257
	% Positive	92.8%	80.0%	94.4%	89.9%
Management by Walking Around	Number	166	103	89	358
	% Positive	86.7%	80.6%	88.8%	85.5%
Open Door Policy	Number	204	121	107	432
	% Positive	90.2%	89.3%	93.5%	90.7%
Staff Advocates	Number	57	44	39	140
	% Positive	77.2%	79.5%	74.4%	77.1%
Common Areas for Meetings	Number	131	71	60	262
	% Positive	87.8%	76.1%	85.0%	84.0%
Open Floor Plan	Number	129	70	54	253
	% Positive	82.2%	82.9%	85.2%	83.0%

IMPACT ON EMPLOYEE BEHAVIOR BY LOCATION OF MAIN OFFICE

Impact on Employee Behavior		Location of Main Office				
		U.S.	Canada	Europe	Other	Total
Interactive Orientation Periods	Number	249	44	13	16	322
	% Positive	88.8%	90.9%	84.6%	87.5%	88.8%
Face-to-Face Conversations	Number	365	67	21	22	475
	% Positive	94.5%	92.5%	100.0%	100.0%	94.7%
Management Meetings	Number	313	63	17	19	412
	% Positive	72.8%	81.0%	76.5%	73.7%	74.3%
Staff Meetings	Number	307	61	16	22	406
	% Positive	84.4%	85.2%	93.8%	86.4%	85.0%
Employee Forums	Number	178	29	4	11	222
	% Positive	87.1%	86.2%	75.0%	72.7%	86.0%
Informal Gatherings	Number	193	36	14	14	257
	% Positive	89.1%	88.9%	100.0%	92.9%	89.9%
Management by Walking Around	Number	288	41	16	13	358
	% Positive	84.7%	87.8%	100.0%	76.9%	85.5%
Open Door Policy	Number	334	60	17	21	432
	% Positive	91.0%	90.0%	94.1%	85.7%	90.7%
Staff Advocates	Number	119	16	1	4	140
	% Positive	78.2%	75.0%	100.0%	50.0%	77.1%
Common Areas for Meetings	Number	204	37	9	12	262
	% Positive	84.3%	83.8%	77.8%	83.3%	84.0%
Open Floor Plan	Number	201	29	12	11	253
	% Positive	81.1%	86.2%	91.7%	100.0%	83.0%

IMPACT ON EMPLOYEE BEHAVIOR BY SECTOR

Impact on Employee Behavior		Sector								
		Profession-al/Scientific/ Technical	Manufac-turing	Finance	Infor-mation Services	Retail	Construc-tion	Health Care	Other	Total
Interactive Orientation Periods	Number	125	37	31	28	19	14	11	57	322
	% Positive	90.4%	91.9%	90.3%	82.1%	78.9%	85.7%	90.9%	89.5%	88.8%
Face-to-Face Conversations	Number	185	55	36	40	30	20	15	94	475
	% Positive	95.7%	96.4%	97.2%	100.0%	86.7%	95.0%	86.7%	92.6%	94.7%
Management Meetings	Number	156	47	38	34	30	13	14	80	412
	% Positive	80.8%	61.7%	78.9%	64.7%	73.3%	69.2%	85.7%	70.0%	74.3%
Staff Meetings	Number	164	42	37	34	27	12	15	75	406
	% Positive	88.4%	83.3%	89.2%	79.4%	85.2%	83.3%	86.7%	78.7%	85.0%
Employee Forums	Number	74	30	22	26	15	10	7	38	222
	% Positive	87.8%	93.3%	86.4%	80.8%	86.7%	70.0%	85.7%	84.2%	86.0%
Informal Gatherings	Number	116	21	17	23	13	11	8	48	257
	% Positive	92.2%	95.2%	94.1%	91.3%	84.6%	81.8%	100.0%	81.3%	89.9%
Management by Walking Around	Number	132	51	27	27	28	14	13	66	358
	% Positive	90.2%	94.1%	81.5%	81.5%	78.6%	71.4%	84.6%	78.8%	85.5%
Open Door Policy	Number	169	56	34	33	30	15	15	80	432
	% Positive	91.1%	91.1%	88.2%	93.9%	90.0%	93.3%	100.0%	87.5%	90.7%
Staff Advocates	Number	38	21	13	12	16	5	3	32	140
	% Positive	76.3%	85.7%	69.2%	91.7%	87.5%	60.0%	66.7%	68.8%	77.1%
Common Areas for Meetings	Number	113	25	16	19	22	11	12	44	262
	% Positive	86.7%	80.0%	62.5%	89.5%	81.8%	90.9%	100.0%	79.5%	84.0%
Open Floor Plan	Number	104	29	16	18	20	9	7	50	253
	% Positive	87.5%	79.3%	68.8%	72.2%	90.0%	88.9%	85.7%	80.0%	83.0%

IMPACT ON EXTERNAL COMMUNICATIONS BY TYPE OF COMPANY

Impact on External Communications		Type of Company				
		Proprietorship	Partnership	Corporation	Other	Total
Interactive Orientation Periods	Number	42	44	171	15	272
	% Positive	78.6%	65.9%	64.9%	66.7%	67.3%
Face-to-Face Conversations	Number	64	67	265	27	423
	% Positive	87.5%	85.1%	81.5%	70.4%	82.3%
Management Meetings	Number	57	59	238	19	373
	% Positive	78.9%	69.5%	74.4%	63.2%	73.7%
Staff Meetings	Number	58	65	226	18	367
	% Positive	69.0%	70.8%	76.5%	77.8%	74.4%
Employee Forums	Number	29	32	121	15	197
	% Positive	72.4%	62.5%	70.2%	60.0%	68.5%
Informal Gatherings	Number	40	44	119	15	218
	% Positive	75.0%	75.0%	70.6%	53.3%	71.1%
Management by Walking Around	Number	43	51	184	18	296
	% Positive	72.1%	68.6%	65.8%	27.8%	64.9%
Open Door Policy	Number	51	65	224	20	360
	% Positive	82.4%	70.8%	67.0%	50.0%	68.9%
Staff Advocates	Number	20	21	80	9	130
	% Positive	85.0%	66.7%	71.3%	44.4%	70.8%
Common Areas for Meetings	Number	35	50	130	11	226
	% Positive	74.3%	68.0%	69.2%	54.5%	69.0%
Open Floor Plan	Number	33	54	134	11	232
	% Positive	54.5%	66.7%	64.2%	54.5%	62.9%

IMPACT ON EXTERNAL COMMUNICATIONS BY NUMBER OF EMPLOYEES

Impact on Profitability		Number of Employees: Up to 50	51 to 200	More than 200	Total
Interactive Orientation Periods	Number	121	77	74	272
	% Positive	72.7%	63.6%	62.2%	67.3%
Face-to-Face Conversations	Number	215	116	92	423
	% Positive	86.0%	79.3%	77.2%	82.3%
Management Meetings	Number	173	107	93	373
	% Positive	78.0%	68.2%	72.0%	73.7%
Staff Meetings	Number	181	103	83	367
	% Positive	77.9%	72.8%	68.7%	74.4%
Employee Forums	Number	89	56	52	197
	% Positive	65.2%	67.9%	75.0%	68.5%
Informal Gatherings	Number	117	56	45	218
	% Positive	74.4%	67.9%	66.7%	71.1%
Management by Walking Around	Number	143	82	71	296
	% Positive	67.1%	65.9%	59.2%	64.9%
Open Door Policy	Number	183	97	80	360
	% Positive	73.2%	62.9%	66.3%	68.9%
Staff Advocates	Number	58	40	32	130
	% Positive	72.4%	70.0%	68.8%	70.8%
Common Areas for Meetings	Number	118	61	47	226
	% Positive	71.2%	67.2%	66.0%	69.0%
Open Floor Plan	Number	125	60	47	232
	% Positive	64.0%	56.7%	68.1%	62.9%

IMPACT ON EXTERNAL COMMUNICATIONS BY LOCATION OF MAIN OFFICE

Impact on External Communications		Location of Main Office				
		U.S.	Canada	Europe	Other	Total
Interactive Orientation Periods	Number	210	35	9	18	272
	% Positive	68.6%	62.9%	77.8%	55.6%	67.3%
Face-to-Face Conversations	Number	323	61	17	22	423
	% Positive	82.7%	82.0%	94.1%	68.2%	82.3%
Management Meetings	Number	284	51	15	23	373
	% Positive	73.9%	78.4%	73.3%	60.9%	73.7%
Staff Meetings	Number	276	55	14	22	367
	% Positive	76.1%	69.1%	85.7%	59.1%	74.4%
Employee Forums	Number	156	27	5	9	197
	% Positive	71.2%	63.0%	60.0%	44.4%	68.5%
Informal Gatherings	Number	163	34	8	13	218
	% Positive	71.2%	73.5%	75.0%	61.5%	71.1%
Management by Walking Around	Number	239	35	10	12	296
	% Positive	66.1%	54.3%	100.0%	41.7%	64.9%
Open Door Policy	Number	279	46	13	22	360
	% Positive	70.6%	58.7%	84.6%	59.1%	68.9%
Staff Advocates	Number	109	16	1	4	130
	% Positive	74.3%	56.3%	0.0%	50.0%	70.8%
Common Areas for Meetings	Number	180	30	7	9	226
	% Positive	69.4%	63.3%	100.0%	55.6%	69.0%
Open Floor Plan	Number	179	29	10	14	232
	% Positive	65.9%	41.4%	80.0%	57.1%	62.9%

IMPACT ON EXTERNAL COMMUNICATIONS BY SECTOR

Impact on External Communications		Sector								
		Profession-al/Scientific/ Technical	Manufac-turing	Finance	Infor-mation Services	Retail	Construc-tion	Health Care	Other	Total
Interactive Orientation Periods	Number	108	29	28	22	19	10	11	45	272
	% Positive	65.7%	55.2%	64.3%	59.1%	78.9%	90.0%	63.6%	75.6%	67.3%
Face-to-Face Conversations	Number	164	46	34	33	32	18	14	82	423
	% Positive	81.1%	78.3%	79.4%	81.8%	81.3%	88.9%	85.7%	86.6%	82.3%
Management Meetings	Number	147	42	32	27	33	11	12	69	373
	% Positive	76.2%	69.0%	75.0%	66.7%	78.8%	72.7%	66.7%	72.5%	73.7%
Staff Meetings	Number	152	39	31	28	29	10	11	67	367
	% Positive	75.0%	69.2%	77.4%	64.3%	82.8%	80.0%	72.7%	74.6%	74.4%
Employee Forums	Number	68	27	19	21	17	7	6	32	197
	% Positive	58.8%	74.1%	84.2%	52.4%	88.2%	71.4%	50.0%	78.1%	68.5%
Informal Gatherings	Number	97	16	16	17	13	11	7	41	218
	% Positive	75.3%	75.0%	50.0%	58.8%	53.8%	81.8%	85.7%	73.2%	71.1%
Management by Walking Around	Number	111	40	23	22	29	9	12	50	296
	% Positive	66.7%	67.5%	56.5%	54.5%	65.5%	55.6%	66.7%	68.0%	64.9%
Open Door Policy	Number	147	42	29	29	31	10	13	59	360
	% Positive	72.1%	57.1%	58.6%	69.0%	71.0%	90.0%	76.9%	67.8%	68.9%
Staff Advocates	Number	40	19	10	11	16	4	3	27	130
	% Positive	67.5%	78.9%	70.0%	45.5%	93.8%	75.0%	66.7%	66.7%	70.8%
Common Areas for Meetings	Number	91	22	14	19	24	8	11	37	226
	% Positive	73.6%	72.7%	71.4%	52.6%	62.5%	100.0%	54.5%	64.9%	69.0%
Open Floor Plan	Number	96	26	15	18	21	7	8	41	232
	% Positive	68.8%	46.2%	66.7%	38.9%	66.7%	85.7%	62.5%	63.4%	62.9%

PRINT COMMUNICATION PRACTICES

PRINT USAGE BY CEO GENDER

Usage		Gender of CEO		
		Male	Female	Total
Formal Grievance Procedures	Number	460	138	598
	% Currently Use	28.7%	18.8%	26.4%
Anonymous Suggestion Systems	Number	460	138	598
	% Currently Use	24.6%	15.2%	22.4%
Public Suggestion Systems	Number	460	138	598
	% Currently Use	34.8%	28.3%	33.3%
Printed Publications	Number	460	138	598
	% Currently Use	40.2%	22.5%	36.1%
Letters Mailed to Employees' Homes	Number	460	138	598
	% Currently Use	25.0%	15.2%	22.7%
Open Book Management	Number	460	138	598
	% Currently Use	42.6%	37.7%	41.5%
Printed Manuals	Number	460	138	598
	% Currently Use	66.1%	47.1%	61.7%

COST-EFFECTIVENESS BY TYPE OF COMPANY

Cost-effectiveness		Type of Company				
		Proprietorship	Partnership	Corporation	Other	Total
Formal Grievance Procedures	Number	17	11	83	7	118
	% Somewhat or Very	82.4%	90.9%	84.3%	100.0%	85.6%
Anonymous Suggestion Systems	Number	18	15	78	5	116
	% Somewhat or Very	94.4%	73.3%	83.3%	100.0%	84.5%
Public Suggestion Systems	Number	22	29	120	10	181
	% Somewhat or Very	86.4%	89.7%	94.2%	100.0%	92.8%
Printed Publications	Number	21	29	128	11	189
	% Somewhat or Very	81.0%	82.8%	88.3%	81.8%	86.2%
Letters Mailed to Employees' Homes	Number	16	18	83	2	119
	% Somewhat or Very	81.3%	72.2%	86.7%	100.0%	84.0%
Open Book Management	Number	29	32	134	17	212
	% Somewhat or Very	89.7%	96.9%	94.8%	88.2%	93.9%
Printed Manuals	Number	32	54	227	16	329
	% Somewhat or Very	81.3%	94.4%	88.5%	75.0%	88.1%

COST-EFFECTIVENESS BY NUMBER OF EMPLOYEES

Cost-effectiveness		Number of Employees			
		Up to 50	51 to 200	More than 200	Total
Formal Grievance Procedures	Number	32	48	38	118
	% Somewhat or Very	84.4%	85.4%	86.8%	85.6%
Anonymous Suggestion Systems	Number	30	52	34	116
	% Somewhat or Very	86.7%	80.8%	88.2%	84.5%
Public Suggestion Systems	Number	75	63	43	181
	% Somewhat or Very	92.0%	95.2%	90.7%	92.8%
Printed Publications	Number	58	67	64	189
	% Somewhat or Very	86.2%	83.6%	89.1%	86.2%
Letters Mailed to Employees' Homes	Number	28	45	46	119
	% Somewhat or Very	78.6%	88.9%	82.6%	84.0%
Open Book Management	Number	80	71	61	212
	% Somewhat or Very	93.8%	94.4%	93.4%	93.9%
Printed Manuals	Number	120	111	98	329
	% Somewhat or Very	90.0%	88.3%	85.7%	88.1%

COST-EFFECTIVENESS BY LOCATION OF MAIN OFFICE

Cost-effectiveness		Location of Main Office				
		U.S.	Canada	Europe	Other	Total
Formal Grievance Procedures	Number	97	10	4	7	118
	% Somewhat or Very	87.6%	80.0%	50.0%	85.7%	85.6%
Anonymous Suggestion Systems	Number	95	16	2	3	116
	% Somewhat or Very	85.3%	87.5%	50.0%	66.7%	84.5%
Public Suggestion Systems	Number	142	21	6	12	181
	% Somewhat or Very	92.3%	100.0%	83.3%	91.7%	92.8%
Printed Publications	Number	145	30	4	10	189
	% Somewhat or Very	89.7%	76.7%	75.0%	70.0%	86.2%
Letters Mailed to Employees' Homes	Number	109	4	2	4	119
	% Somewhat or Very	83.5%	100.0%	50.0%	100.0%	84.0%
Open Book Management	Number	163	32	9	8	212
	% Somewhat or Very	94.5%	93.8%	88.9%	87.5%	93.9%
Printed Manuals	Number	256	43	13	17	329
	% Somewhat or Very	89.8%	86.0%	69.2%	82.4%	88.1%

COST-EFFECTIVENESS BY SECTOR

Cost-effectiveness		Sector								
		Profession-al/Scientif-ic/Technical	Manufac-turing	Finance	Infor-mation Services	Retail	Construc-tion	Health Care	Other	Total
Formal Grievance Procedures	Number	24	23	12	10	9	3	6	31	118
	% Somewhat or Very	83.3%	78.3%	91.7%	70.0%	100.0 %	100.0%	100.0 %	87.1%	85.6%
Anonymous Suggestion Systems	Number	31	20	12	6	12	8	7	20	116
	% Somewhat or Very	93.5%	80.0%	91.7%	66.7%	83.3%	62.5%	85.7%	85.0%	84.5%
Public Suggestion Systems	Number	64	32	15	11	14	8	7	30	181
	% Somewhat or Very	100.0%	96.9%	93.3%	72.7%	85.7%	87.5%	85.7%	86.7%	92.8%
Printed Publications	Number	55	33	19	14	10	10	8	40	189
	% Somewhat or Very	85.5%	87.9%	78.9%	57.1%	100.0 %	100.0%	87.5%	92.5%	86.2%
Letters Mailed to Employees' Homes	Number	34	22	7	8	10	7	6	25	119
	% Somewhat or Very	88.2%	95.5%	85.7%	62.5%	70.0%	85.7%	100.0 %	76.0%	84.0%
Open Book Manage-ment	Number	74	28	25	20	16	11	7	31	212
	% Somewhat or Very	95.9%	96.4%	92.0%	85.0%	87.5%	100.0%	100.0 %	93.5%	93.9%
Printed Manuals	Number	112	50	34	22	27	11	13	60	329
	% Somewhat or Very	86.6%	96.0%	70.6%	72.7%	92.6%	100.0%	84.6%	96.7%	88.1%

IMPACT ON PRODUCTIVITY BY TYPE OF COMPANY

Impact on Productivity		Type of Company				
		Proprietorship	Partnership	Corporation	Other	Total
Formal Grievance Procedures	Number	13	11	71	7	102
	% Positive	69.2%	54.6%	70.4%	71.4%	68.6%
Anonymous Suggestion Systems	Number	16	14	64	3	97
	% Positive	87.5%	78.6%	68.8%	66.7%	73.2%
Public Suggestion Systems	Number	20	27	102	10	159
	% Positive	80.0%	74.1%	76.5%	80.0%	76.7%
Printed Publications	Number	20	25	111	9	165
	% Positive	65.0%	68.0%	74.8%	77.8%	72.7%
Letters Mailed to Employees' Homes	Number	15	16	60	2	93
	% Positive	80.0%	68.8%	70.0%	50.0%	71.0%
Open Book Management	Number	24	24	121	14	183
	% Positive	87.5%	70.8%	83.5%	71.4%	81.4%
Printed Manuals	Number	29	44	183	14	270
	% Positive	86.2%	68.2%	71.0%	64.3%	71.9%

IMPACT ON PRODUCTIVITY BY NUMBER OF EMPLOYEES

Impact on Productivity		Number of Employees: Up to 50	51 to 200	More than 200	Total
Formal Grievance Procedures	Number	30	42	30	102
	% Positive	56.7%	85.7%	56.7%	68.6%
Anonymous Suggestion Systems	Number	24	45	28	97
	% Positive	75.0%	73.3%	71.4%	73.2%
Public Suggestion Systems	Number	68	54	37	159
	% Positive	73.5%	83.3%	73.0%	76.7%
Printed Publications	Number	54	58	53	165
	% Positive	68.5%	74.1%	75.5%	72.7%
Letters Mailed to Employees' Homes	Number	22	38	33	93
	% Positive	72.7%	71.1%	69.7%	71.0%
Open Book Management	Number	73	64	46	183
	% Positive	78.1%	82.8%	84.8%	81.4%
Printed Manuals	Number	104	95	71	270
	% Positive	75.0%	73.7%	64.8%	71.9%

IMPACT ON PRODUCTIVITY BY LOCATION OF MAIN OFFICE

Impact on Productivity		Location of Main Office: U.S.	Canada	Europe	Other	Total
Formal Grievance Procedures	Number	84	8	5	5	102
	% Positive	72.6%	62.5%	20.0%	60.0%	68.6%
Anonymous Suggestion Systems	Number	82	11	2	2	97
	% Positive	76.8%	63.6%	50.0%	0.0%	73.2%
Public Suggestion Systems	Number	126	17	6	10	159
	% Positive	79.4%	58.8%	83.3%	70.0%	76.7%
Printed Publications	Number	127	25	4	9	165
	% Positive	70.1%	84.0%	50.0%	88.9%	72.7%
Letters Mailed to Employees' Homes	Number	83	4	2	4	93
	% Positive	72.3%	75.0%	50.0%	50.0%	71.0%
Open Book Management	Number	143	2	7	5	183
	% Positive	82.5%	75.0%	71.4%	100.0%	81.4%
Printed Manuals	Number	212	31	11	16	270
	% Positive	71.2%	77.4%	45.5%	87.5%	71.9%

IMPACT ON PRODUCTIVITY BY SECTOR

Impact on Productivity		Sector								
		Profession-al/Scienti-fic/Techni-cal	Manufac-turing	Finance	Infor-mation Services	Retail	Construc-tion	Health Care	Other	Total
Formal Grievance Procedures	Number	19	18	10	9	10	3	6	27	102
	% Positive	68.4%	77.8%	70.0%	66.7%	70.0%	66.7%	66.7%	63.0%	68.6%
Anonymous Suggestion Systems	Number	24	19	7	6	12	6	5	18	97
	% Positive	79.2%	73.7%	28.6%	83.3%	83.3%	83.3%	80.0%	66.7%	73.2%
Public Suggestion Systems	Number	53	30	12	10	12	8	7	27	159
	% Positive	79.3%	86.7%	58.3%	80.0%	83.3%	75.0%	71.4%	66.7%	76.7%
Printed Publications	Number	41	26	18	14	11	8	7	40	165
	% Positive	84.0%	77.8%	75.0%	57.1%	66.7%	80.0%	40.0%	60.0%	71.0%
Letters Mailed to Employees' Homes	Number	25	28	4	7	9	5	5	20	93
	% Positive	84.0%	77.8%	75.0%	57.1%	66.7%	80.0%	40.0%	60.0%	71.0%
Open Book Management	Number	58	23	21	21	15	9	5	31	183
	% Positive	77.6%	87.0%	76.2%	85.7%	80.0%	100.0%	80.0%	80.7%	81.4%
Printed Manuals	Number	83	40	29	19	24	10	13	52	270
	% Positive	68.7%	75.0%	65.5%	73.7%	83.3%	50.0%	61.5%	78.9%	71.9%

IMPACT ON PROFITABILITY BY TYPE OF COMPANY

Impact on Profitability		Type of Company				
		Proprietorship	Partnership	Corporation	Other	Total
Formal Grievance Procedures	Number	12	10	59	5	86
	% Positive	75.0%	60.0%	57.6%	60.0%	60.5%
Anonymous Suggestion Systems	Number	15	13	56	2	86
	% Positive	73.3%	76.9%	51.8%	50.0%	59.3%
Public Suggestion Systems	Number	18	24	90	9	141
	% Positive	83.3%	62.5%	70.0%	66.7%	70.2%
Printed Publications	Number	17	23	83	8	131
	% Positive	64.7%	73.9%	67.5%	50.0%	67.2%
Letters Mailed to Employees' Homes	Number	13	14	49	2	78
	% Positive	69.2%	35.7%	57.1%	0.0%	38.5%
Open Book Management	Number	21	23	102	14	160
	% Positive	81.0%	60.9%	75.5%	71.4%	73.8%
Printed Manuals	Number	24	40	146	12	222
	% Positive	66.7%	67.5%	58.9%	50.0%	60.8%

IMPACT ON PROFITABILITY BY NUMBER OF EMPLOYEES

Impact on Profitability		Number of Employees: Up to 50	51 to 200	More than 200	Total
Formal Grievance Procedures	Number	29	33	24	86
	% Positive	51.7%	72.7%	54.2%	60.5%
Anonymous Suggestion Systems	Number	24	41	21	86
	% Positive	62.5%	53.7%	66.7%	59.3%
Public Suggestion Systems	Number	64	46	31	141
	% Positive	65.6%	76.1%	71.0%	70.2%
Printed Publications	Number	51	46	34	131
	% Positive	66.7%	65.2%	70.6%	67.2%
Letters Mailed to Employees' Homes	Number	21	33	24	78
	% Positive	52.4%	57.6%	50.0%	53.8%
Open Book Management	Number	70	55	35	160
	% Positive	72.9%	72.7%	77.1%	73.8%
Printed Manuals	Number	91	84	47	222
	% Positive	58.2%	60.7%	66.0%	60.8%

IMPACT ON PROFITABILITY BY LOCATION OF MAIN OFFICE

Impact on Profitability		Location of Main Office: U.S.	Canada	Europe	Other	Total
Formal Grievance Procedures	Number	73	4	2	7	86
	% Positive	64.4%	25.0%	0.0%	57.1%	60.5%
Anonymous Suggestion Systems	Number	76	5	2	3	86
	% Positive	64.5%	20.0%	50.0%	0.0%	59.3%
Public Suggestion Systems	Number	113	13	5	10	141
	% Positive	71.7%	53.9%	80.0%	70.0%	70.2%
Printed Publications	Number	105	15	3	8	131
	% Positive	66.7%	66.7%	66.7%	75.0%	67.2%
Letters Mailed to Employees' Homes	Number	70	2	2	4	78
	% Positive	55.7%	100.0%	0.0%	25.0%	53.9%
Open Book Management	Number	124	24	6	6	160
	% Positive	76.6%	58.3%	66.7%	83.3%	73.8%
Printed Manuals	Number	181	18	9	14	222
	% Positive	63.0%	61.1%	33.3%	50.0%	60.8%

IMPACT ON EMPLOYEE BEHAVIOR BY TYPE OF COMPANY

Impact on Employee Behavior		Type of Company				
		Proprietorship	Partnership	Corporation	Other	Total
Formal Grievance Procedures	Number	14	12	88	7	121
	% Positive	64.3%	58.3%	67.1%	85.7%	66.9%
Anonymous Suggestion Systems	Number	17	13	77	3	110
	% Positive	88.2%	92.3%	67.5%	100.0%	74.6%
Public Suggestion Systems	Number	24	28	113	9	174
	% Positive	79.2%	92.9%	82.3%	88.9%	83.9%
Printed Publications	Number	18	24	121	10	173
	% Positive	72.2%	87.5%	79.3%	80.0%	79.8%
Letters Mailed to Employees' Homes	Number	14	15	75	2	106
	% Positive	78.6%	73.3%	76.0%	100.0%	76.4%
Open Book Management	Number	26	29	130	16	201
	% Positive	84.6%	86.2%	88.5%	75.0%	86.6%
Printed Manuals	Number	28	46	208	16	298
	% Positive	75.0%	76.1%	73.6%	81.3%	74.5%

IMPACT ON EMPLOYEE BEHAVIOR BY NUMBER OF EMPLOYEES

Impact on Productivity		Number of Employees			
		Up to 50	51 to 200	More than 200	Total
Formal Grievance Procedures	Number	36	48	37	121
	% Positive	58.3%	72.9%	67.6%	66.9%
Anonymous Suggestion Systems	Number	29	50	31	110
	% Positive	79.3%	72.0%	74.2%	74.5%
Public Suggestion Systems	Number	75	61	38	174
	% Positive	84.0%	83.6%	84.2%	83.9%
Printed Publications	Number	54	64	55	173
	% Positive	79.6%	75.0%	85.5%	79.8%
Letters Mailed to Employees' Homes	Number	27	43	36	106
	% Positive	77.8%	72.1%	80.6%	76.4%
Open Book Management	Number	79	67	55	201
	% Positive	84.8%	86.6%	89.1%	86.6%
Printed Manuals	Number	109	110	79	298
	% Positive	73.4%	71.8%	79.7%	74.5%

IMPACT ON EMPLOYEE BEHAVIOR BY LOCATION OF MAIN OFFICE

Impact on Employee Behavior		Location of Main Office				
		U.S.	Canada	Europe	Other	Total
Formal Grievance Procedures	Number	101	10	4	6	121
	% Positive	67.3%	70.0%	25.0%	83.3%	66.9%
Anonymous Suggestion Systems	Number	92	13	2	3	110
	% Positive	77.2%	69.2%	50.0%	33.3%	74.6%
Public Suggestion Systems	Number	139	17	6	12	174
	% Positive	85.6%	70.6%	83.3%	83.3%	83.9%
Printed Publications	Number	133	28	4	8	173
	% Positive	81.2%	78.6%	50.0%	75.0%	79.8%
Letters Mailed to Employees' Homes	Number	96	4	2	4	106
	% Positive	77.1%	100.0%	0.0%	75.0%	76.4%
Open Book Management	Number	154	31	7	9	201
	% Positive	88.3%	80.7%	85.7%	77.8%	86.6%
Printed Manuals	Number	234	38	12	14	298
	% Positive	74.8%	81.6%	58.3%	64.3%	74.5%

IMPACT ON EMPLOYEE BEHAVIOR BY SECTOR

Impact on Employee Behavior		Sector								
		Profession-al/Scientific/Technical	Manufacturing	Finance	Information Services	Retail	Construction	Health Care	Other	Total
Formal Grievance Procedures	Number	27	23	12	10	10	3	8	28	121
	% Positive	59.3%	69.6%	66.7%	60.0%	80.0%	66.7%	87.5%	64.3%	66.9%
Anonymous Suggestion Systems	Number	30	20	10	8	11	8	7	16	110
	% Positive	70.0%	80.0%	70.0%	62.5%	81.8%	87.5%	85.7%	68.8%	74.6%
Public Suggestion Systems	Number	62	29	13	11	14	8	8	29	174
	% Positive	85.5%	93.1%	61.5%	90.9%	92.9%	75.0%	87.5%	75.9%	83.9%
Printed Publications	Number	50	29	17	14	11	8	7	37	173
	% Positive	76.0%	82.8%	88.2%	71.4%	90.9%	87.5%	85.7%	75.7%	79.8%
Letters Mailed to Employees' Homes	Number	30	22	6	9	9	4	5	21	106
	% Positive	76.7%	81.8%	66.7%	77.8%	66.7%	75.0%	60.0%	81.0%	76.4%
Open Book Management	Number	69	27	22	21	16	8	6	32	201
	% Positive	88.4%	88.9%	81.8%	85.7%	75.0%	100.0%	83.3%	87.5%	86.6%
Printed Manuals	Number	98	48	31	20	26	10	12	53	298
	% Positive	73.5%	77.1%	74.2%	55.0%	80.8%	70.0%	83.3%	77.4%	74.5%

IMPACT ON EXTERNAL COMMUNICATIONS BY TYPE OF COMPANY

Impact on External Communications		Type of Company				
		Proprietorship	Partnership	Corporation	Other	Total
Formal Grievance Procedures	Number	14	10	67	4	95
	% Positive	28.6%	50.0%	46.3%	75.0%	45.3%
Anonymous Suggestion Systems	Number	16	13	69	2	100
	% Positive	62.5%	69.2%	53.6%	0.0%	56.0%
Public Suggestion Systems	Number	22	25	105	8	160
	% Positive	86.4%	68.0%	58.1%	50.0%	61.3%
Printed Publications	Number	19	28	110	10	167
	% Positive	63.2%	75.0%	70.9%	90.0%	71.9%
Letters Mailed to Employees' Homes	Number	15	16	66	2	99
	% Positive	53.3%	37.5%	43.9%	0.0%	43.4%
Open Book Management	Number	21	27	118	13	179
	% Positive	42.9%	,5556	63.6%	61.5%	59.8%
Printed Manuals	Number	27	41	182	12	262
	% Positive	63.0%	48.8%	50.6%	50.0%	51.5%

IMPACT ON EXTERNAL COMMUNICATIONS BY NUMBER OF EMPLOYEES

Impact on External Communications		Number of Employees			
		Up to 50	51 to 200	More than 200	Total
Formal Grievance Procedures	Number	34	36	25	95
	% Positive	35.3%	50.0%	52.0%	45.3%
Anonymous Suggestion Systems	Number	28	44	28	100
	% Positive	64.3%	50.0%	57.1%	56.0%
Public Suggestion Systems	Number	70	57	33	160
	% Positive	70.0%	56.1%	60.6%	63.1%
Printed Publications	Number	55	62	50	167
	% Positive	80.0%	58.1%	80.0%	71.9%
Letters Mailed to Employees' Homes	Number	24	42	33	99
	% Positive	58.3%	35.7%	42.4%	43.4%
Open Book Management	Number	72	64	43	179
	% Positive	56.9%	57.8%	67.4%	59.8%
Printed Manuals	Number	97	99	66	262
	% Positive	52.6%	44.4%	60.6%	51.5%

IMPACT ON EXTERNAL COMMUNICATIONS BY LOCATION OF MAIN OFFICE

Impact on External Communications		Location of Main Office				
		U.S.	Canada	Europe	Other	Total
Formal Grievance Procedures	Number	78	6	3	8	95
	% Positive	52.6%	0.0%	0.0%	25.0%	45.3%
Anonymous Suggestion Systems	Number	84	11	2	3	100
	% Positive	60.7%	36.4%	50.0%	0.0%	56.0%
Public Suggestion Systems	Number	129	14	6	11	160
	% Positive	63.6%	50.0%	83.3%	63.6%	63.1%
Printed Publications	Number	130	23	4	10	167
	% Positive	70.8%	78.3%	75.0%	70.0%	71.9%
Letters Mailed to Employees' Homes	Number	91	2	2	4	99
	% Positive	44.0%	50.0%	0.0%	50.0%	43.4%
Open Book Management	Number	141	25	6	7	179
	% Positive	64.5%	40.0%	66.7%	28.6%	58.8%
Printed Manuals	Number	209	30	10	13	262
	% Positive	49.3%	63.3%	50.0%	61.5%	51.5%

ELECTRONIC COMMUNICATION PRACTICES

ELECTRONIC COMMUNICATION USAGE BY CEO GENDER

Usage		Gender of CEO		
		Male	Female	Total
Electronic Mailing List	Number	460	138	598
	% Currently Use	64.8%	45.7%	60.4%
Electronic Newsletter	Number	460	138	598
	% Currently Use	34.6%	21.7%	31.6%
Telephone Hotlines	Number	460	138	598
	% Currently Use	12.6%	9.4%	11.9%
E-mail	Number	460	138	598
	% Currently Use	82.0%	69.6%	79.1%
Employee Blogs	Number	460	138	598
	% Currently Use	9.3%	10.1%	9.5%
Instant Messaging	Number	460	138	598
	% Currently Use	27.83%	25.36%	27.26%
Intranets	Number	460	138	598
	% Currently Use	54.3%	33.3%	49.5%
Company Web Site	Number	460	138	598
	% Currently Use	79.3%	59.4%	74.7%
CRM System	Number	460	138	598
	% Currently Use	32.0%	17.4%	28.6%
Conferencing Systems	Number	460	138	598
	% Currently Use	58.0%	41.3%	54.2%
Portable Devices	Number	460	138	598
	% Currently Use	78.5%	67.4%	75.9%

ELECTRONIC COMMUNICATION USAGE BY LOCATION OF MAIN OFFICE

Usage		Location of Main Office				
		U.S.	Canada	Europe	Other	Total
Electronic Mailing List	Number	466	89	26	28	609
	% Currently Use	58.8%	62.9%	69.2%	71.4%	60.4%
Electronic Newsletter	Number	466	89	26	28	609
	% Currently Use	30.5%	34.8%	30.8%	35.7%	31.4%
Telephone Hotlines	Number	466	89	26	28	609
	% Currently Use	12.7%	7.9%	7.7%	14.3%	11.8%
E-mail	Number	466	89	26	28	609
	% Currently Use	76.2%	87.6%	76.9%	89.3%	78.5%
Employee Blogs	Number	466	89	26	28	609
	% Currently Use	9.2%	6.7%	19.2%	10.7%	9.4%
Instant Messaging	Number	466	89	26	28	609
	% Currently Use	27.7%	18.0%	42.3%	32.1%	27.1%
Intranets	Number	466	89	26	28	609
	% Currently Use	49.1%	50.6%	46.2%	53.6%	49.4%
Company Web Site	Number	466	89	26	28	609
	% Currently Use	73.0%	78.7%	76.9%	85.7%	74.5%
CRM System	Number	466	89	26	28	609
	% Currently Use	29.6%	23.6%	23.1%	28.6%	28.4%
Conferencing Systems	Number	466	89	26	28	609
	% Currently Use	52.1%	62.9%	65.4%	46.4%	54.0%
Portable Devices	Number	466	89	26	28	609
	% Currently Use	73.2%	83.1%	76.9%	89.3%	75.5%

ELECTRONIC COMMUNICATION USAGE BY SECTOR

Usage		Sector								
		Professional/Scientific/Technical	Manufacturing	Finance	Information Services	Retail	Construction	Health Care	Other	Total
Electronic Mailing List	Number	232	67	53	52	39	23	23	120	609
	% Currently Use	66.8%	65.7%	71.7%	57.7%	33.3%	43.5%	69.6%	51.7%	60.4%
Electronic Newsletter	Number	232	67	53	52	39	23	23	120	609
	% Currently Use	31.0%	34.3%	43.4%	32.7%	25.6%	34.8%	34.8%	25.0%	31.4%
Telephone Hotlines	Number	232	67	53	52	39	23	23	120	609
	% Currently Use	8.2%	13.4%	17.0%	7.7%	10.3%	13.0%	26.1%	15.0%	11.8%
E-mail	Number	232	67	53	52	39	23	23	120	609
	% Currently Use	85.8%	74.6%	88.7%	86.5%	53.8%	69.6%	73.9%	69.2%	78.5%
Employee Blogs	Number	232	67	53	52	39	23	23	120	609
	% Currently Use	9.5%	7.5%	9.4%	15.4%	12.8%	8.7%	8.7%	6.7%	9.4%
Instant Messaging	Number	232	67	53	52	39	23	23	120	609
	% Currently Use	34.5%	17.9%	18.9%	32.7%	15.4%	17.4%	30.4%	24.2%	27.1%
Intranets	Number	232	67	53	52	39	23	23	120	609
	% Currently Use	51.7%	55.2%	75.5%	55.8%	28.2%	26.1%	52.2%	38.3%	49.4%
Company Web Site	Number	232	67	53	52	39	23	23	120	609
	% Currently Use	81.5%	82.1%	86.8%	73.1%	53.8%	65.2%	73.9%	60.8%	74.5%
CRM System	Number	232	67	53	52	39	23	23	120	609
	% Currently Use	28.0%	37.3%	32.1%	40.4%	15.4%	17.4%	34.8%	22.5%	28.4%
Conferencing Systems	Number	232	67	53	52	39	23	23	120	609
	% Currently Use	60.8%	70.1%	66.0%	53.8%	25.6%	34.8%	52.2%	40.0%	54.0%
Portable Devices	Number	232	67	53	52	39	23	23	120	609
	% Currently Use	81.5%	85.1%	79.2%	75.0%	64.1%	60.9%	73.9%	64.2%	75.5%

COST-EFFECTIVENESS BY LOCATION OF MAIN OFFICE

Cost-effectiveness		Location of Main Office				
		U.S.	Canada	Europe	Other	Total
Electronic Mailing List	Number	253	53	16	20	342
	% Somewhat or Very	96.8%	100.0%	93.8%	100.0%	97.4%
Electronic Newsletter	Number	134	31	8	10	183
	% Somewhat or Very	93.3%	93.5%	100.0%	90.0%	93.4%
Telephone Hotlines	Number	46	5	2	4	57
	% Somewhat or Very	82.6%	80.0%	100.0%	75.0%	82.5%
E-mail	Number	339	76	20	25	460
	% Somewhat or Very	97.6%	100.0%	100.0%	96.0%	98.0%
Employee Blogs	Number	34	4	5	3	46
	% Somewhat or Very	97.1%	75.0%	100.0%	66.7%	93.5%
Instant Messaging	Number	118	14	10	8	150
	% Somewhat or Very	94.1%	100.0%	100.0%	100.0%	95.3%
Intranets	Number	212	41	11	15	279
	% Somewhat or Very	95.3%	100.0%	100.0%	100.0%	96.4%
Company Web Site	Number	304	66	19	21	410
	% Somewhat or Very	97.4%	98.5%	100.0%	100.0%	97.8%
CRM System	Number	125	19	5	7	156
	% Somewhat or Very	96.0%	94.7%	100.0%	100.0%	96.2%
Conferencing Systems	Number	220	49	15	13	297
	% Somewhat or Very	96.4%	98.0%	100.0%	100.0%	97.0%
Portable Devices	Number	307	68	15	25	415
	% Somewhat or Very	95.8%	98.5%	100.0%	100.0%	96.6%

COST-EFFECTIVENESS BY SECTOR

Cost-effectiveness		Sector								
		Profession-al/Scientif-ic/Techni-cal	Manufac-turing	Finance	Infor-mation Services	Retail	Construc-tion	Health Care	Other	Total
Electronic Mailing List	Number	146	40	36	29	13	9	12	57	342
	% Somewhat or Very	97.9%	97.5%	97.2%	96.6%	92.3%	100.0%	100.0 %	96.5%	97.4%
Electronic Newsletter	Number	70	22	23	16	9	7	7	29	183
	% Somewhat or Very	95.7%	90.9%	100.0%	93.8%	66.7%	85.7%	100.0 %	93.1%	93.4%
Telephone Hotlines	Number	16	8	8	4	4	3	2	12	57
	% Somewhat or Very	81.3%	100.0%	100.0%	75.0%	75.0%	66.7%	100.0 %	66.7%	82.5%
E-mail	Number	192	48	46	45	20	15	15	79	460
	% Somewhat or Very	99.0%	95.8%	97.8%	95.6%	95.0%	100.0%	100.0 %	98.7%	98.0%
Employee Blogs	Number	18	5	4	5	4	2	1	7	46
	% Somewhat or Very	88.9%	100.0%	100.0%	80.0%	100.0 %	100.0%	100.0 %	100.0 %	93.5%
Instant Messaging	Number	73	11	9	15	6	4	5	27	150
	% Somewhat or Very	95.9%	90.9%	88.9%	100.0%	66.7%	100.0%	100.0 %	100.0 %	95.3%
Intranets	Number	113	34	38	26	10	6	10	42	279
	% Somewhat or Very	100.0%	91.2%	100.0%	92.3%	70.0%	100.0%	100.0 %	95.2%	96.4%
Company Web Site	Number	178	51	41	33	18	13	14	62	410
	% Somewhat or Very	98.9%	96.1%	100.0%	97.0%	94.4%	100.0%	92.9%	96.8%	97.8%
CRM System	Number	61	21	16	18	6	4	6	24	156
	% Somewhat or Very	98.4%	95.2%	93.8%	94.4%	83.3%	100.0%	100.0 %	95.8%	96.2%
Conferencing Systems	Number	131	42	29	26	9	8	8	44	297
	% Somewhat or Very	98.5%	95.2%	93.1%	100.0%	88.9%	100.0%	100.0 %	95.5%	97.0%
Portable Devices	Number	174	52	34	35	23	14	13	70	415
	% Somewhat or Very	97.1%	96.2%	97.1%	97.1%	87.0%	100.0%	100.0 %	97.1%	96.6%

IMPACT ON PRODUCTIVITY BY TYPE OF COMPANY

Impact on Productivity		Type of Company				
		Proprietorship	Partnership	Corporation	Other	Total
Electronic Mailing List	Number	35	60	186	20	301
	% Positive	77.1%	78.3%	83.9%	65.0%	80.7%
Electronic Newsletter	Number	21	24	104	6	155
	% Positive	71.4%	79.2%	82.7%	83.3%	80.6%
Telephone Hotlines	Number	8	12	33	3	56
	% Positive	50.0%	75.0%	69.7%	33.3%	66.1%
E-mail	Number	60	73	256	25	414
	% Positive	83.3%	91.8%	87.9%	72.0%	87.0%
Employee Blogs	Number	7	11	22	2	42
	% Positive	57.1%	63.6%	86.4%	50.0%	73.8%
Instant Messaging	Number	25	26	76	7	134
	% Positive	80.00%	88.46%	84.21%	85.71%	84.33%
Intranets	Number	29	38	162	12	241
	% Positive	75.9%	92.1%	84.6%	75.0%	84.2%
Company Web Site	Number	44	59	225	22	350
	% Positive	75.0%	79.7%	76.9%	54.5%	75.7%
CRM System	Number	18	21	98	7	144
	% Positive	88.9%	81.0%	86.7%	71.4%	85.4%
Conferencing Systems	Number	32	40	183	17	272
	% Positive	84.4%	82.5%	89.6%	82.4%	87.5%
Portable Devices	Number	48	68	243	22	381
	% Positive	87.5%	89.7%	93.0%	81.8%	91.1%

IMPACT ON PRODUCTIVITY BY NUMBER OF EMPLOYEES

Impact on Productivity		Number of Employees			
		Up to 50	51 to 200	More than 200	Total
Electronic Mailing List	Number	125	89	87	301
	% Positive	82.4%	83.1%	75.9%	80.7%
Electronic Newsletter	Number	44	57	54	155
	% Positive	72.7%	82.5%	85.2%	80.6%
Telephone Hotlines	Number	19	14	23	56
	% Positive	78.9%	64.3%	56.5%	66.1%
E-mail	Number	196	118	100	414
	% Positive	90.3%	89.0%	78.0%	87.0%
Employee Blogs	Number	17	15	10	42
	% Positive	88.2%	66.7%	60.0%	73.8%
Instant Messaging	Number	66	47	21	134
	% Positive	86.4%	80.9%	85.7%	84.3%
Intranets	Number	75	82	84	241
	% Positive	82.7%	89.0%	81.0%	84.2%
Company Web Site	Number	157	108	85	350
	% Positive	73.2%	77.8%	77.6%	75.7%
CRM System	Number	53	50	41	144
	% Positive	86.8%	86.0%	82.9%	85.4%
Conferencing Systems	Number	106	90	76	272
	% Positive	85.8%	90.0%	86.8%	87.5%
Portable Devices	Number	173	115	93	381
	% Positive	90.2%	93.0%	90.3%	91.1%

IMPACT ON PRODUCTIVITY BY LOCATION OF MAIN OFFICE

Impact on Productivity		Location of Main Office				
		U.S.	Canada	Europe	Other	Total
Electronic Mailing List	Number	222	46	16	17	301
	% Positive	82.0%	78.3%	75.0%	76.5%	80.7%
Electronic Newsletter	Number	115	26	7	7	155
	% Positive	81.7%	84.6%	42.9%	85.7%	80.6%
Telephone Hotlines	Number	46	5	2	3	56
	% Positive	69.6%	40.0%	100.0%	33.3%	66.1%
E-mail	Number	308	67	18	21	414
	% Positive	89.3%	77.6%	77.8%	90.5%	87.0%
Employee Blogs	Number	32	3	5	2	42
	% Positive	75.0%	66.7%	80.0%	50.0%	73.8%
Instant Messaging	Number	108	10	10	6	134
	% Positive	86.1%	80.0%	90.0%	50.0%	84.3%
Intranets	Number	186	33	9	13	241
	% Positive	85.5%	78.8%	100.0%	69.2%	84.2%
Company Web Site	Number	263	52	17	18	350
	% Positive	75.3%	82.7%	82.4%	55.6%	75.7%
CRM System	Number	117	17	4	6	144
	% Positive	84.6%	94.1%	100.0%	66.7%	85.4%
Conferencing Systems	Number	206	43	12	11	272
	% Positive	88.3%	83.7%	100.0%	72.7%	87.5%
Portable Devices	Number	295	56	11	19	381
	% Positive	90.5%	91.1%	100.0%	94.7%	91.1%

IMPACT ON PRODUCTIVITY BY SECTOR

Impact on Productivity		Professional/Scientific/Technical	Manufacturing	Finance	Information Services	Retail	Construction	Health Care	Other	Total
		Sector								
Electronic Mailing List	Number	131	36	28	21	13	7	12	53	301
	% Positive	79.4%	88.9%	67.9%	81.0%	84.6%	85.7%	100.0%	79.2%	80.7%
Electronic Newsletter	Number	57	19	19	13	9	7	5	26	155
	% Positive	78.9%	89.5%	78.9%	69.2%	77.8%	100.0%	100.0%	76.9%	80.6%
Telephone Hotlines	Number	16	7	8	4	4	3	3	11	56
	% Positive	62.5%	57.1%	75.0%	75.0%	50.0%	100.0%	66.7%	63.6%	66.1%
E-mail	Number	173	41	39	41	19	14	13	74	414
	% Positive	89.0%	85.4%	69.2%	87.8%	89.5%	92.9%	92.3%	89.2%	87.0%
Employee Blogs	Number	15	5	4	6	4	2	1	5	42
	% Positive	66.7%	80.0%	25.0%	100.0%	75.0%	100.0%	100.0%	80.0%	73.8%
Instant Messaging	Number	69	9	6	15	6	4	4	21	134
	% Positive	82.6%	77.8%	100.0%	80.0%	100.0%	100.0%	75.0%	85.7%	84.3%
Intranets	Number	100	28	29	23	10	5	8	38	241
	% Positive	83.0%	85.7%	82.8%	82.6%	80.0%	100.0%	87.5%	86.8%	84.2%
Company Web Site	Number	149	41	32	32	19	11	12	54	350
	% Positive	76.5%	80.5%	84.4%	68.8%	84.2%	45.5%	75.0%	72.2%	75.7%
CRM System	Number	51	21	14	19	6	4	5	24	144
	% Positive	92.2%	81.0%	71.4%	78.9%	100.0%	75.0%	80.0%	87.5%	85.4%
Conferencing Systems	Number	114	40	28	25	10	6	7	42	272
	% Positive	91.2%	90.0%	78.6%	92.0%	90.0%	83.3%	85.7%	78.6%	87.5%
Portable Devices	Number	151	49	29	33	25	12	14	68	381
	% Positive	94.0%	87.8%	86.2%	90.9%	92.0%	100.0%	92.9%	86.8%	91.1%

IMPACT ON PROFITABILITY BY TYPE OF COMPANY

Impact on Profitability		Type of Company				
		Proprietorship	Partnership	Corporation	Other	Total
Electronic Mailing List	Number	31	42	149	17	239
	% Positive	74.2%	71.4%	83.9%	70.6%	79.5%
Electronic Newsletter	Number	20	23	79	5	127
	% Positive	65.0%	65.2%	77.2%	100.0%	74.0%
Telephone Hotlines	Number	8	11	28	3	50
	% Positive	50.0%	72.7%	75.0%	0.0%	66.0%
E-mail	Number	52	54	207	19	332
	% Positive	75.0%	87.0%	88.9%	78.9%	85.8%
Employee Blogs	Number	6	12	20	1	39
	% Positive	66.7%	75.0%	90.0%	100.0%	82.1%
Instant Messaging	Number	21	19	66	5	111
	% Positive	66.7%	78.9%	80.3%	40.0%	75.7%
Intranets	Number	24	30	127	11	192
	% Positive	70.8%	80.0%	81.9%	63.6%	79.2%
Company Web Site	Number	41	52	201	18	312
	% Positive	82.9%	84.6%	86.1%	72.2%	84.6%
CRM System	Number	15	20	88	7	130
	% Positive	86.7%	80.0%	85.2%	100.0%	85.4%
Conferencing Systems	Number	26	32	147	13	218
	% Positive	84.6%	81.3%	85.7%	61.5%	83.5%
Portable Devices	Number	41	56	197	19	313
	% Positive	87.8%	85.7%	86.8%	73.7%	85.9%

IMPACT ON PROFITABILITY BY NUMBER OF EMPLOYEES

Impact on Profitability		Number of Employees: Up to 50	51 to 200	More than 200	Total
Electronic Mailing List	Number	103	75	61	239
	% Positive	80.6%	80.0%	77.0%	79.5%
Electronic Newsletter	Number	43	50	34	127
	% Positive	69.8%	78.0%	73.5%	74.0%
Telephone Hotlines	Number	18	13	19	50
	% Positive	77.8%	61.5%	57.9%	66.0%
E-mail	Number	162	97	73	332
	% Positive	86.4%	89.7%	79.5%	85.8%
Employee Blogs	Number	15	14	10	39
	% Positive	86.7%	78.6%	80.0%	82.1%
Instant Messaging	Number	52	41	18	111
	% Positive	71.2%	78.0%	83.3%	75.7%
Intranets	Number	59	70	63	192
	% Positive	78.0%	82.9%	76.2%	79.2%
Company Web Site	Number	146	96	70	312
	% Positive	82.2%	86.5%	87.1%	84.6%
CRM System	Number	46	48	36	130
	% Positive	87.0%	81.3%	88.9%	85.4%
Conferencing Systems	Number	88	77	53	218
	% Positive	85.2%	81.8%	83.0%	83.5%
Portable Devices	Number	145	95	73	313
	% Positive	84.8%	87.4%	86.3%	85.9%

IMPACT ON PROFITABILITY BY LOCATION OF MAIN OFFICE

Impact on Profitability		Location of Main Office				
		U.S.	Canada	Europe	Other	Total
Electronic Mailing List	Number	180	35	10	14	239
	% Positive	81.1%	77.1%	80.0%	64.3%	79.5%
Electronic Newsletter	Number	102	13	5	7	127
	% Positive	72.5%	92.3%	60.0%	71.4%	74.0%
Telephone Hotlines	Number	42	3	2	3	50
	% Positive	69.0%	33.3%	100.0%	33.3%	66.0%
E-mail	Number	254	49	12	17	332
	% Positive	85.8%	89.8%	75.0%	82.4%	85.8%
Employee Blogs	Number	29	3	4	3	39
	% Positive	82.8%	100.0%	75.0%	66.7%	82.1%
Instant Messaging	Number	91	6	9	5	111
	% Positive	76.9%	83.3%	66.7%	60.0%	75.7%
Intranets	Number	154	24	6	8	192
	% Positive	80.5%	66.7%	83.3%	87.5%	79.2%
Company Web Site	Number	239	45	11	17	312
	% Positive	86.2%	75.6%	100.0%	76.5%	84.6%
CRM System	Number	108	13	3	6	130
	% Positive	86.1%	84.6%	100.0%	66.7%	85.4%
Conferencing Systems	Number	171	29	10	8	218
	% Positive	84.2%	72.4%	90.0%	100.0%	83.5%
Portable Devices	Number	240	45	11	17	313
	% Positive	85.4%	86.7%	90.9%	88.2%	85.9%

IMPACT ON PROFITABILITY BY SECTOR

Impact on Profitability		Sector								
		Profession-al/Scientif-ic/Techni-cal	Manufac-turing	Finance	Infor-mation Services	Retail	Construc-tion	Health Care	Other	Total
Electronic Mailing List	Number	104	26	23	18	13	6	10	39	239
	% Positive	75.0%	88.5%	69.6%	83.3%	84.6%	66.7%	100.0%	84.6%	79.5%
Electronic Newsletter	Number	47	17	15	12	9	4	4	19	127
	% Positive	61.7%	88.2%	80.0%	83.3%	55.6%	75.0%	100.0%	84.2%	74.0%
Telephone Hotlines	Number	12	7	6	4	4	3	3	11	50
	% Positive	50.0%	85.7%	66.7%	50.0%	50.0%	100.0%	66.7%	72.7%	66.0%
E-mail	Number	137	36	30	34	17	11	11	56	332
	% Positive	84.7%	86.1%	80.0%	85.3%	82.4%	90.9%	90.9%	91.1%	85.8%
Employee Blogs	Number	13	5	3	5	4	1	1	7	39
	% Positive	76.9%	100.0%	66.7%	80.0%	75.0%	100.0%	100.0%	85.7%	82.1%
Instant Messaging	Number	56	10	5	12	6	3	3	16	111
	% Positive	75.0%	90.0%	80.0%	58.3%	66.7%	100.0%	100.0%	75.0%	75.7%
Intranets	Number	76	24	24	20	10	4	7	27	192
	% Positive	77.6%	79.2%	91.7%	70.0%	80.0%	75.0%	71.4%	81.5%	79.2%
Company Web Site	Number	132	38	28	30	17	9	13	45	312
	% Positive	83.3%	81.6%	96.4%	83.3%	88.2%	55.6%	92.3%	86.7%	84.6%
CRM System	Number	47	21	11	18	6	1	6	20	130
	% Positive	87.2%	76.2%	81.8%	83.3%	83.3%	100.0%	100.0%	90.0%	85.4%
Conferencing Systems	Number	92	37	19	21	7	4	5	33	218
	% Positive	87.0%	86.5%	78.9%	76.2%	85.7%	100.0%	100.0%	72.7%	83.5%
Portable Devices	Number	127	41	22	27	22	9	12	53	313
	% Positive	85.8%	87.8%	81.8%	85.2%	86.4%	100.0%	83.3%	84.9%	85.9%

IMPACT ON EMPLOYEE BEHAVIOR BY TYPE OF COMPANY

Impact on Employee Behavior		Type of Company				
		Proprietorship	Partnership	Corporation	Other	Total
Electronic Mailing List	Number	34	53	186	18	291
	% Positive	64.7%	71.7%	74.2%	72.2%	72.5%
Electronic Newsletter	Number	21	27	110	9	167
	% Positive	71.4%	85.2%	88.2%	100.0%	86.2%
Telephone Hotlines	Number	7	12	33	3	55
	% Positive	71.4%	75.0%	75.8%	33.3%	72.7%
E-mail	Number	58	69	253	23	403
	% Positive	75.9%	84.1%	86.2%	73.9%	83.6%
Employee Blogs	Number	7	12	22	1	42
	% Positive	71.4%	58.3%	95.5%	100.0%	81.0%
Instant Messaging	Number	26	25	82	6	139
	% Positive	76.9%	88.0%	82.9%	100.0%	83.5%
Intranets	Number	30	35	169	14	248
	% Positive	66.7%	88.6%	84.6%	85.7%	83.1%
Company Web Site	Number	47	58	224	21	350
	% Positive	68.1%	70.7%	67.0%	61.9%	67.4%
CRM System	Number	17	20	96	7	140
	% Positive	64.7%	85.0%	80.2%	85.7%	79.3%
Conferencing Systems	Number	30	39	178	15	262
	% Positive	80.0%	79.5%	81.5%	73.3%	80.5%
Portable Devices	Number	50	66	237	18	371
	% Positive	86.0%	83.3%	85.2%	72.2%	84.4%

IMPACT ON EMPLOYEE BEHAVIOR BY NUMBER OF EMPLOYEES

Impact on Employee Behavior		Number of Employees: Up to 50	51 to 200	More than 200	Total
Electronic Mailing List	Number	118	91	82	291
	% Positive	73.7%	71.4%	72.0%	72.5%
Electronic Newsletter	Number	44	65	58	167
	% Positive	75.0%	87.7%	93.1%	86.2%
Telephone Hotlines	Number	18	14	23	55
	% Positive	83.3%	64.3%	69.6%	72.7%
E-mail	Number	190	119	94	403
	% Positive	82.1%	85.7%	84.0%	83.6%
Employee Blogs	Number	17	14	11	42
	% Positive	88.2%	71.4%	81.8%	81.0%
Instant Messaging	Number	64	49	26	139
	% Positive	79.7%	83.7%	92.3%	83.5%
Intranets	Number	72	87	89	248
	% Positive	77.8%	85.1%	85.4%	83.1%
Company Web Site	Number	155	104	91	350
	% Positive	64.5%	65.4%	74.7%	67.4%
CRM System	Number	50	49	41	140
	% Positive	80.0%	73.5%	85.4%	79.3%
Conferencing Systems	Number	98	88	76	262
	% Positive	80.6%	79.5%	81.6%	80.5%
Portable Devices	Number	168	110	93	371
	% Positive	82.7%	85.5%	86.0%	84.4%

IMPACT ON EMPLOYEE BEHAVIOR BY LOCATION OF MAIN OFFICE

Impact on Employee Behavior		Location of Main Office				
		U.S.	Canada	Europe	Other	Total
Electronic Mailing List	Number	215	46	14	16	291
	% Positive	76.7%	60.9%	57.1%	62.5%	72.5%
Electronic Newsletter	Number	122	29	7	9	167
	% Positive	86.9%	82.8%	71.4%	100.0%	86.2%
Telephone Hotlines	Number	45	4	2	4	55
	% Positive	71.1%	75.0%	100.0%	75.0%	72.7%
E-mail	Number	301	64	17	21	403
	% Positive	84.7%	81.3%	82.4%	76.2%	83.6%
Employee Blogs	Number	31	3	5	3	42
	% Positive	77.4%	100.0%	100.0%	66.7%	81.0%
Instant Messaging	Number	108	14	10	7	139
	% Positive	84.3%	78.6%	100.0%	57.1%	83.5%
Intranets	Number	189	36	10	13	248
	% Positive	82.5%	80.6%	80.0%	100.0%	83.1%
Company Web Site	Number	260	54	18	18	350
	% Positive	68.1%	66.7%	72.2%	55.6%	67.4%
CRM System	Number	113	17	4	6	140
	% Positive	79.6%	70.6%	100.0%	83.3%	79.3%
Conferencing Systems	Number	194	44	14	10	262
	% Positive	81.4%	77.3%	92.9%	60.0%	80.5%
Portable Devices	Number	280	57	14	20	371
	% Positive	82.9%	89.5%	85.7%	90.0%	84.4%

IMPACT ON EMPLOYEE BEHAVIOR BY SECTOR

Impact on Employee Behavior		Sector								
		Profession-al/Scientif-ic/Techni-cal	Manufac-turing	Finance	Infor-mation Services	Retail	Construc-tion	Health Care	Other	Total
Electronic Mailing List	Number	130	33	27	21	13	6	12	49	291
	% Positive	69.2%	78.8%	63.0%	85.7%	84.6%	66.7%	83.3%	71.4%	72.5%
Electronic Newsletter	Number	62	21	22	15	9	5	5	28	167
	% Positive	82.3%	95.2%	95.5%	80.0%	66.7%	100.0%	100.0%	85.7%	86.2%
Telephone Hotlines	Number	15	8	6	4	4	2	4	12	55
	% Positive	73.3%	100.0%	83.3%	50.0%	50.0%	100.0%	75.0%	58.3%	72.7%
E-mail	Number	171	41	35	40	21	12	11	72	403
	% Positive	82.5%	90.2%	77.1%	85.0%	85.7%	100.0%	81.8%	81.9%	83.6%
Employee Blogs	Number	16	5	3	6	4	1	1	6	42
	% Positive	75.0%	100.0%	66.7%	100.0%	75.0%	100.0%	100.0%	66.7%	81.0%
Instant Messaging	Number	70	10	7	17	6	3	4	22	139
	% Positive	82.9%	90.0%	85.7%	82.4%	83.3%	100.0%	100.0%	77.3%	83.5%
Intranets	Number	101	32	33	26	10	5	8	33	248
	% Positive	82.2%	84.4%	90.9%	80.8%	80.0%	80.0%	75.0%	81.8%	83.1%
Company Web Site	Number	153	38	35	33	18	12	11	50	350
	% Positive	67.3%	73.7%	71.4%	66.7%	66.7%	50.0%	81.8%	62.0%	67.4%
CRM System	Number	52	21	13	19	5	1	6	23	140
	% Positive	80.8%	71.4%	76.9%	89.5%	80.0%	100.0%	100.0%	69.6%	79.3%
Conferencing Systems	Number	112	38	28	25	9	7	8	35	262
	% Positive	79.5%	81.6%	78.6%	80.0%	88.9%	85.7%	100.0%	77.1%	80.5%
Portable Devices	Number	153	45	30	35	24	13	12	59	371
	% Positive	82.4%	86.7%	80.0%	94.3%	87.5%	92.3%	83.3%	81.4%	84.4%

IMPACT ON EXTERNAL COMMUNICATIONS BY TYPE OF COMPANY

Impact on External Communications		Type of Company				
		Proprietorship	Partnership	Corporation	Other	Total
Electronic Mailing List	Number	33	60	175	18	286
	% Positive	78.8%	65.0%	70.9%	72.2%	70.6%
Electronic Newsletter	Number	18	26	95	7	146
	% Positive	83.3%	73.1%	73.7%	85.7%	75.3%
Telephone Hotlines	Number	6	12	29	4	51
	% Positive	66.7%	75.0%	65.5%	0.0%	62.7%
E-mail	Number	56	71	250	23	400
	% Positive	83.9%	88.7%	85.6%	91.3%	86.3%
Employee Blogs	Number	7	14	20	2	43
	% Positive	85.7%	71.4%	80.0%	50.0%	76.7%
Instant Messaging	Number	19	23	70	6	118
	% Positive	63.2%	65.2%	64.3%	50.0%	63.6%
Intranets	Number	29	34	147	14	224
	% Positive	48.3%	64.7%	51.0%	35.7%	51.8%
Company Web Site	Number	51	65	257	22	395
	% Positive	92.2%	93.8%	94.6%	86.4%	93.7%
CRM System	Number	16	21	97	9	143
	% Positive	87.5%	85.7%	83.5%	88.9%	84.6%
Conferencing Systems	Number	27	40	177	15	259
	% Positive	88.9%	90.0%	80.8%	60.0%	81.9%
Portable Devices	Number	45	68	233	23	369
	% Positive	82.2%	86.8%	83.7%	60.9%	82.7%

IMPACT ON EXTERNAL COMMUNICATIONS BY LOCATION OF MAIN OFFICE

Impact on External Communications		Location of Main Office				
		U.S.	Canada	Europe	Other	Total
Electronic Mailing List	Number	212	42	13	19	286
	% Positive	73.1%	66.7%	69.2%	52.6%	70.6%
Electronic Newsletter	Number	106	25	6	9	146
	% Positive	74.5%	80.0%	100.0%	55.6%	75.3%
Telephone Hotlines	Number	41	4	2	4	51
	% Positive	63.4%	50.0%	100.0%	50.0%	62.7%
E-mail	Number	298	65	15	22	400
	% Positive	86.2%	89.2%	86.7%	77.3%	86.3%
Employee Blogs	Number	32	4	4	3	43
	% Positive	75.0%	50.0%	100.0%	100.0%	76.7%
Instant Messaging	Number	94	8	8	8	118
	% Positive	63.8%	50.0%	50.0%	87.5%	63.6%
Intranets	Number	172	30	9	13	224
	% Positive	55.8%	30.0%	66.7%	38.5%	51.8%
Company Web Site	Number	294	61	17	23	395
	% Positive	94.6%	96.7%	82.4%	82.6%	93.7%
CRM System	Number	116	18	3	6	143
	% Positive	81.9%	94.4%	100.0%	100.0%	84.6%
Conferencing Systems	Number	194	42	12	11	259
	% Positive	82.0%	73.8%	91.7%	100.0%	81.9%
Portable Devices	Number	279	55	14	21	369
	% Positive	80.6%	83.6%	92.9%	100.0%	82.7%

IMPACT ON EXTERNAL COMMUNICATIONS BY SECTOR

Impact on External Communications		Sector								
		Profession-al/Scientif-ic/Techni-cal	Manufac-turing	Finance	Infor-mation Services	Retail	Construc-tion	Health Care	Other	Total
Electronic Mailing List	Number	127	33	23	23	12	6	11	51	286
	% Positive	66.9%	81.8%	69.6%	73.9%	75.0%	50.0%	90.9%	68.6%	70.6%
Electronic Newsletter	Number	54	16	19	16	8	5	4	24	146
	% Positive	72.2%	75.0%	78.9%	81.3%	75.0%	80.0%	100.0%	70.8%	75.3%
Telephone Hotlines	Number	14	7	5	4	3	2	2	14	51
	% Positive	71.4%	57.1%	80.0%	50.0%	66.7%	100.0%	50.0%	50.0%	62.7%
E-mail	Number	172	44	32	39	18	13	11	71	400
	% Positive	90.1%	88.6%	84.4%	84.6%	77.8%	92.3%	81.8%	78.9%	86.3%
Employee Blogs	Number	18	5	3	5	4	1	1	6	43
	% Positive	72.2%	80.0%	66.7%	80.0%	75.0%	100.0%	100.0%	83.3%	76.7%
Instant Messaging	Number	57	10	6	13	5	3	4	20	118
	% Positive	63.2%	80.0%	66.7%	53.8%	60.0%	100.0%	50.0%	60.0%	63.6%
Intranets	Number	91	29	27	26	9	5	5	32	224
	% Positive	51.6%	48.3%	48.1%	42.3%	77.8%	80.0%	40.0%	56.3%	51.8%
Company Web Site	Number	167	51	39	34	19	11	14	60	395
	% Positive	92.8%	92.2%	97.4%	94.1%	89.5%	100.0%	92.9%	95.0%	93.7%
CRM System	Number	52	24	12	19	4	2	6	24	143
	% Positive	90.4%	75.0%	75.0%	84.2%	75.0%	100.0%	100.0%	83.3%	84.6%
Conferencing Systems	Number	117	40	22	24	9	7	6	34	259
	% Positive	87.2%	90.0%	45.5%	79.2%	77.8%	85.7%	83.3%	79.4%	81.9%
Portable Devices	Number	154	48	26	34	22	10	12	63	369
	% Positive	89.0%	83.3%	73.1%	85.3%	63.6%	90.0%	83.3%	74.6%	82.7%

COMMUNICATION RESEARCH PRACTICES

RESEARCH USAGE BY LOCATION OF MAIN OFFICE

Usage		Location of Main Office				
		U.S.	Canada	Europe	Other	Total
Communication Audits	Number	466	89	26	28	609
	% Currently Use	15.7%	14.6%	15.4%	14.3%	15.4%
Employee Opinion Surveys	Number	466	89	26	28	609
	% Currently Use	24.7%	29.2%	23.1%	25.0%	25.3%
Customer Satisfaction Surveys	Number	466	89	26	28	609
	% Currently Use	36.1%	40.4%	38.5%	28.6%	36.5%

RESEARCH USAGE BY SECTOR

Usage		Sector								
		Profession-al/Scientif-ic/Techni-cal	Manufac-turing	Finance	Infor-mation Services	Retail	Construc-tion	Health Care	Other	Total
Communication Audits	Number	232	67	53	52	39	23	23	120	609
	% Currently Use	14.2%	16.4%	24.5%	19.2%	12.8%	13.0%	21.7%	11.7%	15.4 %
Employee Opinion Surveys	Number	232	67	53	52	39	23	23	120	609
	% Currently Use	19.8%	29.9%	39.6%	32.7%	23.1%	26.1%	39.1%	21.7%	25.3 %
Customer Satisfaction Surveys	Number	232	67	53	52	39	23	23	120	609
	% Currently Use	33.6%	41.8%	45.3%	40.4%	43.6%	26.1%	47.8%	30.8%	36.5 %

COST-EFFECTIVENESS BY NUMBER OF EMPLOYEES

Cost-effectiveness		Number of Employees			
		Up to 50	51 to 200	More than 200	Total
Communication Audits	Number	28	24	29	81
	% Somewhat or Very	92.9%	91.7%	93.1%	92.6%
Employee Opinion Surveys	Number	42	44	56	142
	% Somewhat or Very	90.5%	88.6%	92.9%	90.8%
Customer Satisfaction Surveys	Number	42	44	56	142
	% Somewhat or Very	90.5%	88.6%	92.9%	90.8%

COST-EFFECTIVENESS BY LOCATION OF MAIN OFFICE

Cost-effectiveness		Location of Main Office				
		U.S.	Canada	Europe	Other	Total
Communication Audits	Number	61	12	4	4	81
	% Somewhat or Very	93.4%	83.3%	100.0%	100.0%	92.6%
Employee Opinion Surveys	Number	106	24	6	6	142
	% Somewhat or Very	91.5%	83.3%	100.0%	100.0%	90.8%
Customer Satisfaction Surveys	Number	155	34	10	7	206
	% Somewhat or Very	93.5%	100.0%	100.0%	85.7%	94.7%

COST-EFFECTIVENESS BY SECTOR

Cost-effectiveness		Sector								
		Profession-al/Scientif-ic/Technical	Manufac-turing	Finance	Infor-mation Services	Retail	Construc-tion	Health Care	Other	Total
Communication Audits	Number	30	9	13	8	4	2	3	12	81
	% Somewhat or Very	100.0%	88.9%	84.6%	100.0%	75.0%	100.0%	66.7%	91.7%	92.6%
Employee Opinion Surveys	Number	43	19	20	15	9	6	6	24	142
	% Somewhat or Very	93.0%	89.5%	90.0%	100.0%	77.8%	83.3%	83.3%	91.7%	90.8%
Customer Satisfaction Surveys	Number	74	28	22	18	16	6	8	34	206
	% Somewhat or Very	97.3%	92.9%	90.9%	94.4%	87.5%	100.0%	100.0 %	94.1%	94.7%

IMPACT ON PRODUCTIVITY BY TYPE OF COMPANY

Impact on Productivity		Type of Company				
		Proprietorship	Partnership	Corporation	Other	Total
Communication Audits	Number	11	11	52	6	80
	% Positive	72.7%	90.9%	78.8%	66.7%	78.8%
Employee Opinion Surveys	Number	16	20	87	9	132
	% Positive	68.8%	85.0%	81.6%	77.8%	80.3%
Customer Satisfaction Surveys	Number	25	32	127	9	193
	% Positive	84.0%	78.1%	89.8%	100.0%	87.6%

IMPACT ON PRODUCTIVITY BY NUMBER OF EMPLOYEES

Impact on Productivity		Number of Employees			
		Up to 50	51 to 200	More than 200	Total
Communication Audits	Number	26	27	27	80
	% Positive	73.1%	81.5%	81.5%	78.8%
Employee Opinion Surveys	Number	39	40	53	132
	% Positive	76.9%	87.5%	77.4%	80.3%
Customer Satisfaction Surveys	Number	74	56	63	193
	% Positive	87.8%	85.7%	88.9%	87.6%

IMPACT ON PRODUCTIVITY BY LOCATION OF MAIN OFFICE

Impact on Productivity		Location of Main Office: U.S.	Canada	Europe	Other	Total
Communication Audits	Number	63	10	3	4	80
	% Positive	79.4%	90.0%	66.7%	50.0%	78.8%
Employee Opinion Surveys	Number	99	20	6	7	132
	% Positive	85.9%	65.0%	66.7%	57.1%	80.3%
Customer Satisfaction Surveys	Number	144	32	9	8	193
	% Positive	87.5%	93.8%	77.8%	75.0%	87.6%

IMPACT ON PRODUCTIVITY BY SECTOR

Impact on Productivity		Sector: Profession-al/Scientif-ic/Techni-cal	Manufac-turing	Finance	Infor-mation Services	Retail	Construc-tion	Health Care	Other	Total
Communication Audits	Number	28	9	12	10	4	1	4	12	80
	% Positive	75.0%	88.9%	66.7%	80.0%	100.0%	100.0%	75.0%	83.3%	78.8%
Employee Opinion Surveys	Number	37	19	18	14	9	5	6	24	132
	% Positive	70.3%	89.5%	72.2%	78.6%	100.0%	80.0%	100.0%	83.3%	80.3%
Customer Satisfaction Surveys	Number	67	25	22	17	16	4	8	34	193
	% Positive	83.6%	88.0%	86.4%	88.2%	93.8%	100.0%	100.0%	88.2%	87.6%

IMPACT ON PROFITABILITY BY TYPE OF COMPANY

Impact on Profitability		Type of Company: Proprietorship	Partnership	Corporation	Other	Total
Communication Audits	Number	9	11	43	3	66
	% Positive	88.9%	81.8%	79.1%	100.0%	81.8%
Employee Opinion Surveys	Number	14	20	69	5	108
	% Positive	64.3%	80.0%	75.4%	80.0%	75.0%
Customer Satisfaction Surveys	Number	25	32	117	7	181
	% Positive	88.0%	81.3%	87.2%	100.0%	86.7%

IMPACT ON PROFITABILITY BY NUMBER OF EMPLOYEES

Impact on Profitability		Number of Employees			
		Up to 50	51 to 200	More than 200	Total
Communication Audits	Number	24	22	20	66
	% Positive	87.5%	81.8%	75.0%	81.8%
Employee Opinion Surveys	Number	35	38	35	108
	% Positive	74.3%	73.7%	77.1%	75.0%
Customer Satisfaction Surveys	Number	75	51	55	181
	% Positive	85.3%	86.3%	89.1%	86.7%

IMPACT ON PROFITABILITY BY LOCATION OF MAIN OFFICE

Impact on Profitability		Location of Main Office				
		U.S.	Canada	Europe	Other	Total
Communication Audits	Number	52	8	2	4	66
	% Positive	84.6%	75.0%	100.0%	50.0%	81.8%
Employee Opinion Surveys	Number	86	12	4	6	108
	% Positive	77.9%	50.0%	100.0%	66.7%	75.0%
Customer Satisfaction Surveys	Number	137	28	9	7	181
	% Positive	87.6%	82.1%	100.0%	71.4%	86.7%

IMPACT ON PROFITABILITY BY SECTOR

Impact on Profitability		Sector								
		Profession-al/Scientif-ic/Techni-cal	Manufac-turing	Finance	Infor-mation Services	Retail	Construc-tion	Health Care	Other	Total
Communication Audits	Number	23	7	9	8	4	1	3	11	66
	% Positive	78.3%	100.0%	77.8%	87.5%	100.0 %	100.0%	66.7%	72.7%	81.8%
Employee Opinion Surveys	Number	30	15	13	12	9	5	3	21	108
	% Positive	63.3%	93.3%	76.9%	75.0%	88.9 %	80.0%	100.0 %	66.7%	75.0%
Customer Satisfaction Surveys	Number	62	24	19	17	16	4	8	31	181
	% Positive	88.7%	95.8%	78.9%	88.2%	93.8 %	100.0%	100.0 %	71.0%	86.7%

IMPACT ON EMPLOYEE BEHAVIOR BY TYPE OF COMPANY

Impact on Employee Behavior		Type of Company				
		Proprietorship	Partnership	Corporation	Other	Total
Communication Audits	Number	10	12	53	4	79
	% Positive	80.0%	91.7%	84.9%	75.0%	84.8%
Employee Opinion Surveys	Number	15	22	94	8	139
	% Positive	73.3%	77.3%	84.0%	75.0%	81.3%
Customer Satisfaction Surveys	Number	24	35	123	8	190
	% Positive	83.3%	77.1%	88.6%	100.0%	86.3%

IMPACT ON EMPLOYEE BEHAVIOR BY NUMBER OF EMPLOYEES

Impact on Employee Behavior		Number of Employees			
		Up to 50	51 to 200	More than 200	Total
Communication Audits	Number	23	26	30	79
	% Positive	73.9%	88.5%	90.0%	84.8%
Employee Opinion Surveys	Number	39	45	55	139
	% Positive	79.5%	82.2%	81.8%	81.3%
Customer Satisfaction Surveys	Number	71	57	62	190
	% Positive	90.1%	84.2%	83.9%	86.3%

IMPACT ON EMPLOYEE BEHAVIOR BY LOCATION OF MAIN OFFICE

Impact on Employee Behavior		Location of Main Office				
		U.S.	Canada	Europe	Other	Total
Communication Audits	Number	61	11	3	4	79
	% Positive	90.2%	72.7%	66.7%	50.0%	84.8%
Employee Opinion Surveys	Number	103	24	6	6	139
	% Positive	88.3%	62.5%	66.7%	50.0%	81.3%
Customer Satisfaction Surveys	Number	141	33	10	6	190

IMPACT ON EMPLOYEE BEHAVIOR BY SECTOR

Impact on Employee Behavior		Sector								
		Profession-al/Scientif-ic/Techni-cal	Manufac-turing	Finance	Infor-mation Services	Retail	Construc-tion	Health Care	Other	Total
Communication Audits	Number	26	9	12	10	4	2	4	12	79
	% Positive	80.8%	100.0%	83.3%	80.0%	100.0%	100.0%	100.0%	75.0%	84.8%
Employee Opinion Surveys	Number	40	17	18	16	9	5	8	26	139
	% Positive	75.0%	94.1%	77.8%	81.3%	100.0%	80.0%	100.0%	73.1%	81.3%
Customer Satisfaction Surveys	Number	62	26	22	19	16	5	8	32	190
	% Positive	88.7%	80.8%	86.4%	89.5%	81.3%	100.0%	100.0%	81.3%	86.3%

IMPACT ON EXTERNAL COMMUNICATIONS BY TYPE OF COMPANY

Impact on External Communications		Type of Company				
		Proprietorship	Partnership	Corporation	Other	Total
Communication Audits	Number	8	12	47	5	72
	% Positive	75.0%	66.7%	74.5%	60.0%	72.2%
Employee Opinion Surveys	Number	13	20	75	9	117
	% Positive	61.5%	70.0%	64.0%	33.3%	62.4%
Customer Satisfaction Surveys	Number	26	35	128	10	199
	% Positive	92.3%	82.9%	94.5%	100.0%	92.5%

IMPACT ON EXTERNAL COMMUNICATIONS BY NUMBER OF EMPLOYEES

Impact on External Communications		Number of Employees			
		Up to 50	51 to 200	More than 200	Total
Communication Audits	Number	23	26	23	72
	% Positive	82.6%	61.5%	73.9%	72.2%
Employee Opinion Surveys	Number	37	41	39	117
	% Positive	67.6%	58.5%	61.5%	62.4%
Customer Satisfaction Surveys	Number	75	60	64	199
	% Positive	93.3%	93.3%	90.6%	92.5%

IMPACT ON EXTERNAL COMMUNICATIONS BY LOCATION OF MAIN OFFICE

Impact on External Communications		Location of Main Office				
		U.S.	Canada	Europe	Other	Total
Communication Audits	Number	59	8	2	3	72
	% Positive	71.2%	75.0%	100.0%	66.7%	72.2%
Employee Opinion Surveys	Number	89	19	5	4	117
	% Positive	68.5%	36.8%	80.0%	25.0%	62.4%
Customer Satisfaction Surveys	Number	150	33	8	8	199
	% Positive	93.3%	90.9%	100.0%	75.0%	92.5%

IMPACT ON EXTERNAL COMMUNICATIONS BY SECTOR

Impact on External Communications		Sector								
		Profession-al/Scientif-ic/Techni-cal	Manufac-turing	Finance	Infor-mation Services	Retail	Construc-tion	Health Care	Other	Total
Communication Audits	Number	23	8	11	10	4	2	3	11	72
	% Positive	73.9%	100.0%	54.5%	70.0%	100.0 %	50.0%	66.7%	63.6%	72.2%
Employee Opinion Surveys	Number	35	13	16	15	9	3	4	22	117
	% Positive	60.0%	69.2%	56.3%	60.0%	66.7%	66.7%	75.0%	63.6%	62.4%
Customer Satisfaction Surveys	Number	71	25	22	16	16	5	9	35	199
	% Positive	91.5%	96.0%	86.4%	100.0%	93.8%	100.0%	88.9%	91.4%	92.5%

APPENDIX D / Glossary of Terms Used in the Survey

IN-PERSON COMMUNICATION PRACTICES

Common areas for meetings – an informal space with a relaxed atmosphere where employees and management interact and exchange ideas.

Employee forums – a venue for employees to voice any concerns.

Face-to-face conversations – in-person discussions between two or more people.

Informal gatherings – meetings at an off-site location where open, constructive feedback and discussion between management and staff occur.

Interactive orientation periods – when management actively participates in providing briefings of the company's vision, mandates and policies; acquaints the new employee with job duties; and instills a sense of being welcome and valued.

Management by walking around – managers walk through the workplace, interacting with staff to offer positive comments and receive input and feedback.

Management meetings – meetings where the management team discusses strategy and business progress.

Mentorship and coaching programs – new employees are paired with knowledgeable staff members who assist with job training and orientation.

Open door policy – staff with concerns and issues are encouraged to approach management.

Open floor plan/flexible seating – a floor plan with few physical separations in the workplace; staff are able to move freely and collaborate at each other's workstations.

Performance appraisals – an in-person assessment of employee productivity, recognition of accomplishments and discussion of improvement areas; employees are encouraged to discuss issues related to job performance and achievement.

Staff meetings – meetings of staff and management.

Staff advocates – staff members who report matters of concern regarding employees' perceptions.

PRINT COMMUNICATION PRACTICES

Anonymous suggestion systems – an anonymous system where employees can submit concerns, feedback and ideas for improvement.

Customer service manuals – print publications that provide information to employees on customer service.

Employee handbooks – a print publication that provides information on company rules and regulations, policies, and employee benefits.

Formal grievance procedures – print publications that provide information on filing a grievance against other staff members or management.

Journals – similar in content to newsletters and magazines, journals also offer research articles and results of in-house surveys.

Letters mailed to employee's homes – standard correspondence that relays general information and is mailed to employee's homes as opposed to being distributed in the workplace.

Magazines – similar in content to newsletters but with longer features and formatted like a popular magazine.

Newsletters – in-house publications generated by staff that provide information on company activities, employee achievements and news.

Open book management – portions or all of the company's financial figures are shared with employees.

Procedure manuals – print publications that provide information on company procedures relating to health and safety.

Public suggestion systems – a system where employees can submit concerns, feedback and ideas for improvement—anonymity is not assured.

Training manuals – print publications that provide specific information on job descriptions and duties.

ELECTRONIC COMMUNICATION PRACTICES

Cell phones – portable telephones.

Company web site – a web site offering public information about a company.

CRM system – a customer relationship management system that provides electronic information about client's needs and details of interactions with the client.

Electronic mailing list – a list of employee recipients to whom specific correspondence is sent through electronic means.

Electronic newsletter – a newsletter sent to employees via the Internet.

E-mail – correspondence sent and received by employees via the Internet.

Employee blogs – an Internet page that hosts entries written by employees.

Instant messaging – real-time, electronic chatting between coworkers.

Intranets – a computer network using the same technology and protocols as the Internet but with access restricted to employees of the firm.

IPASS – allows the user to make a local connection from almost anywhere in the world.

Laptops – portable computers.

Online conferencing – virtual office meetings enabled by various Web tools and performed over the Internet.

Pager – a portable device that alerts the recipient to an incoming call or message.

Personal digital assistant (PDA) – portable device that manages information and e-mail and is word processing and Internet capable.

Teleconferencing – meetings with three or more participants at remote locations by means of the telephone.

Telephone hotlines – an answering service where employees can voice concerns or suggestions via the telephone.

Videoconferencing – meetings with two or more participants at remote locations by means of transmitted audio and visual signals.

VPN – a Virtual Private Network, which allows a connection to the network at a workplace from a person's home PC or anywhere else the person has an Internet connection. It's called virtual because the employee is not directly connected to the network, and private because the channel between the PC and the company network is secure and encrypted.

Webcam – camera operating from a computer that allows the user's image to be projected.

COMMUNICATION RESEARCH

Communication audits – surveys that assess the effectiveness of internal communication.

Customer satisfaction surveys – surveys that assess levels of customer or client satisfaction with a firm's services.

Employee network analysis – research methods that reveal communicative connections between employees.

Employee opinion surveys – surveys that assess levels of employee satisfaction with their work and the company, and their attitudes toward new policies and strategies.

COMMUNICATION SKILLS TRAINING

Communication skills training – training to enhance communication and listening skills.

Conflict resolution – methods of diffusing hostility and resolving conflict.

Customer relations training – training to enhance relationships and/or communication with customers or clients.

Diversity training – training that promotes tolerance and a respect for differences between people.

Documentation – planning a project and gathering and organizing information.

Forms of writing – letters, memos, proposals, reports, etc.

Gender sensitivity training – education to facilitate effective communication between men and women.

Group facilitation – instruction on conducting meetings and group collaboration.

Language instruction – training that promotes proficiency in specific languages.

Listening skills – listening ability.

Negotiation skills – skills in dispute resolution and issues related to bargaining.

Presentation skills – skills in public speaking, leading discussions or delivering presentations.

Writing skills – skills in sentence structure, paragraph design and word choice.